Adult Transformat

Overcoming Life Stressors
and Healing Emotional Wounds

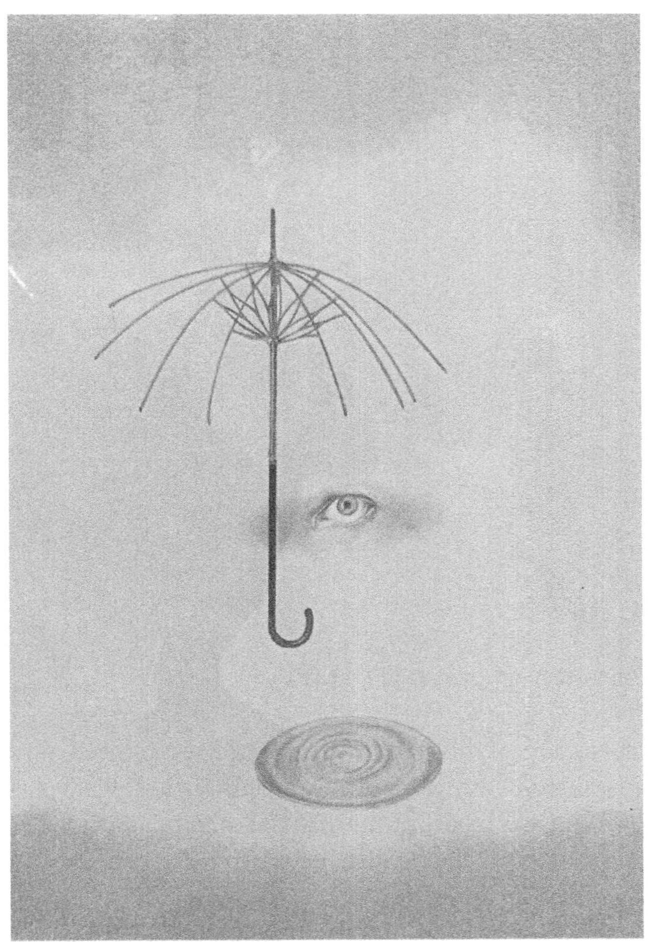

Above art by Gerald Tomal

First printing January 2024

For permission requests, contact:
Dr. Marsha Mathews, PsyD, LMFT

To My Daughter, Merissa

*For her therapeutic work with others
who are healing from trauma.
She is a warrior.*

Foreword

Dr. Marsha Mathews' book, *Adult Transformational Change*, is a source by which those in pain—psychological, emotional, and physical pain—can get out of the rut to which they believe they are condemned for the foreseeable future. The reason this book is a cut above the usual psychological approaches to healing our souls is thanks to the author's personal experiences in coaching her clients over many years, and her time-tested means of teaching others to break old patterns and develop new ones.

The desire to change begins with the recognition of a problem, whether it is between people, within a person as an individual, or in a situation that may seem permanent and inescapable. Each chapter of this book contains the description of how we might be approaching our present and our future and coming to terms with the realities of desperation and sadness. Those who find this book will likely identify with thoughts, conditions, and perceptions of life where it meets them. Mathews' clear content lets you focus and recognize personal conditions and symptoms to then find positive, achievable solutions toward desired outcomes.

Those who are fortunate enough to have a personal psychologist, counselor, or therapist will find this as a useful companion to do self-work at home. All readers can take to heart the path of learning to "unlearn" patterns of behavior and shed our false beliefs. In the best-case scenario, an individual who finds themselves standing in the aisles of a bookstore can obtain this book, go home, read, think, list, and go through the book in programmatic fashion and initiate healing.

The book is organized according to feelings, potential barriers, solutions to overcoming those barriers, and willingness to change. The central therapy described is cognitive behavioral therapy, which includes the interaction between basic environment, emotions, cognitions (your thoughts), behaviors and associated physiology. Modifying any one of these may have a profound impact on your life. Successful change can be permanent or sustainable, given the right conditions.

We all need a "safe place" to exist, as our home base. If we are to grow and leave behind self-doubt, fear, complacency, and negativity, then we are more likely to seek new truths, find reinforcements for those truths, and change our path. This process or journey is an important part of our healing. Before we can accomplish any mission to leave behind a harmful script, we may need affirmation. The tone of this book is that of a trusted friend standing beside you when you need it and encouraging you onward.

Change can be hard, but not impossible. With *Adult Transformational Change* as your partner in healing, you can leave the pain of the past behind and begin a new life. Every day we make a series of choices on how to react to life's mysteries. Armed with a positive self-concept, we recognize our inner and outer resources, and life can be transformed. Dr. Mathews' contribution to these personal resources is valuable to every adult as they mature, grow, change, adapt, and thrive.

Dawn Lee Wakefield, MS, MEd, PhD
West Communications, Bryan, Texas
December 2023

Acknowledgments

I must begin by acknowledging the courageous men and women who have come to me for psychotherapy during a time where they were experiencing the emotional pain and suffering brought upon by life circumstances. These individuals experienced personal growth that transformed their existing life into a new and different way of being in the world.

Whether overcoming a predisposition toward anxiety or depression or overcoming a life situation that has caused emotional distress, each person has worked toward self-improvement through their willingness and commitment. One definition of courage is *"practicing faith in the face of fear."* Having faith in the process of change and maintaining the commitment in the face of challenges, fears, and difficult life experiences is one of the necessary ingredients for transforming one's life. I acknowledge this courage.

I would like to give special thanks to Katelyn Pfaff for her editorial expertise. I also thank Darden Dodge for providing me with support, mentorship, and valuable formatting and design contributions.

Introduction

My work as a psychotherapist has brought me to the decision to write this book on adult transformation and change that occurs when an individual has made the decision to get help and initiate the journey toward personal growth. I have observed so many brave and courageous men and women engage in therapy and alter their behaviors, perceptions, and emotional responses to life circumstances. Working with people who desire change and want a life that is more valuable has inspired me to use many different approaches and orientations to psychotherapy. I have found that many of these methods are core strategies for transformation.

The chapters of this book correspond to processes that are part of the journey I have watched individuals take. When people make the decision that there is too much pain to stay the way they are, they are ready to do the work. My hope is that if you are reading this book, you have decided to begin your journey of personal growth.

Practicing psychotherapy in the 21st century has brought an awareness of the prevalence of depression, anxiety, and traumatic injuries. For this reason, I have dedicated chapters with interwoven information specific to the spectrum of these disorders. I have also written on interpersonal problems that are prevalent in people who make the decision to come to therapy.

There are many core areas of healing that are needed by all people who are struggling to find their way to feeling healthier again despite their diagnoses. My goal is to reach individuals who are experiencing mild, moderate, or more severe levels of emotional pain. I hope to walk with you toward transforming your life into a new way of thinking and living.

My practice of psychotherapy has provided insight into the challenges of today's world. Individuals seek treatment because of a variety of personal problems and an array of situational stressors that are accelerated by external world issues. These problems weigh heavily on each courageous person who makes the decision to get help. I see such bravery in the individual seeking help. The decision can be blocked by the stigma our culture has for someone who is experiencing "*emotional problems*" or "*mental health problems.*"

Seeking help in psychotherapy, however, is a ***healthy decision***. To deny that a person will experience grief, loss, anxiety, sadness, or hurtful experiences on life's journey is to deny a significant part of our human experience. Another barrier to the decision to seek therapy is the idea of having to bare one's soul to another person. It takes courage to become vulnerable and trust another person to gain insight into one's problems. My patients are my heroes.

I decided on the title of *Adult Transformational Change* because of the dramatic transcendence I have observed in those individuals who choose to seek therapy. The idea of transformation has been used in a variety of contexts including spiritual and metaphysical. Change that occurs in therapy is seen in emotions, cognitions, behaviors, and in a spiritual nature. Transformation and change are likely to happen "*if and when*" a person ***decides*** to embark on the journey of personal growth.

This book is intended to be a handbook for people who are walking the path from brokenness toward healing. There are multiple life experiences that can block or hamper an individual's ability to grow and develop personally and interpersonally. Dislodging those barriers to living a joyous and fulfilling life can be liberating. Establishing passion in life through the identification of *purpose* may be blocked because of false narratives and erroneous decisions made earlier in life. Expressions of healthy thoughts may have been derailed because of old ideas about lack of personal value or worth.

This book will cover many aspects of our human experience with the intention of helping you to overcome the self-imposed barriers to living a full and meaningful life. I utilize a variety of therapy interventions, and this book will incorporate some variations of therapeutic orientations such as cognitive behavioral therapy (CBT), dialectical behavior therapy (DBT), and therapies that are associated with trauma such as Eye Movement Desensitization and Reprocessing (EMDR) therapy, Trauma Resilience Model (TRM), and Cognitive Processing Therapy (CPT). Other therapies associated with attachment and information associated with brain functioning will be included also.

The journey must begin with a *desire to change*. Embracing the present is significant in your ability to transcend life's difficulties. The path toward wholeness can be filled with indecision and cluttered with negativity that can alter your course. Your perseverance will be important in making changes that can enhance your life. You may be faced with *recommitting* to change along your way. Ultimately, your journey is your own and it is up to you to stay on course.

I trust that your deepest desire for change will motivate you to stay on the path toward freedom. The path is different for everyone. The result is often increased insight and self-awareness.

Note that the Workbook (orange cover) and Handbook (blue cover) have the same content. In the Workbook, the self-inventories and exercises are in the body of the text and in the Handbook the exercises are in the Appendix at the end of the book. I strongly suggest that you complete some or all the self-inventories and reflection prompts that are associated with each chapter.

Table of Contents

Chapter 1

Beginning the Journey Toward Change

Every Journey Has a Beginning

"That's life: Starting over, one breath at a time."

— *Sharon Salzberg, Real Happiness: The Power of Meditation*

The above quote reminds us that the potential for starting over and embarking on a new beginning is possible. The desire to re-establish our intention about our life can be transformational and can be the gateway toward change. At any given moment of any day, we can make a decision to alter the course of our life and move beyond the self-imposed shackles that have kept us from living.

Personal freedom will depend upon our ability to examine our lives and courageously alter what needs to be changed. You have this freedom. Claim it. Accept it.

Every journey has a starting point, and the start of a transformational experience begins with a decision. Transformation is a term that may sound mysterious or have connotations of being in line with a spiritual metamorphosis. Although I do not discount that this can happen through the course of therapy, I have my definition of transformation for the purpose of this book. I have identified transformation as ***"change that occurs with adults who are pursuing a new and better life or an end to suffering."***

I have observed the gradual process of change happen with people who come to therapy and make the decision that they no longer want to endure the emotional pain they are experiencing. Many have been suffering since childhood and some have endured the pain of an adult life experience. The challenges may come from a lifetime of a biological predisposition to having a mental health diagnosis. The common ground is the desire for change. The common result is a transformational process that provides new insight, awareness, perspectives, and ultimately change.

> *"You are writing a new page of your life story that is free of past beliefs."*

Transformation is often the word used to describe the metamorphosis that a caterpillar experiences in becoming a butterfly. In many ways this is like what people experience as they go through a therapeutic process and begin to investigate layers of themselves. And it begins with the decision to seek help. It begins with the growing awareness that life can be better or more satisfying than their current state. If you are reading this book, there is the chance that you are feeling the need for change in your life. I welcome you to the choice of pursuing transformation.

You Decide

Every journey has a starting point. Throughout the day you are making decisions about your life. Some are big and some are small. Some decisions may involve things such as what to eat for lunch and some decisions may be much more consequential such as a career choice. Each decision involves you as the individual standing at a crossroads where you have two or more paths that you can take. Each decision has some impact on your life. You are the "*decider*." You are the primary "*shot caller.*" You are the author of your day-to-day choices.

Imagine that you have a clean piece of paper every day and you have the option of writing a new page to your story. Or imagine that you have a canvas and each day you are painting a new picture that represents your day's choices. All your collective decisions create a picture of your choices. You can choose to succumb to old patterns and routine behaviors or you can choose a new path. The new path may represent risk, and you may feel fearful about trying something new and different.

It also represents the realm of possibility and breaking free of unhealthy patterns of behavior. If you have decided that you want a new and different way of being in the world, or if you have chosen to get therapy, you are stepping out of your rut of routine behavior and stepping into the possibility of a new way of being in your world. You are writing a new page of your life story that is free of past beliefs. You are painting a new picture on your canvas that has potential for a happier outcome.

The Canvas

Imagine that your life is like a canvas of a picture you are painting. You possess the ability to create and paint whatever picture you desire for yourself.

If your life was represented by a canvas and you were the primary artist painting the picture, I think you might agree that parts of the canvas have already been painted for you. Part of your story has already been written. You did not pick your parents, nor the country or socioeconomics you were born into. You did not select other parts of the "backdrop" of your painting.

Let's think about some of the things that may be a part of your canvas that you did not choose:

- Parents
- Socioeconomic status
- Ethnicity
- Country and neighborhood where you were born and raised
- Childhood abuse (neglect, emotional, physical, sexual abuse)
- Loving, nurturing, and caring family environment
- Loss of those close to you
- Traumatic natural disasters (earthquakes, fires, hurricanes, etc.)
- Cultural values imposed early on

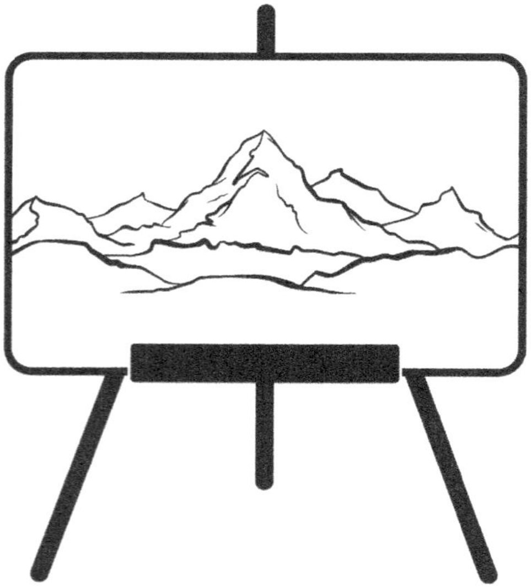

These items that you did not choose may have a positive or negative influence on the choices you make for yourself. They could be part of your story that you did not author but were there in the backdrop of the choices you have made for yourself (like the background mountains in the canvas). These layers are not necessarily painted or written by us, but by others. That will forever be a part of our story or canvas, but it won't ever be the only part. We will be adding layers to our story according to our conscious desires, goals, and values, as we wield the power to create.

1.a The Canvas

In the space below write some of the things that are a part of your canvas that you did not choose. What is the "backdrop" of your canvas that was already written for you?

Did the above things that you did not choose encourage positivity or contribute to negativity in the choices you have made for yourself?

What early life decisions did you make about yourself based upon the backdrop of your canvas?

Have those early decisions about yourself changed over time?

Influences and Influencers

In addition to the backdrop of your canvas, which includes things that you did not choose and things that were not a part of your selection for your life, are *influences* and *influencers*. The influences and influencers of your canvas we will be referring to in this section are the ones with which you are consciously aware. In future chapters we will be discussing the unconscious influences that you may not be aware of that become a part of your belief system.

Influences to age 18: Influences are life experiences that affect the decisions you make in life. They may include a trip to a doctor's office as a child where you were given a shot that was painful. This experience made you avoidant of future inoculations. Another example of an influence may be a trip with your grade school class to the opera house where you observed a symphony orchestra. This experience made you decide to play a musical instrument. Other examples of influences on your personal decisions are:

The *situations to age 18* that shaped my future decisions	The *influence* this had on me was
Growing up in a neighborhood with crime and violence	This has made me more cautious, and I place high value on safety over risk in my decisions
Growing up in a neighborhood where I was an ethnic minority	This has made me more aware of prejudice and I surround myself with safe people
Attending gifted classes in school or college prep classes	This has made me feel more confident in my decisions about career and college
Playing team sports and learning lessons on sportsmanship	This has made me aware of sportsmanship and I make decisions based on fairness
Observing domestic violence in my home while growing up	This has made me aware of anger and I make decisions to protect myself from violence
Enduring the pain of observing parental divorce during childhood	This has made me distrustful of relationships and I am guarded in my decisions about love
Experiencing neglect or abuse by my parents while growing up	This has made me look for very secure relationships and I make decisions based on fear

The list goes on, and there are many life circumstances that may influence who you have become and the decisions you have made for yourself. Many of these circumstances may have different influences on the decisions you make in your life. The situation of *"growing up in a neighborhood with crime and violence"* may have made you *"more cautious"* or perhaps it caused you to become *"aggressive."* Much depends upon your defenses and responses, which we will explore in more detail in later chapters. Initially, let's identify life circumstances that have influenced the decisions that affect the story you have written for yourself.

1.b

1.b Influences Chart

Use following space to describe influences in your life to the best of your understanding:

Situation to age 18: ______________________

____

Influence: ______________________

____

____

Situation to age 18: ______________________

____

Influence: ______________________

____

____

1.b

Situation to age 18:

Influence:

Situation to age 18:

Influence:

Situation to age 18:

Influence:

Influencers

Influencers in your life to age 18 include the people that had an impact on who you became and decisions you made about yourself because of them. Influencers may involve close family members or extended family. They may include friendships or people in your life with whom you were close. They may be teachers, the neighborhood grocery store clerk, or anyone who impacted your life and the decisions you made about yourself. Following are examples of influencers:

People **who had an impact on me and what I observed that stood out to me**	**The** ***influence*** **this person had on my decisions about myself**
Mother – A hard worker, worked long hours, and did not engage in fun or enjoyment	I didn't want to be like this, so I chose work with limited hours and time for lots of fun
Father – Daily alcohol drinker who had many angry outbursts toward mother, me and family	I decided I didn't want to deal with a violent relationship, so I found a passive partner
Older brother – Drank and used drugs and got into legal trouble for crimes	I decided I liked alcohol but that I would not use drugs and become like him
Joey the bully in elementary school – said mean things to me and called me fat	I decided that I was not pretty and that I was overweight
8th grade English teacher – told me I was a good student and a good writer	I decided that I was good at writing and always did well on writing assignments
Age 14 – first boyfriend Carl – lasted two months and then he dated my girlfriend	I decided that I didn't trust friends and wasn't worthy of love from an exclusive partner
Age 18 – First boss fired me for being late on three days	I decided I was not a very good employee

Notice that the decisions that were made in the examples could have been very different. For example, with the first influencer (*"Mother – a hard worker..."*), a person may have decided that hard work was a value and made a decision that working hard was the only way to be successful in life. In the second example (*"Father – angry alcoholic..."*), a person may have decided that they would never marry someone like their father but unconsciously selected someone that was just like him.

1.c

We are all so very different in how we respond to life situations. The decisions we make are significant to the development of our belief systems. (Belief systems will be explored in Chapters 4, 5, and 6.)

1.c Influencers Chart

Identify some of the influencers to age 18 in your life. I suggest starting with your mother and father even if you never met them. What decisions did you make about yourself?

Person: ____________________

Influence: ____________________

Person: ____________________

Influence: ____________________

Person: ____________________

Influence: ____________________

1.c

Person: ______________________________

Influence: ______________________________

____

____

Person: ______________________________

Influence: ______________________________

____

____

Person: ______________________________

Influence: ______________________________

____

____

Re-decisions

In 1965, Mary and Robert Goulding began using interventions called "*Redecision Therapy*" (Lennox, 1997), which identified decisions we make as adults that are based upon the messages we hear from our parents and caregivers. The decisions we make about our lives are often based upon what we have heard and incorporated into our beliefs about ourselves. Consider the impact of messages we receive from our primary caregivers when we are children.

I suggest that you begin your list of influencers (Exercise 1.c) with your parents even if you did not know them or grow up with them. The message of an absent parent can be just as influential as the verbal messages we receive from parents. When you were a small child, you looked up to your parents for information about yourself and about the world around you. There was a tremendous imbalance of power of the adults in your life in contrast with you as a small, growing, and developing child.

The influence of your primary caregivers is significant, and their messages are powerful. Everything you heard them tell you about yourself was processed by your brain whether you believed what they said was true or not. Your brain as a small child is much like a computer gathering data and it does not screen for false statements. Over time, we learn to filter for false statements; however, the incoming information continues to challenge our self-perception. The messages are persuasive and become a part of our identity. Unfortunately, the negative messages can create a very dark false narrative about self.

Now as you look at the canvas, you can start to see more. The backdrop of the canvas (backdrop is represented by the lower mountains) may include more things that you did not have a choice about. Many aspects of your life represented by the mountains may have also influenced who you have become. The things we experience in life, whether they were out of our control or within our control, potentially have an impact on who we become and the ideas we have about ourselves.

Looking at the canvas now, the choices you have made throughout your life may be more apparent. You may begin to see that ***influences*** and ***influencers*** have driven some of your choices and life decisions. The trees in the preceding canvas may represent the choices you made that were influenced by experiences or people.

As you are beginning your journey into change, you have started to identify your personal decisions that may not match what you really want for yourself. Your initial decision, however, to want to change and embark on a transformational process is important. Your decision will require a willingness. Your willingness may originate from your experience of emotional pain.

It may be that you just want more for yourself. Your willingness may stem from being tired of the choices you have made. What do you think about your canvas? Is it driving the story you want for yourself or are you not satisfied with the picture you are painting based upon your decisions? Do you want to navigate a different story than the one you have been living? Let's explore further.

1.d

1.d Reflection

- In what ways have your influences and influencers changed your story or altered the direction of your canvas?

- If you could "redecide" your direction in life, what new picture would you want to paint for yourself?

- Do you have the willingness to begin a journey into a new and different path for yourself?

Chapter 2

Cognitive Dissonance

What Are You Doing That Does Not Match What You Value?

"Open the window of your mind. Allow the fresh air, new lights, and new truths to enter."

— Amit Ray, Walking the Path of Compassion

Amit Ray reminds us of how open-mindedness is crucial to developing new awareness and insight. As we engage in self-examination, there is the potential to see truth from a new perspective. Self-reflection provides us with the ability to identify the discomfort that comes from not living our values.

Consider the migration of many bird species. Their need for food and comfortable weather drives their journey thousands of miles. Are you willing to go the distance? Your journey is just beginning.

The introductory quote by Amit Ray reflects the need to open the *"window of your mind,"* to allow for new ideas to enter. The path of change begins with an open-minded attitude. The ability to see things from a new perspective begins with a desire to move beyond the barriers of fear of change. New truths will emerge with the willingness to be open. This chapter will explore cognitive dissonance, or internal conflict that leads to change.

Cognitive Dissonance

Prior to a decision about change, a person usually experiences some type of internalized motivational crisis. The conflict a person may feel is often reflective of a life circumstance that does not match an individual's goal or vision of their desired life. This type of discomfort often stems from thoughts or actions that are inconsistent with what they believe. Oftentimes personal goals will send a "red flag" to the recipient and provide cause for either denial or "making a decision" to change. This is called **cognitive dissonance.**

Festinger (1957) identified the theory of **cognitive dissonance** as a condition people experience where there is lack of consistency between attitude and behaviors, resulting in a feeling of disharmony. This causes an internalized conflict for a person. ***Cognitive dissonance indicates that the way you are living your life is not congruent with what you want, need, or value.*** Feeling the internal tension of dissonance is a signal for you to consider that you need to begin painting a new picture for yourself. Feeling internal conflict is an indicator that it is time to get help to find a new perspective.

Some examples of the life circumstances that do not match a person's goal or vision are:

Life Circumstance	Does not match	Individual's Goal or Vision for Themselves
A person is engaged in unhealthy relationships (romantic or friendships)	Does not match	Vision is for a fulfilling, happy life with loved ones and friends
A person finds that they are lacking close and valuable friendships	Does not match	Vision is for friendships of different levels that provide support and comfort
A person is unable to separate self from unhealthy family dynamics	Does not match	Vision is to establish close and healthy relationships with family members
A person is unable to control anger or negativity toward those close to them	Does not match	Desire is to have fulfilling close relationships and to feel supported
A person is in a work environment that is unsupportive and unrewarding	Does not match	Desire is to feel content, happy, and a sense of purpose from career and work
A person finds dissatisfaction with primary life partner (or marriage)	Does not match	Vision is to be happy with a "soulmate-life-partner" that is mutually rewarding
A person feels ineffective as a parent and resorts to conflict in the home	Does not match	Goal is to be an effective and trusting parent to all children
A person is using drugs or alcohol excessively to change how they feel	Does not match	Goal is to live a drug-free lifestyle that supports personal growth

These are only a few examples of *cognitive dissonance,* when the way you are living your life does not match your goals, desires, or vision. You may have your own unique ways that you feel conflict with circumstances in your life that do not match what you really want for yourself.

You may only have a few life circumstances with which you are unhappy, or you may find many areas of your life that are not satisfying. It is up to you to be thorough with your inventory of things and situations that conflict with what you would like for your life to look like. This is the beginning of determining what you would like to change about your life that is at odds with what you are doing.

2.a

2.a Cognitive Dissonance Chart

Complete your personalized examples of your cognitive dissonance:

Life Circumstance:

(does not match) My Goal or Vision:

Life Circumstance:

(does not match) My Goal or Vision:

Life Circumstance:

(does not match) My Goal or Vision:

Life Circumstance: ______________________________

____

(does not match) My Goal or Vision: ______________________________

____

____

Life Circumstance: ______________________________

____

(does not match) My Goal or Vision: ______________________________

____

____

2.a

You may only have a few life circumstances with which you are unhappy, or you may find many areas of your life that are not satisfying. It is up to you to be thorough with your inventory of things and situations that conflict with what you would like for your life to look like. This is the beginning of determining what you would like to change about your life that contrasts with what you are doing.

Change, Desire, and Emotional Pain

Change begins with a desire. The desire may be fueled by emotional pain. You may find yourself content with the status quo of your life if there is minimal pain or discomfort caused by cognitive dissonance. It does not need to get to a point of devastation or insurmountable emotional suffering for you to change.

But when the pain of any situation becomes great enough, there is usually motivation to make some changes. You can look at your personal list of ***cognitive dissonance*** and make the decision that you want your life to be in greater alignment with your values. You can make the decision that your canvas is not portraying the life you really want for yourself.

Remember that you are at a crossroads. At any moment you can make the decision to alter the narrative of your life from *complacency and dissatisfaction* to ***fulfillment and purpose***. Ask yourself what a more purposeful life would look like and what you need to put on your canvas to create the picture you want. What contradictions are you seeing?

Barriers to Change

There are many barriers to change that can be within your conscious awareness. Future chapters will deal with unconscious barriers that block you from living a better and more satisfying life. Let's look at some of the things that may be preventing you from resolving the cognitive dissonance you are experiencing.

Barriers to change may include:

- *not wanting to leave the familiar or comfort zone*
- *fear of change*
- *fear associated with the uncertainty of the outcomes of change*
- *fear of failure or making mistakes*
- *fear of risk*
- *Anxiety*
- *Depression*
- *other factors*

Familiarity

Possibly the things that are familiar to you provide you with a false sense of safety. Avoiding the *risk* of trying something new can be a barrier. Risk can be seen as problematic when it represents reckless or dangerous behavior. But the risk of trying something new could have fewer consequences. The risk of doing something that coincides with your values and what is important to you is not the same as the risk of driving carelessly down the freeway or engaging in an addictive behavior.

Risk as it applies to investments is a matter of degree. The higher the level of risk on an investment, the higher the potential for larger returns on your investment. There is also a high potential for loss with greater risk.

My suggestion for change is not about high-level risk. I suggest that taking steps toward something new and different in your life will dislodge you from the status quo or comfortable state of a "rut." The rate of return is likely to be something greater than the pain of staying the same.

Helen Keller was a remarkable woman who lost her ability to see and hear as an infant. She became an author and advocate for disability rights. She said, "*Life is either a daring adventure or nothing. To keep our faces toward change and behave like free spirits in the presence of fate is strength undefeatable*" (Keller, 1940, pp. 50-51).

Helen Keller would certainly know about taking risks and seeing life as a daring adventure. She also stated that having a sense of security is a superstition. The fantasy of feeling safe and secure by not taking personal risks to try something new is not necessarily preventing danger, according to Ms. Keller. And she lived her life accordingly. I would agree that an illusion of safety can block our ability to live in freedom from our self-imposed barriers.

The root of the word "*familiarity*" is family. Perhaps you continue to do something that does not fit what you really want or value for yourself because you are doing what your family has always done. An illustrative example is of a woman I worked with in psychotherapy:

> *A 25-year-old adult woman wanted to break free of the family tradition of becoming a teacher. She did not like the idea of teaching or working with children. This did not match what she really wanted for herself. However, her mother and grandmother were teachers, and they applauded her sister for taking the same path. Her mother encouraged her throughout her life to become a teacher.*
>
> *For her, law enforcement was appealing, and she found it difficult to break free of the family rules and traditions. She felt that it would be a betrayal to her family to do what her heart spoke to her to do for her career. She started her college education with the goal of obtaining a teaching credential, then began to re-evaluate her decision. In therapy, she was able to identify this barrier and eventually break free.*
>
> *She changed course in college and began studying criminal law. She is now in law enforcement, and she loves doing the work of a police officer. Her barrier was family tradition. Breaking free of tradition to embark on a different career path meant living outside the lines of self-imposed parameters she saw as barriers.*

Breaking free meant honoring her true desires and living her values. Breaking free meant living in possibility rather than in the confines of the "*familiar or family zone*." She now is living her life according to her values. She is happy and she is free.

Fear

There are so many different fears that may be part of a barrier for change. It is important for you to determine the type of fear that may be preventing you from stepping outside of your comfort zone. Fear of change is something that is a part of the human experience. Most of us appreciate routines and this gives us a false sense of being in control. Remember that control is an illusion, as we are never really in control. But routines can make a person believe that their life is in order and predictable. Predictability, unfortunately, does not equal control and does not provide for the safety that is being sought.

> *"The rate of return is likely to be something greater than the pain of staying the same."*

The most extreme fear of any situation can be described as a "*phobia*." There is a name for the phobic response to fear of change called "*Metathesiophobia*." This very extreme form of fear of change will cause physiological responses and possibly panic attacks. This is an irrational response to the idea of change. It is a phobia seen in some anxiety disorders. Most of you who are reading this book do not have *Metathesiophobia*, which can be helped through therapy and desensitization techniques. However, the resistance to change is present for most people.

The issues underlying the fear of change are very personal to the individual. Some people fear failure or making mistakes and therefore do not want to risk error in their decision to change. A perfectionistic person may want to avoid mistakes, and this can be a deterrent to change or making choices that allow for a freedom of choice. Perfectionism often leads to procrastination in making decisions, which goes against the ability to make choices.

If the fear of mistakes and failure is underlying your fear of change, it is time for a new mindset so that you can experience the *freedom* of "***possibility***." Possibility allows for infinite options and choices that are potentials for life improvement. Possibility opens the door to an array of new beginnings.

"*Fear of unknown outcomes*" can also be a barrier for change. The comfort of knowing what to expect in your actions can be a reason for resistance to change. It is true that you cannot predict the outcome of any new adventure, but to maintain the safety of not making any new choices is more likely to cause lack of satisfaction in life. One definition of courage is the ability to practice faith in the face of fear. Practice faith in yourself or a Higher Source in the face of your fear of change and uncertainty.

Anxiety

Anxiety is associated with excessive worry and fear about the future. In some of the examples related to phobia of change (*Metathesiophobia*), anxiety is at the core of the barrier to change. Any person with an anxiety disorder is prone to being fearful of venturing out or having new experiences because of associated anxiety and worry. The decision to not engage in anything new or different may be stemming from an underlying anxiety disorder.

Despite the source of your decision to not change, you are not living your life according to what is most important to you. The barrier you possess to making changes in your life is a part of your cognitive dissonance. Consider what you are doing versus what you really value.

Depression

Depression is known to cause a *lack of motivation*, which is one of the criteria for the diagnosis. Lack of energy and motivation to make changes in your life may stem from depression. If you know that you have depression, you may have been resistant to change due to lack of motivation for change. But the condition itself is a barrier. If you are depressed, it is important to seek outside help so that you can find relief through therapy and/or medication.

Barriers

Barriers are the things that will potentially block you from progressing or advancing your desire to change. Most people internalize ideas or thoughts that are potential blockages to reaching a goal or a desired outcome. Some of the barriers may be real. The aforementioned fears are examples of common barriers. Some barriers may be valid and reality-based. An example of a valid barrier would be that of a person who is very short and uncoordinated who has a desire to become a professional volleyball player. This barrier is not perceived but is a reality. The likelihood of this person becoming a professional volleyball player is slim.

Other barriers may not be valid or reality-based. For example, a person perceives themself as unlovable and sees this as a barrier to finding a fulfilling relationship. This is a perceived reality or a ***false reality*** that poses a barrier to healthy relationships.

Consider a self-imposed barrier of believing, "*I'm not good at relationships.*" There is a strong likelihood that you will not be good at relationships with this negative self-fulfilling prophesy looming over you. Fear of change or not wanting to leave familiarity or your comfort zone is a common irrational barrier to change. When this presents as conflict or tension in what you really want for yourself, it is an example of *cognitive dissonance.*

Following are some examples of barriers to change and how they might manifest:

Barrier to Change	**Specific Barrier**
Fear of change	"I want to discontinue a friendship that has been draining and non-reciprocal. I fear this change."
Depression	"I want to become more active and work out more and my depression causes a loss of motivation."
Not wanting to leave my comfort zone	"I want to leave a job that is no longer satisfying, but I don't want to leave what I am familiar with."
Fear of failure or making mistakes	"I want to go to school for my life dream of becoming a nurse, but I fear I won't get A's or will fail classes."
Fear of uncertainty of outcomes of change	"I want to start dating again but I am so afraid I will meet the wrong person and get hurt so I stay safe."
Anxiety	"I want to go out with my friends, but I am afraid I will have a panic attack, or just wish I was home instead."
Fear of risk (low, non-reckless risk)	"A friend invited me to travel to a resort in Mexico with her, but I fear the risk of leaving my country."

2.b Barriers to Change Chart

Now is your opportunity to make your list of barriers. You may only identify a few or you may identify with barriers in every category and more *(fear of change, depression, leaving comfort zone, fear of failure, fear of change, anxiety or fear of risk)*:

2.b

Barrier to Change (select from above categories):

My Specific Barrier to Change:

Barrier to Change:

My Specific Barrier to Change:

Barrier to Change:

My Specific Barrier to Change:

Barrier to Change: ______________________________

____

My Specific Barrier to Change: ______________________________

____

____

Barrier to Change: ______________________________

____

My Specific Barrier to Change: ______________________________

____

____

Barrier to Change: ______________________________

____

My Specific Barrier to Change: ______________________________

____

____

Discontent

I want to mention that in some situations a person may feel discontent with one's life. Discontent may present as an extreme dissatisfaction with life or with specific aspects of one's life. It may be that a person is discontent with their employment, their marriage or partner, or extended family members. If malcontent is from one area of a person's life, it can be worked on. For example, where there is discontent with employment, there is the option of changing jobs. Therapy is also an option for working through these issues.

When there is discontent in a relationship or a marriage, therapy can assist in resolving or dissolving the problem. I have worked with individuals who struggle with members of their extended family who bring pain and distress and dissatisfaction with family member relationships. This is resolvable.

Overall discontent with one's life can stem from a state of depression. When a person has an overwhelming feeling of hopelessness and an inability to see anything positive about life, there is a chance that depression is driving discontent. It is important to realize that the feeling of hopelessness, which is a symptom of depression, is often a result of brain chemistry driving the feeling and emotion. A depressive episode can also be reactive where a *situation* is triggering feelings of hopelessness.

Discontent may also be coming from cognitive dissonance. Feelings of discontent with life often emerge when aspects of one's life do not match what their values or goals are, as described in the previous section of cognitive dissonance. Discontent has the potential to immerse a person in a sea of negativity. The result is often to "*give up*" or not try to change one's life. The resulting attitude of "*why bother trying*" can create a sense of self-imposed hopelessness.

A friend of mine was speaking to how much he hated change. Then he joked by saying, "*The only thing I hate more than change is when everything stays the same.*" Although this was funny at the time I heard it, I also appreciated that the joke reflected the pervasive discontent with life that many people experience.

It is important to personally assess your level of negativity and discontent with life. Do you maintain an attitude of wanting to "*give up*?" Do you hear negative self-talk such as, "*Why bother trying*," or other narratives that provide you with an excuse to not try painting a better picture for yourself?

Keep in mind that if you are the artist creating your canvas, you can change the course of your life at any time. If you are the primary author of the story of your life, you can decide to write a new chapter.

2.c Negativity & Willingness Scales

Rate yourself on the following negativity scale. On a scale of zero to ten, where would you rate yourself in terms of your negative outlook on life? Place a dot on the negativity scale to self-assess your negativity:

0---1---2---3---4---5---6---7---8---9---10

(Low negativity) (High negativity)

Now let's rate your willingness to change. How willing are you to break free of the barriers and negativity that may be impeding your ability to live outside the box? How willing are you to move beyond the confines of your familiar and safe zone into the realm of possibility? Does your dissatisfaction with aspects of your life motivate you to want more? Or are you stuck in your old ways and former patterns that no longer serve you? Do you have a desire to change and are you willing to put forth the effort? Rate yourself in willingness for change by putting a dot on the following willingness scale:

0---1---2---3---4---5---6---7---8---9---10

(Low willingness) (High willingness)

2.c

If you have found yourself above a 5 on the negativity scale: It may help to work on altering your attitude and mindset. Your negative narratives or private conversations of discontent may be stemming from a belief system that is reflecting mistaken beliefs about yourself, others, or the world around you. **In the following space, journal about your negative narratives that block you from change:**

If you have rated yourself below a 5 on the willingness scale: It may help to work on altering your mindset and personal narratives. In the space below, journal on your willingness or lack of willingness to put forth the effort toward change.

2.c

If you are low on the negativity scale and high also on the willingness scale: There is greater hope for change. Your willingness is essential for new and different things to happen in the realm of possibility and you more than likely have a more positive perspective on the ability to change. In the space below journal about how your negativity and willingness encourage or block you from reaching goals.

Do you have a desire to change and are you willing to put forth the effort? This will make a difference in the outcome of your efforts to change course. Remember that you are the master artist in charge of your canvas. You are the author of your novel.

Sometimes the *internalized false narratives* that block us from change stem from an internalized reality that is based on *mistaken beliefs*. The belief system can be a powerful influence over our ability to break free from distorted realities. The following chapter will introduce you to cognitions followed by a chapter on belief systems and the power they have over your life.

2.d Reflection

- What barriers to change do you most identify with (familiarity, fear, depression, anxiety or others)?

- Do you feel that you are at a crossroad between making a change and staying the same regarding something in your life? If so, write about that.

2.d

- Write a few sentences about your willingness to move from complacency to change:

____

____

____

____

____

____

____

____

Chapter 3

Cognitions and Perceptions

Thinking, Perceptions, Learning and Understanding

"I think; therefore, I am"

— *Descartes, Discourse on Method*

Our human ability to have conscious thought separates us from the rest of the animal kingdom. Creative thinking can be transformational and can be the bridge that brings dreams to reality. Negative thoughts can affect perspective and be the dark cloud of misperception that looms over your life.

Whether you see your thinking as a gift or a curse, it is important to acknowledge the power that thoughts have over your daily decisions. Your thoughts are actively painting your canvas and writing the next page of your story. How will you choose to write the next page of your story? How will you choose to paint your canvas today?

The seventeenth century French Philosopher René Descartes made this chapter's opening statement in certainty, and it reflected his knowledge of human existence. He suggested that our conscious thought is the evidence we have of our existence. The depth of this philosophy will not be discussed in this book; however, there is significance in the fact that our ability to think provides us with an array of perceptions and cognitive processes.

Cognitions

Cognitions refer to the multiple mental processes that include thinking, perceptions, learning, and understanding. The outer portion of the brain, or the gray matter that has folds and "*convolutional neural networks*," is the part of the human brain that is different from other animals due to being more highly advanced.

The outer portion of the brain in humans is sometimes referred to as the evolved portion of the brain where our ability to think, reason, and make decisions is centered. "*Executive function*" is a set of skills that involves complex processes and allows for abstract thinking. It is called the executive functioning portion of the brain because it is involved with processing information such as memory, thinking, and self-control throughout your day.

Executive function is the management system within the brain. This part of the brain is packed with *neurons*, or brain cells that work overtime to provide an individual with the ability to gain perspective about any situation at hand. (The brain will be discussed in further detail in Chapter 8 of this book.)

The frontal lobe is a part of the outer portion of the brain which contains the executive functioning or higher-level thought processes. Your thoughts are constantly at work. Your brain is constantly at work. This process is perpetual and does not stop. Your thoughts are also called your "cognitions."

Cognitive Behavioral Therapy

Cognitive behavioral therapy (CBT) is the primary therapeutic orientation that I use throughout this book. CBT was developed by Dr. Aaron Beck (1976) with roots in behavior and cognitive theories. CBT incorporates behavioral interventions as well as a focus on maladaptive thinking patterns that underly emotions (Beck, J., 2011).

Beck identified that a person's thought processes were often erroneous and were driven by mistaken beliefs. In cognitive behavioral therapy, automatic thoughts or private conversations can help to identify beliefs that are otherwise difficult to access.

One important concept in understanding CBT is the interconnectedness of thoughts, emotions, and behaviors (Early & Grady, 2017). In the following ABC model, CBT is demonstrated through three major components of an individual: (a) Affect/Emotion, (b) Behaviors, and (c) Cognitions.

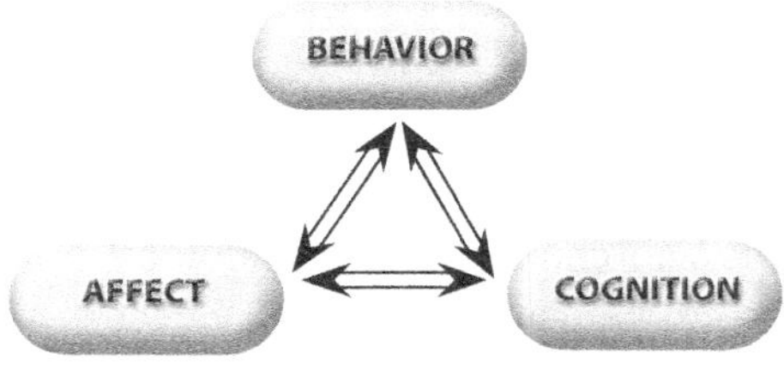

Thoughts (or cognitions), feelings (or affect), and behaviors are very much interconnected and are constantly influencing one another. Another model for demonstrating the interconnectedness of thoughts, feelings, and behavior that I like to use includes physiology:

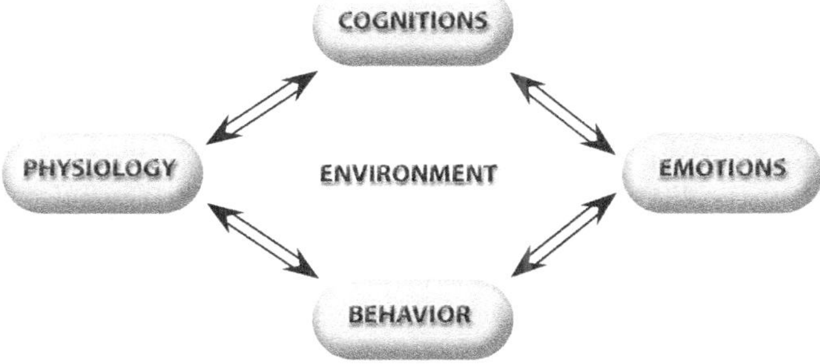

Thoughts, Emotions, Behavior, and Physiology

Thoughts, emotions, behaviors, and physiology are constantly interacting and affecting one another within the context of a person's environment. They are like the four wheels of a car, and when all four wheels are working well, the car will drive smoothly.

If one wheel breaks or one tire goes flat, however, it will affect the whole car's ability to run. This is true for your thoughts, emotions, behaviors, and physiology. If your thinking becomes negative, it will affect your behavior, emotions, and physiology. If your emotions are heavy and sad, the other three wheels of your car will be affected. On the other hand, you can change one of the four wheels of your car, and the whole vehicle can be affected in a positive way.

Let's say you are feeling depressed, and your doctor provides you with an antidepressant. The prescription provides you with a change in your physiology and brain chemistry. This affects your thinking in a positive way, your emotions are lifted, and your behavior may change in that you now have more energy and motivation to become more active.

Or possibly you decide to change a behavior and begin going to the gym for an hour every day of the week. This will change your physiology in that you will be releasing more endorphins (*"feel good"* neurotransmitters). Because you feel elevated, you are likely to have more energy all day long. This is also likely to alter your thinking in a more positive way. You can alter all four wheels of your car by changing any one of the four wheels.

Cognitive behavioral work incorporates changing your cognitions, or the way you think about things. Changing your thinking and your behaviors will allow for your perceptions to change and your mood will shift to a more positive state. This will also alter your physiology. An analogy would be going to a tire store and changing two of the tires that are underperforming. Your car will ride much smoother.

Environment

Environment in this context is defined as where you are physically at any given moment (at work, at home, at the beach, etc.). Environment also includes the people that are present. So, you may be at your place of employment and your environment consists of your workplace with three coworkers present. Consider how different you would feel if you were at the beach with a good friend. Your environment influences your thoughts, feelings, behavior, and physiology.

It is important to consider that your environment at any given moment can affect all four wheels of your car. Imagine yourself in a place that you consider to be your "*safe place*." Your safe place is wherever you feel calm, relaxed, and free of judgment, fear, and anxiety. Your safe place may be on a mountaintop, on a beach, or in a wooded area.

> *"Your thoughts, feelings, and physiology will align to the environment you are experiencing."*

Your safe place may also include a place with your dog or cat. Animals will often represent a safe environment because they are so unconditional and loving. Or your safe place may include a parent, grandparent, child, or friend. Any people or animals in your safe place should bring you a sense of serenity, peace, and nonjudgment. (Establishing your defined "*safe place*" will be covered again in Chapter 12 on The Brain, Mind/Body Attunement, and Energy-Shifting Solutions.)

When your environment is safe, you are likely to feel a greater sense of calm and peace reflected in the four wheels of your car. Your thoughts, feelings, behaviors, and physiology will align in direct proportion to the environment you are experiencing. When your environment is in a stressful place with difficult people, your thoughts are more than likely to be laden with worry or fear. Emotions are likely to reflect the anxiety-producing emotions. Your physiology will be tense. Your behaviors will align with the stressors at hand.

Ask yourself which of the four wheels of your car are most vulnerable. Are your thoughts, feelings, behaviors or physiology more likely to be the flat tire that has your car malfunctioning? You may also want to ask yourself what environments tend to change you in an affirming or defeatist way. What people and places affect you?

Your thoughts are often reflecting your ***belief system***. If you have excessively critical thoughts about yourself or the world around you, your belief system is often behind these thoughts. The next chapters will look at belief systems and how they are related to negative thoughts. The formulation of your perceptions and ***maladaptive core beliefs*** will also be discussed.

3.a Reflection

3.a

- Which of the four wheels of your car are most vulnerable? Thoughts, feelings, behaviors, or physiology?

- Are there people or places in your environment that trigger you into emotional distress or negative thinking?

- Are there any behavior changes that you can make (exercise, healthy food choices, staying away from negative influences) that can help the four wheels of your car to run smoother?

Chapter 4

Belief Systems

That Which I Believe About Myself, I Will Manifest

"If our thinking is bogged down by distorted symbolic meanings, illogical reasoning and erroneous interpretations,we become, in truth, blind and deaf."

— *Aaron T. Beck, Love is Never Enough*

The unconscious process of establishing beliefs is complex and is derived from many aspects of our life experiences as well as our perceptions of those events. We have the potential to distort or misinterpret situations and this can affect our present-day response to events that we encounter. In contrast, other animals with which we share the planet have a much more simplistic experience.

They are not "bogged down" by distorted perceptions and erroneous interpretations. Consider the potential of simplifying your life through mindfully seeing and hearing with intention. Embrace the present moment. Attune yourself to the truth. What can you learn from other animals?

In the introductory quote, Dr. Beck speaks to how we can find ourselves in a world of illusions because of our misperceptions. We are *"blind and deaf"* when we do not see the truth or hear what is being said due to distorted narratives. These false narratives come from our mistaken core beliefs. This chapter will introduce you to your belief system and will begin to provide an understanding of how we develop our core beliefs. (Chapters 5 and 6 will also cover aspects about your personal beliefs.) This topic is significant to understanding what is often navigating our lives and what often colors our perspective about people, situations, and the world around us.

Your ***beliefs***, or the things that you believe to be true about yourself, are things that you will demonstrate to the world through your decisions, actions, and behaviors. For example, if you have a belief about being a good cook, you will create opportunities to receive validation. You will likely work hard at being a good cook and demonstrate your talent.

> *If you believe you are a good cook, you will unconsciously attempt to prove it to the world. You will usually always cook good food about which people compliment you. People will express content with your cooking and ask for recipes. You have proven to the outside world what you believe to be true about yourself. This is followed by validation of your belief that comes from others.*

The concept of being a good cook is a belief that you have within your conscious awareness. *Is it true or is it just an idea that you have about yourself?* Do you have a natural affinity for cooking, or do you just believe it is true? We ***manifest*** that which we believe to be true about ourselves. As human beings, we can create and manifest what we believe to be true. Then through our actions, we receive validation from others that it is true. Being a good cook is a positive and conscious belief.

Imagine, however, if you have negative unconscious beliefs about yourself. What decisions and actions might you take to get validation from those mistaken beliefs?

All of us have ***conscious*** beliefs and ***unconscious*** beliefs about ourselves. We have beliefs that we are consciously aware of and beliefs that run our decisions and actions at an unconscious level. Some of these beliefs are valid and some are inaccurate or mistaken beliefs. Let's start by talking about how your internalized belief system was formed.

Your Internalized Belief System

Your internalized belief system began when you were born. When you began interacting with the world around you, your belief system was beginning to formulate. From the time that you were first communicated to by your caregivers, you began to establish beliefs about yourself and the world around you. Your initial communication with the world was likely a cry as an infant, and you were either responded to or not.

Your communication in the form of a cry most likely was a request to be held, comforted, or fed, or was an expression of a basic need. Basic needs for food, comfort, safety, and love continue to be significant to our well-being throughout our lifetime. Our beliefs begin to formulate from our initial communication with the world. Access to those sometimes-hidden beliefs can be found through our thoughts or *cognitions*. Let's first begin to visualize this concept.

Consider whether a baby can have positive or negative thoughts at the time of birth. There is evidence from research on brain development that suggests that a developing fetus has experiences in utero that may involve stress, emotions, or trauma that the mother has experienced. This is all recorded in the brain, although we cannot retrieve that information consciously. But for the most part, I think we can all agree that a newborn does not yet have negative thoughts or beliefs about themselves and the world around them.

As stated earlier, however, from the first time this infant interacts with the world around them, they will begin to formulate ideas about themselves, others, and the world. This infant cries as a request to be held, comforted, fed, or to relieve any discomfort they may be feeling. The newborn will get responded to or neglected and through these early interactions with the primary caregivers, they will begin to establish beliefs about themselves and their world. Are they safe? Are they loved?

The initial relationship between a child and parent is significant to how we relate to who we are in the world and what type of a world it is. This initial or primary relationship may be with just one parent, a grandparent, or an adoptive parent. This relationship is significant to the beginning of establishing core beliefs.

This initial relationship is also where the parent/child bond takes place and where *attachment* begins to form. (Attachment will be discussed further in Chapter 7 of this book.) An individual's attachment may be secure or insecure. The three *insecure attachment styles* are avoidant, ambivalent, and disorganized. All attachment styles may also contribute to a person's core beliefs about themselves and the world.

Imagine if an infant is born to parents that are neglectful or abusive in the first year. The beliefs that will begin to formulate will most likely reflect that they are not loved or not important. Their beliefs about the world will probably reflect that the world is not a safe place.

From a biological standpoint, much will depend upon the baby's neurochemistry and constitution. From an environmental standpoint, *cognition* (or thoughts) will play a huge role in the resulting perspective of the situations they experience. Cognitions involve what they understand to be happening and their perception of those events. Two people may experience the same situation and have very different perceptions of that event.

Cognitions

Recall from Chapter 3 that cognitions refer to multiple mental processes including thinking, perceptions, learning, and understanding. Learning is one aspect of cognition, as our brain is making connections from what we see and hear in the external world, and this becomes our thoughts or perspectives.

A newborn begins the process of learning about themselves and the world around them through what they experience. This continues throughout our lifetime. We see, hear, and experience life circumstances. Then we translate what we see and experience into our thoughts and perceptions of those situations.

Formulation of Memory

All your *preverbal communication* and verbal communication is stored as memory in your brain. You are not able to access *preverbal memory*. Preverbal memory comes to you in sensations, feelings, or fragmented images, but not as a retrievable memory. Preverbal memory is also sometimes referred to as somatic memory, or memory we carry in our body. Trauma is also often written into somatic memory. Most people can only access memory that is associated with words. Most people can access memory from the age of three, four, or five when vocabulary begins to form.

Your early childhood and lifetime experiences are all stored in your brain whether they are preverbal, connected to words, retrievable, somatic, or buried memories. These life experiences become transformed into your beliefs about yourself and the world around you.

Let's look again at the newborn baby interacting with the world around them. Through the process of growth and development, this individual is gradually developing words and language to describe their experience. Memory is stored in words, and this is retrievable unless the process is interrupted. So as a person develops, they may respond to what people say and develop perceptions of what they say.

As a child begins to understand language, kind words or angry critical words can make a difference in how they perceive themselves. Also, the child's world begins to expand with extended family and eventually people outside of the family.

An Individual's Unique World

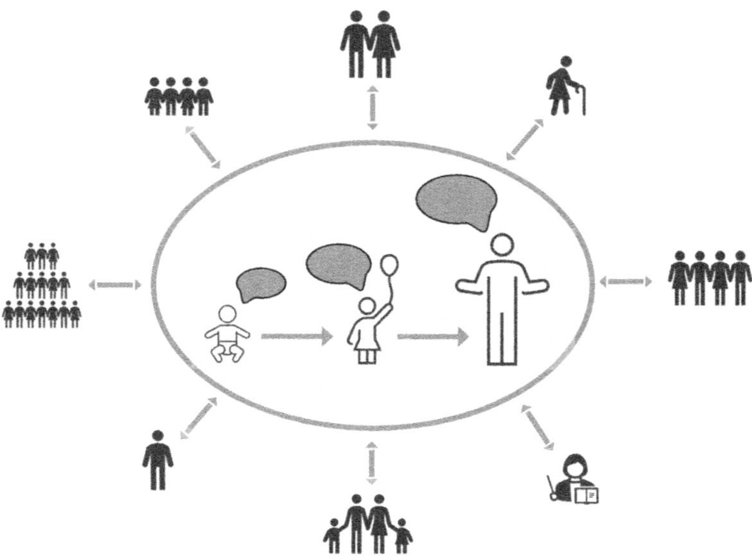

Every person has a unique perspective of the world. This is based upon interaction with the world around them, communication with the people they encounter, and experiences that may or may not be chosen by them. We really don't have much choice over our parents, natural disasters, our socioeconomics, our culture, or our overall environment that we are born into.

As we get older and mature into adulthood, we can choose our partners, friends, workplace environments, and love relationships. It is through the interaction with the world around us and our perception of those people and the events in our lives that we begin to develop a belief system about who we are in the world.

The preceding diagram indicates that there are many life experiences and many people who we interact with that have the potential to plant seeds of strength or negativity. Additionally, our *perception* of those situations, people, and events will also contribute to our understanding of who we are and what type of a world this is.

Internal Reality

There is a need for individuals to develop an understanding of their internal and external world. When a person grows up in a healthy environment where there is love, nurturing and caring, they develop a more accurate internal and external world view. When people grow up in chaotic environments or homes where there is violence, addiction, or other major distractions, they often lose touch with what is going on internally because they are focused on the unstable and unpredictable environment.

This can lead to lack of self-awareness and an inability to identify feelings and other internal cues. Ask yourself what types of life experiences you had during childhood, and what distractions you experienced. Were there relational problems, difficulties with parents, violence, addiction, or major illness that distracted you from being in touch with *your* internal self?

4.a Internal Reality Inventory

Consider how your life experiences shaped who you are and your beliefs about yourself. Were there relational problems or situations that distracted you from being in touch with your internal self?

Family problems: (e.g., parental conflict, violence, addiction, terminal illness, etc.)

Life experiences: (positive and negative)

Past emotional injuries:

Myths I was taught to believe:

4.a

Socioeconomic values:

Cultural and/or Religious values:

Bias, prejudice, insensitivity, or hostility I was taught:

____

____

____

____

Other internalized information:

____

____

____

____

Consider how family problems, life experiences, past emotional injuries, socioeconomics, and cultural and religious values have contributed to your unique world and how these things have created your internal reality. Were you taught myths, bias, prejudice, or hostility in your family of origin? Question yourself on how accurate your lifetime of information feels to you at this point in your life and whether your initial understanding of yourself and the world around you is based upon reality or false information. These early forms of information are the building blocks of your belief system.

Self-awareness contributes to healthier present-day relationships by helping to avoid personal emotional reactivity. It also helps to maintain a more objective perspective in interpersonal relationships. As you become aware of your motivation, your sensitivities, and the origin of your responses to your environment, you will also have greater freedom to be authentically who you are.

It is also important to become aware of the barriers that block you from your true motivations and desires for your life. As your barriers to being your authentic self are reduced, you are also more open to having relationships that are rewarding and reciprocal.

Your Personal Canvas and Story

As you begin to formulate your personal canvas of who you have become from life experiences, influences and influencers, and your perceptions of those significant events, you will see things that you like or do not like. You may see manifestations of your life experiences that have altered your personality or character. Perhaps you will identify things that you have tried to hide about yourself. Are there aspects of who you have become that you do not like?

Your *personal canvas and related story* are uniquely who you are and what you believe to be true about yourself. Can you decide to change the story that you have created about yourself? In Chapter 1, we discussed the "canvas" and the contribution you make to painting the picture of your choices in life. There are things already determined in the backdrop of your canvas (remember the mountains in the background). But there is also a lot of space for you to create your life based upon the choices that you make (remember the trees that stand in front of the mountain, in the foreground, that add to the scenery). Are there places in your *personal canvas* that you hope to change or alter as you visualize your life canvas?

If there are things that you don't like about yourself, can you begin to "re-imagine" yourself as a different person? Think about the power you possess over your life. Along with choices about what you want for yourself are actions that can enhance your ability to be emotionally present and attuned to others. This may mean removing the barriers that are preventing you from being your authentic self. These barriers block your freedom to love others, connect fully, and be mindfully present.

4.b Your Personal Canvas and Story

Are there aspects of who you have become as a result of your life experiences that you do not like?

- Are you able to "re-imagine" yourself? If so, what would you like to see?

Vulnerability. The ability to be vulnerable and the ability to take the risk of opening yourself up to others is something that is valuable in relationships. Vulnerability allows you to connect with others, learn about others, and allows for others to get to know you. Many people become afraid of being vulnerable due to life experiences where the trust from others has been violated. *Trust* is something that we have for others until we learn that others cannot be trusted. Many people learn to put walls up around trust and vulnerability because of their experiences in early relationships.

Our mothers, fathers, and primary relationships are powerful influences in our lifetime sense of safety. Your parents or caregivers have had the power to make you feel that the world is a safe or unsafe place. Parents can create a sense of trust or distrust in their children.

Think about the household you grew up in and whether it was stable and predictable, or if it was chaotic and unpredictable. Our sense of safety as children involves the stability and predictability of our environment. Did your primary caregivers provide you with a sense of safety and security? Think about the people who raised you and your feelings of safety and security as a child.

4.c Trust and Safety with My Primary Caregivers While Growing Up

In what ways did your primary caregivers shape or influence your sense of safety and trust and how does that affect your present-day relationships? Reflect and expand on this idea:

Complete the following sentences regarding your primary caregivers. **Regarding trust and safety:**

My mother (or primary caregiver) was...

My father (or primary caregiver) was...

Allowing yourself to be vulnerable involves the need to trust others. Past hurt and emotional injuries by people you have trusted can often lead to feeling "exposed" when vulnerable. Past emotional injuries may not necessarily have been committed by parents or caregivers. Think about others you have trusted that violated your sense of safety. If your caregivers were kind and loving and nurturing, you may have blindly trusted people who were abusive, aggressive, or hurtful.

Romantic relationships can also lead to feelings of violation of trust. Consider if you have had relationships where you were hurt. Or consider relationships where your trust was violated.

4.d

4.d Trust and Safety with Other Relationships

How have other relationships either restored your trust or violated your trust and how does that affect your present-day relationships?

___

___

___

___

___

___

___

◂ How easy or difficult is it to feel vulnerable considering these past relationship experiences?

Complete the following sentences by naming people who affected your sense of trust and safety.

(name) *affected my trust by ...*

affected my trust by ...

affected me by ...

4.d

affected me by ...

Whatever your unique situations were with people who violated your trust, it is important to know that you are safe today. Establishing safety in current day relationships allows for healing. Know that you are deserving of whole and healthy relationships despite what barriers you have built to block others. Know that being vulnerable is a gift and that your barriers and blockages are no longer serving you.

Today you can choose who to have in your life and who to allow access to that vulnerable part of you. You don't have to let everyone in, but it is important to allow some into your safe place. You are deserving and you are lovable despite what beliefs about yourself you may have formulated at a previous time.

What You Believe About Yourself

You may have begun to identify some mistaken beliefs that you have about yourself based upon earlier childhood experiences or later life hurtful experiences. Recall in the beginning of this chapter, it was identified that "*what you believe to be true about yourself, you will attempt to demonstrate to the world.*"

In the beginning of the chapter, it was mentioned that if you believe you are a good cook, you will attempt to prove it to the world and will probably always cook delicious food that provides you with validation through people complimenting you. We demonstrate to the world what we believe to be true about ourselves. Then we get ***validation*** from the environment that it is true.

- The good cook receives compliments on their cooking and requests for a recipe.
- The person who believes they are good at math receives high scores on math tests.
- The person who believes they are an excellent gardener will get compliments on their garden.

These examples are positive beliefs that get validated and reinforced by others. The negative beliefs we have can also get validated and reinforced by others. It may be difficult to conceptualize that we seek to validate our negative beliefs.

Consider a negative belief that is associated with "*not being lovable.*" If I believe I am unlovable, I will probably choose a partner who will eventually validate this. Or I may begin pushing my partner away or creating conflict in the relationship. I will manifest this belief by acting in ways where my partner will eventually leave me or treat me in a way that makes me feel unlovable.

It is frightening to consider how our beliefs may be driving behaviors that create our unhappiness. ***Our beliefs are powerful. They can be a strength, or they can be a strong source of misinformation***. Either a positive or a negative belief has power over how we see ourselves and what we manifest in our life. The first step toward change is identifying the negative mistaken beliefs that are affecting our ability to live and love freely.

Think about the people who you have placed trust in throughout your lifetime. Have they encouraged a belief about yourself as being lovable and safe? Or have they validated a belief about being unlovable and unsafe? Have you manifested barriers to love and relationships because you do not feel worthy of love? Or do you allow yourself to be vulnerable in your relationships? Who have you chosen to be in your life and what aspects of your worthiness do they validate? Or do they invalidate you?

These ongoing interactions between you and the world around you with caregivers, family, friends, and other influencers are the beginning of understanding your individual belief system and your unique perception of yourself. Some of your relationships have been more significant to manifesting thoughts and self-perception, such as those with parents, primary caregivers, and close family members.

As stated earlier in this chapter, your beliefs about yourself began to formulate in your earliest interactions with the outside world. At birth you began to formulate ideas about your ability to be loved, cared for, and nurtured. At the beginning of your life, you began to establish beliefs about your lovability, your worthiness, and your safety. Throughout your life you continued to establish beliefs about yourself. The following chapter will continue this discussion with respect to "***private logic,***" or our personal reality.

4.e Reflection

- What are some of your initial thoughts about your strengths that may be a part of what you believe to be true about yourself?

- What are some of your initial thoughts about your negative self-perceptions that may be a part of your belief system?

- What helps you to feel safe in your present-day relationships?

4.e

Chapter 5

Private Logic

My Unique Evaluation of Self

"Meanings are not determined by situations, but we determine ourselves by the meaning we give to situations."

— Alfred Adler, What Life Should Mean to You

As we walk through our journey in life, there are infinite opportunities to interpret our experiences. There are situations that we allow to define us through the meaning we give to those moments. These junctures along our path are but fleeting winks of time where we make decisions about ourselves that may have lifelong residual effects.

Engaging in the question of the accuracy of self-perception is a daunting task. It breaks down the walls of self-deception and promotes the ability to access the unvarnished truth of who we are. Are you willing to look deeper into the memories that have formed the meaning you have given to situations?

Dr. Alfred Adler was a colleague of Sigmund Freud, and he developed a theory that was associated with social relationships. His established theory about a person's individual reality was called "private logic." This *private logic* is an individual's unique evaluation of themselves that has been influenced by their interaction with the world around them (Adler, 2013; Ferguson, 2001). An individual will also evaluate the world around them and what they will need to do to make a place for themselves based upon this information.

Private logic may consist of false narratives about self and the world, and this is based upon the early interactions with primary social figures and the *perception* of those interactions. This chapter's introductory quote by Dr. Adler suggests that we determine who we are by our perception of life experiences and the meaning we give to them. Whether or not you have developed distorted realities based upon your perception of being loved and cared for, we all develop a private reality of self.

According to private logic, there are three questions we ask ourselves and continue to answer throughout our life. These questions are:

- Who am I?
- What kind of a world is this?
- What does someone like me need to do in a world like this in order to make a place for myself?

If you consider your life experiences from birth onward, the answers to these questions may have changed over time. As an infant, you may not have consciously asked yourself these questions; however, your needs were either met or unmet, which can give you a perspective on whether you are loved and cared for, and worthy of being nurtured by your caregivers.

Neglect or abuse at an early age can affect your self-perception as well as your perception of how safe the world is. If you were nurtured and cared for at an early age, and then neglected or criticized as a youth, your answers to these questions could change during that time. This will also affect what you feel you need to do to survive in the world, which is different for everyone.

- Do you need to isolate from others to avoid hurt and pain, or are you aggressive when you experience hurt?
- Do you need to be kind to others to establish trust?
- Do you need to intellectualize situations to avoid your feelings?
- Do you censor yourself and avoid speaking your truth?

These are just some of the responses you may have in consideration of who you are and what type of a world this is. Early life experiences can affect your beliefs about yourself and are the initial building blocks of your belief system. Later in life, your answers may change to these questions. Perhaps you had a nurturing childhood and then during adolescence or early adulthood experienced hurtful relationships. Every human life is unique. The experiences and perception of those experiences shape who we become.

Private Logic

Part 1: Who am I?

The answer to this question takes form over time, from birth onward. Consider the diagram a few pages back regarding the *individual's unique world*. Your interactions with the world around you and your interpretation of those events from your initial caregivers to siblings to peers in school will begin to provide you with an idea about your perception of who you are. Teachers, close relationships, romantic relationships, and later work experiences will continue to contribute to your concept of who you are.

The early years, however, are the most significant regarding the formulation of your belief system. Did you feel loved, cared for, and nurtured? Did you feel worthy of love just for who you were at face value? Was your love and nurturing inconsistent or disrupted by family chaos or violence? How did you internalize those early relationships?

Let's start with the question of your experience of your early years. Although preverbal memory is not retrievable for the most part, what information do you have of your life from birth to toddler years? What stories have you been told by parents, caregivers, grandparents, or siblings? Feeling a sense of secure attachment or disrupted attachment happens at these early vulnerable years. (Attachment will be discussed further in a Chapter 7.)

When you were a child, it is likely that you felt less powerful than your parents. What did you do with these feelings? What roles did you establish in your family because of the interactional patterns within your family system? Understand that family dynamics and interactional patterns are very influential.

"Although your retrievable memory may begin at age 4 or 5, your sense of self began at birth."

Parental influences are very significant to how you perceive yourself and are also a very dominant force in your early formulation of the answer to the question, "Who am I?" Although your retrievable memory may begin at age 4 or 5, your sense of self began at birth. What memories do you have of early childhood that may shed light on your earliest self-perception?

Keep in mind that you have trillions of memories from childhood onward. If you think of each moment of your life as a slide in a movie, there are many slides that you have blocked, many slides that you have buried, and some slides that you are able to retrieve. The ones that you can see today usually represent something significant to your life presently.

Sometimes those memories can represent a happy or fulfilling moment in time, and sometimes the memories can represent a hurtful or painful moment in time. Our brains often work for us to eliminate things that are too hurtful or traumatic. The ability to "*dissociate*" from extremely painful memories is an effort by our brains to block what would potentially feel unbearable. Although we are capable of blocking things that are too painful, there are many memories that stand out.

5.a My memories - birth to age 5

There are many memories that stand out throughout your lifetime that are significant to who you are today. In the space below, or in a journal, jot down a few of the memories that you have from birth to age 5. (***Warning: If you have had severe trauma during these years, skip this part and consider working on this section with a therapist.***)

My Age: Memory:

My Age: Memory:

My Age: Memory:

My Age: Memory:

My Age: Memory:

5.a

As you have identified memories to age 5, what thoughts have come up for you regarding your ideas about "self?" In what ways have these memories shaped your answer to the question, "who am I?" Reflect and journal in the space below.

You may have only a few memories that are retrievable, but they may be significant to your answer to the first question of, "Who am I?" In early childhood you may have developed an idea about yourself that is what we would refer to as *private logic*. This private logic may not be logical or rational, but it is meaningful in terms of your earliest self-perception.

Access to your ideas about "self" in early childhood can be found in the stories you have been told by family and friends. Sometimes these external accounts from others can influence how we see ourselves. Parents, caregivers, and siblings often have stories or memories of our childhood that may or may not reflect what you remember about childhood experiences.

Some of the stories you have heard may be from unreliable sources, and some may be from trustworthy sources. Some of the stories you heard about yourself are things that you remember also, or that you remember in a different way than others remember. The stories from others are only allegations and are pulled from other family member perceptions. If you don't agree with the stories of others about you, then the source of the stories may be unreliable.

This can also provide insight into how you perceive yourself. If you disagree with the narrative another family member has of you, then your concept of self probably doesn't match their story. You can confirm or deny their information about the idea of, "Who am I?"

Stories and memories from infancy to age 5

Some of the important stories told by family are stories related to your earliest infant years. Learning about relationship disruptions during the first few years of life may give clues regarding attachment and disrupted attachment. If you are adopted, finding out the date that your parents received you is significant to attachment. What do you know about your earliest years? Do you suspect that your primary caregivers were warm and nurturing, or is there suspicion that there was limited connection by your mother, father, or primary caregivers?

Present day difficulties in relationships can often be traced back to attachment bonds between you and your primary caregivers. The infant bonding process is significant to our ability to be in healthy adult relationships. Are your present-day relationship difficulties reflective of being overly distancing, fear of closeness, or fear of abandonment? Look into your relationship with your primary caregivers in the early years. The first year of life encourages a sense of trust or distrust with others.

Other stories you may hear about yourself are about early development, such as talking, walking, and your toddler stage. This can provide clues to whether your early year independence was welcomed or considered difficult to family members. Early development may have been encouraged and it may have been discouraged depending upon the dynamics of the relationships within the household. Early developmental tasks foster a sense of autonomy or dependence.

Stories from family about your early childhood to age 5 may be reflective of whether you were able to take initiative in your developmental tasks or if you felt guilt or shame for your curiosity and inquisitiveness. Were you active and mobile, and did you act when you were motivated to seek new experiences?

5.b Accounts from family members – birth to age 5

External accounts from family members may or may not reflect what you remember about childhood experiences. Take a few moments below or in your journal to jot down a few of the stories you heard from family members about you from birth to age 5. These stories are significant to your self-perception. Circle **Y/N** to confirm or deny each story:

Family Member: My Age:

Their story about me:

(Y/N)

Family Member: My Age:

Their story about me:

(Y/N)

Family Member: My Age:

Their story about me:

(Y/N)

Family Member: My Age:

Their story about me:

(Y/N)

Family Member: My Age:

Their story about me:

(Y/N)

5.b

What thoughts have emerged as a result of thinking about the stories told about you by other family members? The stories are significant to your self-perception and that is why it is important to confirm or deny the memories of others.

Reflect in the space below on how the stories of family have shaped your self-perception:

Stories and memories from ages 5 to 10

Your personal memories and family reports of you from ages 5 to 10 are the beginning of school experiences and increased interactions with peers. This period is likely when you were interacting with people other than your immediate family. Teachers may influence this period. Academic performance may play a part of whether you felt a sense of competence or incompetence.

What are your memories of this period, and what memories do family members provide you with to fill in the blanks of what you recall? Do you have memories that reflect success or failure in school, and do you recall feelings of ineffectiveness? This stage of development can produce a sense of inferiority. This is also a time where you may have gotten information from friends, classmates, or neighbors.

5.c My memories - age 5 to 10

5.c

In the space below, or in a journal, jot down some of the memories you have from age 5 (when you started school) to age 10. This includes the kindergarten and elementary school age. Some school memories may overlap from the previous section.

My Age: Memory: ______________________________

____

____

My Age: Memory: ______________________________

____

____

My Age: Memory:

My Age: Memory:

5.c

My Age: Memory:

As you have identified memories to age 10, what thoughts have come up for you regarding your ideas about "self?" In what ways have these memories shaped your answer to the question, "who am I?" Reflect and journal in the space below.

5.d Accounts from others - age 5 to 10

The space below is for memories of you that have been described by people other than your family (friends, classmates, others). Circle **Y/N** to confirm or deny each story:

Name: My Age:

Their story about me:

(Y/N)

Name: My Age:

Their story about me:

(Y/N)

Name: My Age:

Their story about me:

(Y/N)

5.d

Name: My Age:

Their story about me:

(Y/N)

Name: My Age:

Their story about me:

5.d

(Y/N)

Name: My Age:

Their story about me:

(Y/N)

These are the years (ages 5 to 10) when you expanded your interactions with people other than your family. Again, the stories that others have may not be what you feel represents truly who you are. The perspective of a school bully or a dishonest neighbor may not represent who you are. However, their opinion or statements can influence your sense of self-worth. The opinion of others can influence a sense of inferiority in you.

Keep in mind that these are merely stories, and perceptions of others that may or may not be accurate. Whether or not they are accurate, they can still influence your questions about, "Who am I?"

As you have identified memories to age 10, what thoughts have come up for you regarding your ideas about "self?" In what ways have these memories shaped your answer to the question, "who am I?" Reflect and journal in the space below.

As you have identified memories to age 10, what thoughts have come up for you regarding your ideas about "self?" In what ways have these memories shaped your answer to the question, "who am I?" Reflect and journal in the space below.

____

____

____

____

____

____

Memories from adolescence

You are likely able to retrieve more memories from your adolescent years in contrast to early childhood. Adolescence is a time when you begin to have greater cognitive ability, and you develop what is called *metacognition.* This means that you are beginning to examine your own thoughts and the thoughts of others. You begin to compare your ideas and thoughts with others.

Additionally, you are establishing your identity. Identity usually comes from peer groups and during adolescence your identity is very much about your role in life. When a person lacks the ability to establish identity with a peer group, there is often a sense of role confusion.

From ages 11 to 19, there is an emphasis on social relationships, and this becomes significant to one's perception of self. The answer to the question of "Who am I?" may shift as peers may influence the answer to this question.

5.e My memories - age 11 to 19

In the spaces below, list any memories that you have during adolescence that shaped your answer to the "*Who am I?*" question.

My Age: Teen Memory:

My Age: Teen Memory:

My Age: Teen Memory:

My Age: Teen Memory:

My Age: Teen Memory:

5.e

Your memories during adolescence may indicate that you shifted your self-perception based upon social relationships. Were you popular or isolated and unpopular? Were you a part of a group or team, or did you feel like a loner? Did you pride yourself on being unique, or did you feel awkward and *"weird"?* During this period, what others thought of you can significantly influence your self-perception. This is especially true if there were things said or done by your peers.

5.f Accounts from others - age 11 to 19

The next section asks you to pull up memories of what others said or thought about you (friends, classmates, others). Circle **Y/N** to confirm or deny each story:

Name: ____________________ My Age: ________

Their story about me: ____________________

____

____

____________________ (Y/N)

Name: ____________________ My Age: ________

Their story about me: ____________________

____

____

____________________ (Y/N)

Name: ____________________ My Age: ________

Their story about me: ____________________

____

____

____________________ (Y/N)

Name: My Age:

Their story about me:

(Y/N)

5.f

You may have been a quiet introverted person and others called you *"weird"* or *"lame"*. You may have been a high achiever and others thought you were *"smart"* or *"talented"*, but you feel that you were attempting to cover up your feelings of inadequacy. You have the opportunity now to confirm what they said about you according to your truth. Despite whether you believe what they say is true, it may have influenced your answer to the question of, ***"Who am I?"***

As you have identified memories during adolescence, what thoughts have come up for you regarding your ideas about "self? In what ways have these memories shaped your answer to the question "who am I?" Reflect and journal in the space below.

Memories from adulthood

As an adult, there are many things that occur from age 20 onward that can influence the answer to the question of ***"Who am I?"*** During adulthood there are many life experiences that can alter your self-concept. Higher education, career, employment, health, and relationships are the biggest highlights of adult years. Did a career overshadow intimacy in relationships, or did relationships distract you from your career? Have you felt fulfilled during adult years, or do you feel stagnant and unfulfilled?

5.g My memories from adulthood

In the chart below, list any memories you have of adult life that reflect on the answer to the *"Who am I?"* question. Include memories of career, education, employment, and primary relationships.

My Age: Adult Memory:

5.g

My Age: Adult Memory:

My Age: Adult Memory:

My Age: Adult Memory:

5.g

My Age: Adult Memory:

The memories that stand out to you currently are things that probably affect your present perspective of self and provide answers to the question of, *"Who am I?"* Your adult memories have a tremendous influence on your self-perception. If you felt insecure and inferior as a youth, you may have established greater self-worth as an adult through career development. A *"nerdy"* youth may become quite successful in the technology field or academic field.

The opposite may be true also. You may have been a very popular and successful athlete in high school, but as an adult found challenges in career development. Or an unhealthy relationship may have lowered your sense of self-worth. Your story is your own, and the important thing is to ***own your identity*** as it stands today. This way you can look honestly at the answer to the question of, *"Who am I?"* Although your self-perception may have changed over the years, it is important to embrace this first question.

5.h Who am I?

5.h

Provide a short summary of your answer to the first question of:

"Who am I ?": ______________________________

____

____

____

____

____

Part 2: What kind of a world is this?

As you have taken the time to gather your memories from childhood onward, you have established that certain flashbacks of your life stand out. Remember that of all the trillions of memories that you have experienced throughout your lifetime, there are only some that stand out. These are the memories that apply to your current self-perception. Take a few moments to review all the memories from childhood to present, and think about how all your life experiences have contributed to your sense of what type of a world you live in.

- Is this world one that you can trust?
- Has this been a safe world for you?
- Has your perspective on safety and trust changed over the years?
- Do you feel a sense of belonging or do you feel isolated and rejected?
    - Has the world been abundant for you, or do you feel you have had to fight for every penny earned?
    - Do you feel that your voice has been heard by others, or do you feel dismissed and discounted?

5.i

5.i

After you have reviewed the primary memories that have impacted your life, take some time to write a short summary of your thoughts about what kind of a world is this (consider trust, safety, belonging, being "heard", and love).

"What Kind of World is this":

____

____

____

____

____

____

Part 3: What does a person like me need to do in a world such as this in order to make a place for myself?

As you consider your life experiences that have shaped your self-perception and your perspective of the world, you may begin to see that you have made ***decisions*** for yourself about what you needed to do to make a place for yourself. Your decisions may have been based upon overcoming earlier challenges or they may have been based upon a positive outlook on the future.

Whatever your decisions have been, they belong to you. Take some time to think about the decisions you have made in the past about "*what a person like you needs to do in a world such as this in order to make a place for yourself.*" You will have an opportunity to "redecide" what you want to do in the future.

5.j

After you have reviewed your answers to Private Logic Parts 1 & 2, take some time to write a short summary of your thoughts about the question: "*What does a person like me need to do in a world such as this?*"

5.j

What decisions have I made about what I need to do to make a place for myself based upon how I see myself and the world?"

Re-deciding

You now can look at the decisions you have made regarding your self-perception and your perspective of the world around you. Now is your chance to "***re-decide***" what you need to do to make a place for yourself. You now can think about a *potential better path* toward making a place for yourself.

In the past if you have hidden in relationships or jobs that were safe but did not allow you to expand your abilities, you may want to think about what types of things you want to do in the future. In the past you may have gotten into unhealthy relationships and are now looking for something different. Think about the ***re-decision***s you might want to make in order to create a place for yourself.

5.k Re-deciding

Write about what you want to do from this point onward to make a place for yourself:

5.k

___

___

___

___

___

___

___

This chapter has taken you through a process to examine your self-perception, your view of the world around you, and what you have done to try to make a place for yourself. You have also been able to design your ***re-decisions*** about how you want to make a place for yourself in the future. Remember that you are the artist of your life, and you can create the next layer of your canvas in a positive way or a negative way. You can paint paradise or despair.

In the next chapter we will further examine belief systems and look at your core beliefs, which have been formulated by your life experiences.

5.1 Reflection

- What specific memory stands out to you in terms of those that have shaped your self-perception?

____

____

____

____

____

____

____

- What are your strengths that will help you to move forward with redeciding?

5.1

- What stands out to you in terms of the next page of your story or the next part of painting your canvas?

- Is your "re-decision" of what you want to do to make a place for yourself on the next page that you write in your story, or the next picture you paint on your canvas?

____

____

____

____

____

____

____

Chapter 6

Identification of Core Beliefs

Getting to Know What Has Been Navigating My Life

"The most fundamental aggression to ourselves, the most fundamental harm we can do to ourselves, is to remain ignorant by not having the courage and the respect to look at ourselves, honestly and gently."

— *Pema Chodron, When Things Fall Apart: Heart Advice for Difficult Times*

The willingness to reach beyond what we already believe to be true about ourselves takes courage. This path sometimes begins with a discomfort with how our life is unfolding. Or we may have developed invisible armor to protect ourselves from seeing the truth and remain numb to the pain of our present existence. Moving apart from the familiar may be uncomfortable.

There is also a freedom that emerges as a result of change. Harm may come from not looking at the truth about ourselves because we are likely to be held hostage to the past. Courage is needed to explore the decisions we have made about ourselves. Are you ready to release the shackles and contemplate your past with courage?

You have been introduced to beliefs and belief systems. Now we are going to venture into identifying your *"core beliefs."* Your core beliefs are *"navigating your life"* in your daily responses to life situations. It may seem frightening that this entity called your ***"belief system"*** is in the backdrop of your everyday decisions in life. It may be scary to think that something that you cannot see or concretely identify is directing the course of your actions.

In Chapter 5, the questions associated with private logic involve, "*Who am I?*", "*What kind of a world is this?*" and "*What does a person like me need to do in a world like this in order to make a place for myself?*" The summaries of these three questions can allow you to evaluate how you perceive yourself and the world. In your personal inventory of answering these questions, you can begin to see that some ***core beliefs*** have emerged.

Your central ideas about yourself and the world around you are your ***core beliefs***. These beliefs direct your thoughts, perceptions, feelings, and behaviors in daily life encounters. If these beliefs are positive, your outlook on life is most likely optimistic and will provide you with motivation to take positive actions. It is the negative erroneous beliefs about self that can create negative thought patterns, and emotional plunges. Unfortunately, these beliefs are running you at an unconscious level, and your belief system is something that you cannot see or touch.

In Chapter 4 you explored your belief system and in Chapter 5 you explored the private logic associated with your formulation of ideas about your self-perception. In this chapter, we will be putting together some of what you have learned about safety, trust, and beliefs about yourself.

Conscious Beliefs: The Tip of the Iceberg

If you have ever seen a picture of an iceberg, you have a good visual of how just a small portion of the iceberg is visible. This is the part of the iceberg that you see above the water line. Most of the iceberg is below the water. This visual is like the concept of your belief system. Your *conscious beliefs* are small in proportion to the *unconscious beliefs* that are the backdrop of your daily interactions.

For this reason, your ***unconscious mistaken beliefs*** are difficult to identify. Your best access to your unconscious beliefs is through your negative self-talk or private conversations. The following diagram will help you to visualize this.

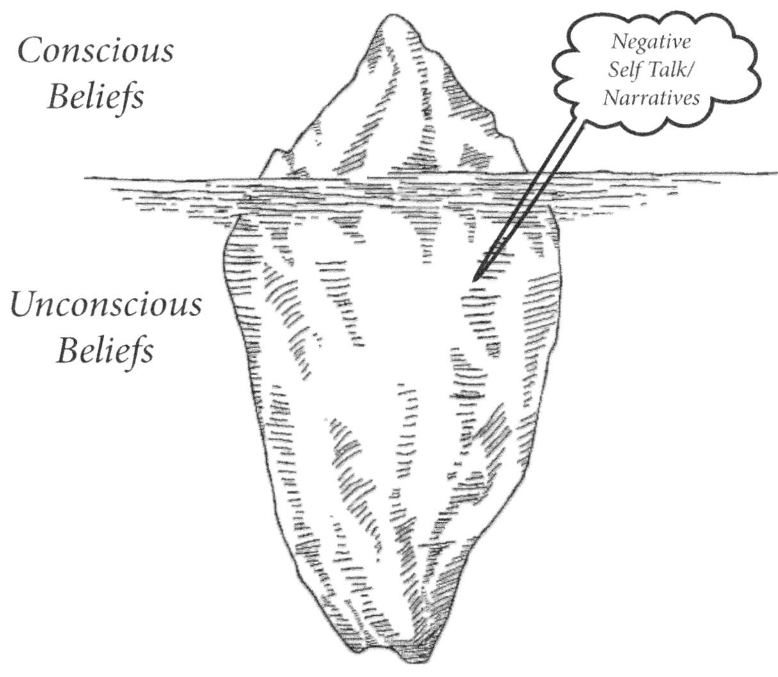

What you believe to be true affects your perception of yourself and the world around you. Quite often, when you see yourself as someone who does not measure up, you will look out at the world, and it will seem to fall short of your expectations. Your perspective of the world can often be like a mirror to yourself. If you are feeling happy and liking yourself, the world and other people will feel happy to you. If you see yourself as a failure, the world and other people will seem like they have also failed you.

Your beliefs are always affecting your perspective on your day-to-day situations. It is as if you have a bubble around you that is your personal reality of yourself, others, and situations. It is as if you have a ***personal filter*** through which you see the world and situations. This filter is comprised of life experiences, things you have been told about yourself, and things your primary caregivers have said to you that have left impressions.

In the previous chapter, you made assessments associated with memories of your life that stand out to you. These memories correspond with your core beliefs and fuel your thoughts about yourself. These memories are likely to be a part of your personal *"filter"* through which you see the world. It is as if you have a personal set of lenses that you look through that reflects your core beliefs and that influences your perception.

The most difficult part of this is that your core beliefs often involve ***mistaken negative beliefs*** about yourself. Mistaken negative beliefs are sometimes referred to as ***self-defeating beliefs***. This is appropriately named because negative core beliefs can be very damaging to your self-worth. These core beliefs can cast a dark shadow over your outlook in life and cause a feeling of worthlessness. These negative core beliefs can be the *false narratives* in your head talking to you in your own voice. These false narratives can include berating yourself for mistakes, reinforcing feelings of unworthiness, or turning a life experience into a narrative of being a failure.

6.a Self-Defeating Beliefs Exercise

Let's begin by identifying what some of your self-defeating beliefs are. Following is a list of common mistaken self-defeating core beliefs. ***Circle the mistaken core beliefs that you have heard or felt about yourself:***

- *"I don't deserve love."*
- *"I am a bad person."*
- *"I am unimportant."*
- *"I can't trust myself."*
- *"I cannot trust others."*
- *"I am a failure."*
- *"I am unworthy."*
- *"I am weak."*
- *"I am worthless."*
- *"I am stupid."*
- *"I am unlovable."*
- *"My needs don't matter."*
- *"I don't measure up to others."*
- *"I am not good enough."*
- *"I am different and an outsider."*
- *"I don't belong."*
- *"I am defective."*

6.a

There are potentially many more mistaken negative core beliefs that you may have that are *"navigating your life."* ***The statements that you have circled are a part of your beliefs.*** Most of these negative beliefs relate to a sense of low self-worth or not measuring up to others. You may not directly hear these beliefs, but you may hear a ***"false narrative"*** in your head about yourself when a situation arises where you question your capability or worth.

> *"What you believe to be true affects your perception of yourself and the world around you."*

False Narratives

A false narrative is an erroneous private conversation that you have in your head about a situation. We will often judge ourselves based upon a life experience in which we feel an extreme emotional response. The emotional response triggers thoughts that surface from the pool of mistaken beliefs we have that are running us at an unconscious level. Keep a journal and jot down any false narratives you may hear in your thoughts about yourself or others. This will help you to tap into the mistaken unconscious beliefs that are running your daily responses to life encounters.

6.b False Narrative Exercise

You may hear your private conversations in your head that sound something like the following narratives. Circle any statement that you have heard in a similar way:

- *"I'm just not good at anything." (I am worthless)*
- *"Relationships just don't seem to work for me." (I am unlovable)*
- *"I don't fit in with these groups." (I don't belong)*
- *"Everyone seems to have friends but me." (I am different and an outsider)*
- *"I can't believe that I made that same mistake again." (I am stupid)*
- *"They are all smarter than me and better than I am." (I don't measure up to others)*
- *"I can never make a good decision." (I can't trust myself)*
- *"I cannot count on anyone to help me." (I cannot trust others)*
- *"I guess others are lucky in love, but not me." (I am not worthy of love)*
- *I would ask for help, but it's not that important." (My needs don't matter)*
- *"I'm afraid to say anything because it really doesn't matter." (I am unimportant)*
- *"I can never do anything right." (I am a failure)*
- *"I have always been horrible, even as a child." (I am a bad person)*

The false narratives that you say about yourself in your own voice reflect your core mistaken beliefs. These mistaken beliefs can direct your choices in life and set limitations on your ability to be the best version of yourself. It is difficult to be your best self when your core beliefs are narrating commentary about your low self-worth and low confidence. It is time to challenge these ideas and create affirmations that are the opposite of these thoughts.

False narratives and corresponding mistaken beliefs

Following are examples of ***false narratives*** or ***private conversations*** you may have inside of your head that reflect a mistaken belief:

False Narrative	Corresponding Mistaken Belief
"I'm just not good at relationships; they always leave me."	I don't deserve love
"My mother called me a problem child…I guess she is right."	I am a bad person
"What I have to say and what I think don't really matter at all."	I am unimportant
"It is so hard for me to make a decision. I may make the wrong choice."	I can't trust myself
"There are so many people out there who want to hurt me. I need to keep to myself."	I can't trust others
"Everything I do turns out wrong. Why even bother?"	I am a failure
"Nothing good happens to me. I just don't deserve to have good things."	I am unworthy
"I can't ask for what I want because my voice doesn't matter."	I am weak
"I am not worthy of good things. Other people get what they need but not me."	I am worthless
"I always make poor choices. I have a broken brain."	I am stupid
"I don't do well in relationships. They never seem to work out."	I am unlovable

False Narrative	Corresponding Mistaken Belief
"I feel awkward expressing what I need to others. I don't deserve anything special."	My needs don't matter
"Everyone is better than me. They all seem to know more and do more than I can."	I don't measure up to others
"I don't quite make the grade. I just don't have what it takes."	I am not good enough
"I just don't seem to fit in no matter how hard I try. Others don't see me as one of them."	I am different and an outsider
"I have tried so hard in relationships and yet I don't ever feel the connection with others."	I don't belong
"There are parts of me that are broken and cannot be fixed."	I am defective

6.c

6.c False Narrative Inventory

Using the items you've circled in 6.a. and 6.b, take this time to list your **false narratives** *(the negative thoughts you hear in your head)* or **private conversations** and the **corresponding mistaken belief** that is consistent with the narrative.

False Narrative:
"They are all smarter than me and better than I am."

Mistaken Belief: I don't measure up to others.

False Narrative:

Mistaken Belief:

False Narrative: ______________________________

____

Mistaken Belief: ______________________________

____

False Narrative: ______________________________

____

Mistaken Belief: ______________________________

____

False Narrative: ______________________________

____

Mistaken Belief: ______________________________

____

False Narrative: ______________________________

____

Mistaken Belief: ______________________________

____

Messages of your primary caregivers

Your parents or primary caregivers that raised you have had a tremendous influence on your thoughts about yourself. We ***internalize*** our parents' values, beliefs, and messages and they become a part of us and what we believe to be true about ourselves. Our parents or primary caregivers have a tremendous influence on our self-perception and the establishment of our core beliefs.

If you think about the power differential between you as a child and your parents, it makes sense that they influenced what you believe to be true about yourself. The size difference between your child self and your parents is an example of a power differential. The fact that you depended upon them for support, guidance, food, shelter, and everything else sets up a disparity of power between you and them.

Sometimes you may hear your parents' words in your head speaking to you in your own voice. Did you receive harsh criticism or judgments from your primary caregivers? Or did you receive some unintentional criticism from parents that has stuck with you? The following are examples of a parent or caregiver's words and how they become a mistaken core belief.

Parent/Caregiver Narrative	Corresponding Mistaken Belief
"Stop talking to me right now. I am too busy to listen to you."	I am unimportant
"You are a problem child... you are always causing trouble."	I am a bad person
"Why are you feeling angry? You have no reason to be angry right now."	I don't trust myself or my emotions
"The world is a dangerous place. You are not to go anywhere without me."	I cannot trust others
"I wish you were never born. I have had nothing but problems with you."	I am worthless
"You should be more like your sister or your cousin."	I don't measure up to others
"All you ever think about is yourself. You are selfish."	My needs don't matter

6.d False Narratives from Parents & Caregivers

6.d

Write some of the negative or judgmental messages you received when you were younger from your parents. Then identify a corresponding core mistaken belief that may reflect that negative message. You can start by writing any negative messages you received, then select from the list of mistaken core beliefs in 6.a.

Caregiver False Narrative: "My mother called me a problem child...I guess she is right."

Mistaken Belief: I am a bad person

Caregiver False Narrative:

Mistaken Belief:

Caregiver False Narrative: ________________

____

Mistaken Belief: ________________

____

Caregiver False Narrative: ________________

____

Mistaken Belief: ________________

____

6.d

Caregiver False Narrative: ________________

____

Mistaken Belief: ________________

____

Caregiver False Narrative: ________________

____

Mistaken Belief: ________________

____

Seeking external validation of what you believe to be true about yourself from the outside world

You unconsciously seek validation for the things that you believe to be true about yourself. Let's explore this idea by identifying just a few things you believe to be true about yourself. You have conscious beliefs that you know to be true about yourself. These things may include your beliefs about subjects in school, things you do well, or aspects of your character. For example:

> *You may believe you are a good cook. If you affirm this to be true about yourself, you probably always cook well and then people say to you that they think your cooking is the best. They ask you for recipes and tell you they love your cooking. You are* ***validated*** *for your belief about being a good cook and your belief gets* ***reinforced****.*
>
> *Is it true that you have an aptitude for cooking creatively, or is this a belief that has gotten reinforced over the years through validation? Is this belief something that you have manifested into reality by your actions of creating tasty foods? This belief is something that may represent a strength in the things you believe to be true about yourself. It is a part of your conscious beliefs about yourself.*

What about validation for a mistaken belief that is ***self-defeating***? What if your mistaken core belief is, "*I am unlovable*?" What would validation of this mistaken belief look like? Unfortunately, it may present as unconsciously selecting partners who would confirm the belief of, "*I am unlovable*."

Imagine that you are looking for a life partner and have been dating several candidates. Your process for selecting a person to date long-term will involve picking someone that you are attracted to and to whom you are drawn. If your mistaken belief is, "*I am unlovable*," you may unintentionally pick someone that will treat you in a way that validates this belief. Or you may also pick someone that you inadvertently push away until they leave the relationship which will also validate the mistaken belief, "*I am unlovable*."

Most of us have a desire to be happy in our primary romantic relationships, so it is hard to believe that we would pick someone to abandon us or validate, "*I am unlovable.*" However, our ***belief system is powerful*** and can affect our decisions to unconsciously validate mistaken beliefs. Consider the following example of a person that came to me for therapy:

> *Alice was a 43-year-old married woman who was soon to be divorcing her second husband of 8 years. She was devastated that her husband, Mel, had cheated on her and now was asking for a divorce. She felt he had never really loved her and always felt she came as "second best" to his work, friends, and others.*
>
> *Her previous marriage to a man named Craig was equally as hurtful. Craig was married to Alice for 4 years and he was verbally abusive, degraded her, and he eventually told her that he did not love her. Alice began to think that she had "bad luck with relationships." Was it bad luck? Or was Alice manifesting this type of unhealthy relationship because of a mistaken belief?*
>
> *In therapy we explored her narratives, and then accessed her core beliefs. Her **narratives** about relationships were, "I have bad luck with relationships," and "Men just don't like me very much," and "No matter how hard I try, I get disappointed in my relationships."*
>
> ***These narratives were explored to identify her mistaken core belief which was, "I am unlovable."*** *Alice's history: Alice was sent to a state residential care facility in the first year of her life due to her father's abuse and mother's alcoholism. At age five, Alice was transitioned to multiple foster care homes where she stayed for a maximum of 5 months before getting rejected again and going to another home. At age 11, Alice was adopted by a very loving and caring woman.*

However, during Alice's earlier years, she established a core belief of, "I am not lovable," and "I am not worthy of love." ***These core beliefs eventually had Alice choosing men that would validate these core mistaken beliefs.*** *Alice's two marriages validated her belief about not being lovable. Alice began to see how she manifested unhealthy marriages due to her core belief established as a child. These two hurtful marriages with Craig and Mel validated her mistaken belief that she was not worthy of love. She was repeating her earlier life experiences.*

In therapy we worked through the process of challenging those beliefs and establishing Alice's worthiness of happiness and healthy relationships. Alice began her journey of reclaiming her positive attributes and self-love. She began using affirming thoughts to replace the old false narratives.

Your Belief System is Powerful

Keep in mind that when referring to the idea of *your belief system making decisions for you or affecting your life choices*, there is an indication that a force within you is creating your personal reality. This can be a frightening thought and can give you a feeling that you are not in the *"driver's seat"* of your life. Although this is true, you can reclaim control of your life and begin to dismantle your belief system through identifying the mistaken beliefs.

By using false narratives to assist you to identify beliefs and through challenging these old ideas about yourself, you can begin a new narrative that is more life-supporting and valuable for you. You can try replacing the old ideas with new affirming thoughts about yourself. The following examples will assist you in finding replacement affirmations that will assist you in beginning to challenge your mistaken beliefs.

Old Mistaken Narrative and Belief	Corresponding New Affirming Belief
"I'm just not good at relationships; they always leave me." ***(I don't deserve love)***	"I am worthy of relationships and love. I give and receive love freely and easily."
"My mother called me a problem child…I guess she is right." ***(I am a bad person)***	"I have made some mistakes in life, and I am a worthy and good human being."
"What I have to say and what I think don't really matter at all." ***(I am unimportant)***	"I have value and I am important to myself and others. I use my voice to affirm this."
"It is so hard for me to make decisions. I have made bad choices." ***(I can't trust myself)***	"I trust my decisions despite the outcomes. I trust myself to learn from mistakes."
"There are so many people out there who want to hurt me." ***(I cannot trust others)***	"I make good judgments about who to trust."
"Everything I do turns out wrong. Why even bother?" ***(I am a failure)***	"I am a success in my life's adventure. My mistakes are guidelines for future action."
"Nothing good happens to me. I just don't deserve to have good things." ***(I am unworthy)***	"I am a worthwhile human being. I deserve all good things in life."
"I can't ask for what I want because my voice doesn't matter." ***(I am weak)***	"I am strong and I speak up for myself despite what others think."
"I am not worthy of good things. My needs do not matter." ***(I am worthless)***	"I am worthy and my needs matter. I freely ask for what I want."
"I always make poor choices. I have a broken brain." ***(I am stupid)***	"I am competent, knowledgeable, and make good choices based upon my needs."
"I don't do well in relationships. They never seem to work out." ***(I am unlovable)***	"I am a loving human being. I give love and receive love easily."
"I feel awkward asking for what I want. I am undeserving." ***(My needs don't matter)***	"I freely ask for what I want, and I deserve to get my needs met."
"Everyone is better than me. They all seem to know more." ***(I don't measure up to others)***	"I am equal to others. I am smart enough and nobody is better than me."
"I don't quite make the grade. I just don't have what it takes." ***(I am not good enough)***	"I am as good as others, and I have everything it takes for me to be successful in all areas."

Old Mistaken Narrative and Belief	Corresponding New Affirming Belief
*"I just don't seem to fit in no matter how hard I try." (**I am different and an outsider)***	"I am a part of the whole of life. I am unique and a perfect creation of God or my Higher Source."
*"I have tried so hard in relationships and yet I don't ever feel connection." (**I don't belong)***	"I belong to my family, friends, and other relationships. I easily connect with others."

6.e Rewriting my Beliefs

Now let's try replacing the old beliefs with a Corresponding New Affirming Belief. ***Example follows.*** Now put your Old Beliefs and New Affirming Beliefs:

Old False Narrative and Mistaken Belief: "I'm just not good at relationships. They always leave me." (I don't deserve love)

Corresponding New Affirming Belief: I am worthy of relationships and love. I give and receive love freely and easily.

6.e

Old False Narrative and Mistaken Belief: ______________________

____

Corresponding New Affirming Belief: ______________________

____

____

____

Old False Narrative and Mistaken Belief:

Corresponding New Affirming Belief:

Old False Narrative and Mistaken Belief:

Corresponding New Affirming Belief:

6.e

Old False Narrative and Mistaken Belief:

Corresponding New Affirming Belief:

Next Steps

The next steps on this journey of exploration of your core beliefs are to:

1. Find the affirmations that are the opposite of your negative narratives and mistaken core beliefs.
2. Challenge the negativity to a positive affirmation every time you hear it in your head. The negativity and false narrative are not true, and they are not you.
3. Identify the new affirming beliefs that contradict your mistaken core beliefs and write at least one down per week.
4. Post it on you mirror or on the visor of your car so that you can read it every day.
5. Set an intention to remind yourself of the ***strength, courage, and determination*** you possess to overcome the negativity and false narratives in your head.
6. Commit to a new mindset and make a promise to yourself associated with the new affirming thoughts.
7. Remember that you are powerful, brave, and beautiful.

6.f Reflection

- What negative core belief stands out to you that has held you hostage to your past experiences?

- What affirmation have you identified that is the opposite of your most prominent negative core belief?

6.f

- What will it take to practice self-love and self-acceptance?

Chapter 7

Attachment

Primary Relationships and My Primal Wounds

"We do as we have been done by."

— *John Bowlby, Attachment*

As each human being makes the journey from the safety of the womb to the hands of their caregiver, there are countless experiences a newborn will face. The safety or the insecurity of the new human will depend upon the bond or distress of that initial relationship. The lioness provides comfort to her cub. The mother eagle provides a cone shaped next with soft feathers on the bottom for her babies to feel safe and comforted. All mammals and birds have a period of bonding time before preparing the new arrivals for survival.

The newborn human is faced with absolute dependence on their caregivers. That initial bond is significant to a long-term sense of security. There are multiple factors and relational tasks that are needed to establish a secure bond between infant and caregiver. Consider the fragility of the relationship and environmental circumstances in your early years. Was yours predictive of misfires or consistency in the bonding process?

The social and emotional bond between a primary caregiver and an infant is a significant relationship that has the potential to affect a person's initial sense of trust, safety, and connection. This bond is called ***attachment***. During this process of attachment, networks of neural connections are being formed in the infant and caregiver (usually the mother) and this develops further throughout a person's lifetime.

Early attachment, however, is significant to future social development and impacts relationships. The previous chapter presented aspects of the development of core beliefs. An individual's insecure attachment may contribute to core beliefs about trust and safety. This chapter will have you exploring and thinking about your personal attachment style.

Primal Wounds

I refer to ***primal wounds*** as the injuries experienced by primary caregivers, especially in early childhood. The relationship with our primary caregivers is significant to who we become. The ruptures in these relationships cause wounds that we carry with us throughout our lifetime until we begin to examine the experiences. We internalize our parents (or caregivers) in a way that is unlike any of the other relationships in our life.

As small developing humans, we look up to our caregivers. They provide us with our sense of love and safety in the world. There is a tremendous power differential between a small child and their parents, and the child is dependent upon this relationship even when it is dysfunctional or unhealthy. We wear these primal wounds just beneath the surface of our day-to-day experiences. These wounds are often behind our unexplained emotional reactivity or behaviors toward others.

You could also say that these wounds become a part of our belief system and sometimes are a part of formulating our mistaken beliefs about ourselves. As we look at attachment, you can see how attachment issues are woven into your belief system about self. Attachment wounds can present as barriers to healthy adult relationships.

What is *secure attachment*?

It is important to start with speaking to the idea of ***secure attachment*** and what that looks like in a growing and developing individual. A healthy relationship with a child's primary caregiver creates a sense of safety and security in the world. A child with secure attachment feels a strong connection and feels comfort from their primary caregiver. A primary caregiver may be the mother, father, grandparent, adoptive parent, or foster parent with whom a child is being raised.

If that primary caregiver is present from birth and if the relationship is consistent and stable, there is a greater likelihood of the attachment bond being secure. When a person is *securely attached* as an infant through early childhood to their primary caregiver without disrupted bonding, the person is likely to be able to develop trusting, long-term relationships as adults. In addition to the ability to develop intimate romantic relationships, a person with secure attachment will likely have high levels of self-worth and have connections with a network of social support.

Trust is known to be established in the first year of life. Consider an infant's inability to verbalize what they need. An infant will cry if they are uncomfortable, hungry, cold, or have a wet diaper. ***The infant has the need to establish trust with their primary caregiver for food, comfort, warmth, and emotional caregiving.*** This feeling of trust transfers to adulthood and a securely attached adult will be well suited to trust others in relationships.

An adult who has secure attachment in early childhood is comfortable in close relationships with others and can connect with others because of their ability to trust. They are comfortable with independence and with building healthy relationships. A securely attached adult can also be comfortable with being alone, and they will seek emotional support if it is needed.

A securely attached individual may find it difficult to understand people who have the insecure attachment styles. They may find it difficult to understand when others push them away for no reason or become clingy. They may have a belief system that dictates a sense of wholeness and completeness. The securely attached person may have a narrative that says "*the world is a safe place*" or that "*people can be trusted.*" This narrative can get jolted when encountering someone who they trust indiscriminately and then get hurt by them. Through this, a securely attached individual will learn discernment in the trustworthiness of others. They can easily recover from conflict with another person.

The securely attached individual has an integrated flow of energy between the ability to be logical and emotionally sensitive. This means that the right and left hemispheres of the brain are both flowing well and that one has access to logic and reason, and emotions. They are comfortable with making connections and being attuned to others.

Emotion Regulation and Attachment

Emotion regulation describes a person's ability to effectively respond to a situation that may cause surges of feelings. A person that can emotionally regulate can respond competently during a situation that arouses emotions. Attachment plays a role because emotion regulation is learned in early childhood. If a child has a *secure base* or stable primary caregiver attachment, they will be able to explore, learn, and adapt to various situations. The ***attachment bond*** provides the neural programming for an emotion regulation mechanism (Ainsworth, 1989; Bowlby, 1969; Porges, 2010).

Early infant and parent bonding is significant. A disrupted attachment bond can lead to insecure attachment styles. Research has demonstrated that these early childhood bonding experiences create attachment circuits in the brain, and this circuitry may be modified depending upon the quality of care. Trauma is known to also affect these neural circuitries and, depending on the mother's availability to the infant, may cause problems later in life.

Basically, the early life experiences may alter the number of complex neurons that are developing during this time that are associated with attachment to the primary caregiver. An infant or child attaches to the primary caregiver despite the quality of care that they receive, and the brain circuitry adapts to the individual's relationship. Emotional deficits may occur because of a less than healthy relationship experience.

A secure attachment will happen as the result of the optimal bonding experience between the caregiver and child. Optimal bonding will cause the brain to develop in a healthy way. Secure bonding will result in an individual's ability to function with quality programming (Bowlby, 1969; Porges, 2010; Sullivan, 2012).

Let's look at three other ways that attachment may develop that are associated with insecure styles. The three types of insecure attachment styles are ***avoidant attachment*** *(dismissive or anxious avoidant)*, ***anxious attachment*** *(preoccupied or anxious ambivalent)*, ***and disorganized attachment*** *(fearful avoidant)*.

Avoidant Attachment *(dismissive or anxious avoidant)*

Avoidant attachment begins in infancy and early childhood with caregivers who demonstrate instability and unreliability. When the child seeks emotional support from the primary caregiver, they are rejected or dismissed. Or the caregiver may not be attuned to the child and the caregiver displays an inability to provide healthy emotional responses to the child. The caregiver may be physically present, but unable to meet the emotional needs of a child by providing appropriate emotional responses to the youngster.

A child needs to be able to reach out to their primary caregiver and receive a welcoming and loving response. However, with a caregiver that blocks closeness and expression of feelings, the natural desire for reaching out for emotional support is interrupted. The child stops seeking connection and support from caregivers and this transfers to adulthood.

An adult who displays avoidant attachment has relationships that are more surface-level, rather than in-depth intimate relationships. The avoidantly attached individual will often reject intimacy. They may have difficulty with close relationships and people will often say that they cannot get close to them.

An avoidantly attached adult may be social on the surface and be seen as independent. Displays of independence may be present for the avoidant adult. This may be an attempt to avoid reliance on others. Close romantic relationships are often difficult. They may push partners away if they get too close. Or they may choose partners that they will eventually reject. In long-term relationships, they will often say that their partner wants more physical closeness than what feels comfortable to them.

In terms of belief systems, as discussed in previous chapters, an avoidantly attached adult may have established mistaken beliefs associated with being "*not good at relationships*" or say "*I am a loner.*" They may live by a rule that it is "*easier to be alone*" or that "*my life is simpler without being in a relationship.*" These types of narratives will most often manifest a life of alienation and isolation unless help is sought.

The avoidant individual is more oriented to the left hemisphere of the brain and is logical, rational, and deals easily with reason. However, when it comes to emotion or the ability to be empathic, they may struggle. They may have difficulty with emotional expression or being sensitive to the emotions of partners and others.

Anxious Attachment *(preoccupied or anxious-ambivalent)*

Anxious attachment is another type of insecure attachment style. The development of anxious attachment begins in infancy and early childhood and is usually a result of inconsistent or disrupted bonding with primary caregivers. Anxious attachment may also be due to a perception by the child that the parent is ambivalent to their needs.

The anxiously attached child often fears abandonment, lacks the ability to do self-care, and is in excessive distress when separated from the caregiver. The parent of an anxiously attached child is likely to use the child to satisfy their own needs for physical and emotional closeness. At other times, the parent may be unresponsive to the child.

In some situations, the anxiously attached child has had periods of separation from the caregiver which provides that inconsistency of the bonding process. The caregiver is often self-absorbed and preoccupied with their own wounds. The caregiver to the anxiously attached individual may have very poor boundaries with their children. The child is often parentified or takes on the role of the parent.

The anxiously attached adult will seek closeness from their partner or friends and feel insecure when they do not receive the closeness they are craving. They are often found to feel insecure about their worthiness in a relationship. Perceived rejection is very difficult for the anxiously attached adult and they often need an excessive amount of reassurance of their worth.

When an anxiously attached adult feels rejection from friendships or romantic partners, they will often pursue the partners harder due to their dependency needs. The anxiously attached adult may be prone to questioning the love that their partner feels for them, and they need more reassurance than a securely attached person. Low self-worth of the anxiously attached person leads to fear of abandonment and wanting to hold their partner hostage to their emotional needs.

The anxiously attached individual may have a belief system that dictates unworthiness, a belief that they are unlovable or not measuring up to others. They may have a mistaken belief that they "*will be abandoned*" or a false narrative that they "*get rejected when they fall in love.*" These types of mistaken beliefs can manifest what a person fears the most. This insecurity and potentially "*clingy*" behavior may inadvertently push others away and validate the belief that they will be abandoned or rejected. The anxiously attached adult may be very talkative and overly emotional.

> *"Low self-worth leads to fear of abandonment and wanting to hold their partner hostage to their emotional needs."*

The anxiously attached person is more oriented to the right side of their brain and may become flooded with feelings and emotions. Dominance in the right hemisphere of the brain often leads to a person being a fountain of feelings and lacking logic and reason.

Disorganized Attachment *(fearful avoidant)*

The lack of bond between caregiver and infant is especially prominent in the ***disorganized,*** or fearful-avoidant attachment style. The bond between caregiver and infant that should establish a sense of safety instead becomes dominated by fear. The disorganized attachment style incorporates components of anxious and avoidant attachment styles.

Often *childhood trauma* or *extreme abuse* can result in ***perceived fear*** instead of a sense of safety due to unpredictable parenting. The child has difficulty trusting their primary caregiver and has difficulty adapting to how the parent will act. The child may gravitate between seeking closeness with the caregiver and sometimes distancing themselves from the primary caregiver. *Fear is the basis for their attachment behavior.*

The parent of the disorganized child will often set their child up for failure. They may threaten their child with abandonment or things that are frightening to the child. The parent is often abusive (emotionally, physically, or sexually) and will utilize shaming for punishment.

The disorganized *(fearful avoidant)* adult has a pervasive sense of fear associated with their personal safety and in relationships. They have a *fear of intimacy* and find difficulty in building relationships. They may unconsciously sabotage relationships or end them if they become fearful of rejection in the relationship. They will often doubt that anyone will love them and when faced with the need to trust, they will often find evidence of rejection and opt out of the relationship.

A belief system that characterizes a disorganized adult may dictate mistaken beliefs that state "*people cannot be trusted*" or "*I cannot trust anyone, even myself*." The narrative may be, "*I prefer to stay away from relationships, or I will get hurt*." This can be a lonely and isolative ideology and can lead to feeling fear instead of love. The disorganized adult may choose someone that causes them to feel fear, or invoke anger in another to validate their belief that they cannot trust others.

The brain of the disorganized individual often will lack important linkages in the neo-cortex of the brain due to lack of important bonding. Their brain is often stuck in a trauma response rather than being able to effectively respond to existing situations.

Your Attachment Style

Exploring the Possibilities

After reading the descriptions of the various attachment styles, you have probably already guessed at whether you are secure, anxious, avoidant, or disorganized. Because we cannot usually retrieve memory from the first few years of life (pre-verbal memory), we cannot know how we were treated during infancy or early toddler years. We may have some clues based upon stories we heard from others who were there.

For example, if you know that you were adopted but not placed with a family for some time, there is a good chance you had a disruption in your bonding process as an infant. If you were placed in foster care at birth or in early childhood due to problems your parents were having such as substance abuse or violence, there may have likely been an *interruption in bonding* with your parent. These would be disruptions in the bonding process. Or you may have had a parent that worked a lot in early childhood, and you can guess that you may have been bonding with whomever cared for you.

> *A person that I saw in therapy stated that as an early adolescent, she was put in charge of her infant sister for a good amount of her early years. This may be an indicator that Mom did not see the bonding process as important or significant.*

You may have clues about what your early years were like. You may just know that your mother is not affectionate or a "*cuddly*" type. You may just know that your mother is caught up in her personal drama, conflict, or mental health problems, and parenting you as an infant may have been overwhelming. You may be aware that your mother has anger problems and that her fuse is short. Parenting an infant may have been difficult for her. Was there a surrogate parent such as a grandparent present during infancy and early childhood that was nurturing and loving?

Take some time to reflect on your attachment to primary caregivers throughout infancy, toddlerhood, and early childhood.

7.a Childhood Bonding Activity

Provide your best guess at the following infancy and early childhood bonding questions.

- **Infancy:** Provide your best guess at how well you were bonded with your primary caregiver based upon the things you know about your caregiver, pictures, or stories you were told.

____

____

____

____

- **Toddlerhood:** Provide your best guess at how well you were bonded with your primary caregiver based upon the things you know about your caregiver, pictures, or stories

____

____

____

____

- **Early Childhood:** Provide any memories you have from your earliest recollection of interactions with your primary caregivers.

____

____

____

____

Putting the Information Together Regarding Caregivers

Now you have some clues about your earliest years. These thoughts may provide information about your earliest years and childhood years where bonding and attachment take place. Remember that during this time, your brain is making neural connections with whatever circumstances you experience. These experiences shape your attachment style, create core beliefs about yourself, and have significant impact on your adult relationships.

The following questions may provide more clues regarding your attachment style:

7.a

1. Did you feel safety and trust with the primary caregiver that was present in infancy and early childhood? YES *(secure)* or NO
2. Was the primary caregiver that was present at infancy and early childhood consistently present, emotionally supportive, and affectionate? YES *(secure)* or NO
3. Do you feel a bond of closeness and caring from your primary caregiver present during infancy and childhood? YES *(secure)* or NO
4. Was your primary caregiver prone to addiction during your infancy or early childhood? YES *(avoidant)* or NO

5. Was your primary caregiver dealing with mental illness during childhood and unable to provide emotional support? YES *(avoidant)* or NO

6. Did your primary caregiver have difficulty providing emotional support to you? YES *(avoidant)* or NO

7. Did your primary caregiver that was present during infancy and childhood have difficulty providing physical touch? YES *(avoidant)* or NO

8. During infancy or childhood, did your caregiver change or were they inconsistent? YES *(anxious)* or NO

9. During infancy or childhood, was there divorce or conflict between parents? YES *(anxious)* or NO

10. Did you have a helicopter caregiver or someone who is emotionally needy or smothering? YES *(anxious)* or NO

11. During infancy or childhood, were there any traumatic events that you are aware of? YES *(disorganized)* or NO

12. Are you aware of any physical, emotional, or sexual abuse by older adults during early childhood? YES *(disorganized)* or NO

13. Do you recall feeling fear toward one or both caregivers due to their anger? YES *(disorganized)* or NO

Be easy on yourself, as these questions can bring up emotions and memories. Remember that we are merely conducting an inventory so that you can further identify mistaken beliefs and their origin. Attachment issues can highlight insight into the developing belief system.

The concept of attachment is very complex, and these questions may provide you with clues. They are not absolute indicators of your attachment style. If you have questions or concerns, you may want to initiate some therapy to ascertain attachment issues. First and foremost, just consider this an inventory and not an absolute confirmation of your attachment style. And do not berate yourself. Be aware that you have had the courage to look within and initiate reflection on your bond as a child.

Next, we will discuss your relationships that will provide further clues into your attachment style. Your adult relationships and your interactive responses may indicate more about your attachment. Let's explore further.

Putting the Information Together Regarding Adult Relationships

The following questions will seek to explore your tendencies in adult relationships and how attachment issues have created a basis for who you are in relationships. Consider friendships and romantic relationships. Consider that you may have had different responses to various people based upon your sense of safety and trust in those relationships. The following questions may be indicators of your attachment style. The "yes" responses reflect the italicized attachment style.

Answer the following questions based upon your adult friendships and romantic relationships:

1. Are you receptive to relationships? Do you welcome new people into your life, and feel safety and trust with others overall? YES *(secure)* or NO

2. Are you able to show romantic partners how you feel deep inside of you? YES *(secure)* or NO

3. Do you find it easy to discuss your life problems with your partner and friends? YES *(secure)* or NO

4. Do you try to work through problems in a relationship before leaving the person? YES *(secure)* or NO

5. Do you feel worthy of healthy, happy relationships? YES *(secure)* or NO

6. Do you feel uncomfortable opening up to friends and romantic partners? YES *(avoidant)* or NO

7. When you feel insecure in a relationship, do you push them away so they cannot hurt you? YES *(avoidant)* or NO

8. Do you keep friends at "arm's length" distance to keep from being hurt or disappointed? YES *(avoidant)* or NO

9. Do you feel distressed when friends and partners infringe on your alone time and space? YES *(avoidant)* or NO

10. Do you feel that you don't need much in the way of comfort or affection from your romantic partner? YES *(avoidant)* or NO

11. When you feel insecure in a relationship, do you try to pursue the person and get closer? YES *(anxious)* or NO

12. Do you worry that your partner does not love you as much as you care for them? YES *(anxious)* or NO

13. Do you find yourself worrying that others do not really care for you? YES *(anxious)* or NO

14. Do you put the needs of others before your own and then become upset or resentful? YES *(anxious)* or NO

15. Do you feel that you want or need to be closer to your friends and romantic partners than you are? YES *(anxious)* or NO

16. Do you have difficulty trusting your relationships, and fear abandonment? YES *(disorganized)* or NO

17. Do you fear abandonment and rejection by romantic partners? YES *(disorganized)* or NO

18. Do you fear that friends will eventually leave you, reject you, or abandon you? YES *(disorganized)* or NO

19. Do you have difficulty setting boundaries, and then get angry and push those same people away? YES *(disorganized)* or NO

20. Do you feel emotional turbulence with family members and your romantic partners through the relationships? YES *(disorganized)* or NO

Looking at Attachment in Terms of How You Communicate with Others

The following categories are related to how you communicate and interact with others verbally. Attachment styles will often predict characteristics of how an individual articulates themselves in their communication with others. Interpersonal communication functioning often is set up in the neural connections made during early bonding experiences with the primary caregiver. Keep in mind that we are also genetically "prewired" to lean toward certain strengths in brain functioning. However, attachment styles can also create a style of communication.

Answer the following questions based upon your communication and narrative style:

1. Are you easy to follow in dialogue? Do you easily engage in communication with others? YES *(secure)* or NO

2. Do you have appropriate voice inflections that indicate emotional expression in your communication? YES *(secure)* or NO

3. Do people say that you communicate in a coherent, sequential, and fluent style? YES *(secure)* or NO

4. Do you communicate in a direct way and "stick to the facts" when sharing with family or at work? YES *(avoidant)* or NO

5. When you talk do you limit the amount of words you use?
   YES *(avoidant)* or NO

6. Are you monotone in your communication, using minimal voice inflection to express the emotional content of what you say?
   YES *(avoidant)* or NO

7. Are you "chatty" or talkative? YES *(anxious)* or NO

8. Do you become overly emotional when you express yourself or communicate with a family member or partner? YES *(anxious)* or NO

9. Do you dwell on negativity and tend to see a glass as "half empty" rather than "half full"? YES *(anxious)* or NO

10. Do you speak in an incoherent way that is difficult for others to follow? YES *(disorganized)* or NO

11. Are there long gaps of verbalization that happen when you are asked a question? YES *(disorganized)* or NO

12. Do you have difficulty finding words to express what you want to say? YES *(disorganized)* or NO

Looking at the three groups of questions, tally the categories that you responded "yes" to:

____ Secure ____ Anxious ____ Avoidant ____ Disorganized

Did you have a frequently scored "yes" category of *secure, anxious, avoidant, or disorganized*? Again, please do not consider this an absolute regarding your attachment style. However, you can begin to identify which style you lean toward. Most people have a primary attachment style with some leaning toward other styles as well.

This inventory can provide you with greater insight into your core beliefs about yourself. This may provide you with understanding in how you may answer the questions: "*Who am I? What kind of a world is this? What does a person like me need to do in a world like this in order to make a place for myself?*"

The important consideration for this chapter has been the idea that there are other factors that often lead to the establishment of mistaken core beliefs that are running you at an unconscious level. Attachment is one of those considerations because of the beliefs that can emerge from feeling the inability to trust others or having thoughts about self that foster low self-worth.

Thoughts such as "I am unworthy" or "I am unlovable" or "I am not important" can be reflections of mistaken beliefs that must be challenged. Today is a new day. You can affirm yourself despite these dark and mistaken self-perceptions.

Polyvagal Theory and Attachment

Early infancy and childhood bonding are aspects of brain development and neural connections that may affect relationships throughout our lifetime. Neuroscientist Dr. Stephen Porges (2017; 2022) established a fascinating theory about the vagus nerve and how it relates to early childhood bonding and attachment. (More information on the vagal nerve will be discussed in the next chapter).

Infants are learning to cope with stress such as feeding needs, attention needs, and emotions. The vagal nerve has significant involvement in attachment and social engagement. Evolved vagal nerve development happens in a safe and consistent environment. This is sometimes referred to as ***co-regulation***, which allows the developing person to establish a sense of safety from a biological perspective.

We begin to learn how to ***co-regulate*** in infancy and this is through the attachment bond between caregiver and infant. The infant is learning to emotionally regulate in this process. When the environment is not safe during infancy and early childhood, the vagal nerve becomes more stress sensitive, and a developing person has limited ability to cope with stress throughout their lifetime. *Co-regulation* can happen in adulthood, however, with a safe and supportive partner or relationship.

The next chapter will speak to the brain and the neurological connections that affect our response to life experiences. Gaining an understanding of the various neural networks in the brain can provide a pathway toward healing as we work to reconstruct our self-perception. Remember that ***you are worthy, you are important, and you are lovable.***

7.b Reflection

- What emotions come up for you as you have reviewed your possible attachment style? What thoughts emerge?

____

____

____

____

____

____

- What awareness do you have of how you deal with insecurity in your adult relationships?

____

____

____

____

____

____

- In what ways has your attachment bond been a part of your canvas?

Chapter 8

My Brain is My Friend

Getting Familiar with My Old Brain, Midbrain, and Executive Network

"The human brain has 100 billion neurons, each neuron connected to 10 thousand other neurons. Sitting on your shoulders is the most complicated object in the known universe."

— Michio Kaku, *The Future of the Mind*

The average human brain weighs a little over 3 pounds. The human brain has been elegantly designed to think, reason, pursue dreams, create, logically apply information, emote, and move your body just to name a few things. The capability and multiple processes are powered by microscopic cells called neurons. The brain is designed to help you pursue your vision and paint new pictures on your canvas or write the next page of your story. It is also designed to protect you.

In your brain's effort to keep you safe, it will sometimes create barriers, blockages, or have you responding emotionally to a situation. Your brain's intention is to serve you and preserve your life. Are you willing to take the journey to explore your brain?

This chapter will not teach you intricate specifics about the brain, but it will provide you with some basic information about brain functioning. This is significant when referencing ***mental health issues, cognition, emotions, behaviors, and physiology. The brain controls it all.*** The brain is so vital to understanding behavioral health that most recent research has highlighted neuroscience psychology. This is because of the connection between brain, mind, and body.

Historically, the focus of human behavior has been on social issues and theory behind why people think, feel, and behave the way they do. The connection to brain functioning, however, provides a much greater understating of behavior, as the brain mechanisms are driving most all human interactions. Additionally, the scientific understanding of brain actions provides validity to findings about human behavior.

As you begin to understand how your brain works to protect you or to advance your motivations, you will see that learning about the brain can help you to become *"smarter than your brain."* This provides you with the ability to create change in a positive direction. Your brain has been designed to provide you with ways to deal with your life situations. It is an organic, highly advanced computer that responds to the data it is provided. In addition, however, its complex mechanisms have incredible potential for adaptation to your life and your interactions with the world around you.

Brain Basics

I will explain the brain by describing its three major parts: ***the brain stem, the midbrain*** *(or limbic regions)*, ***and the neocortex.*** Each of these areas has complex duties, responsibilities, and mechanisms far too complicated for my purposes. However, I intend to provide a brief and basic understanding of the three major regions which will help you to understand this amazing organ that you possess. Each of these areas has much to do with your behavioral, emotional, and cognitive responses to the people and world around you.

Your brain is designed in a very phenomenal way that works to protect you. It helps you to forget and to remember, provides you with energy, provides you with the ability to think, feel, and choose your next move. The following description of brain and nervous system functioning will give you information to help you understand the miraculous organ that you hold in your head. It will help you to see that your brain is not working against you but working for you, and has your best interests as the basis for its actions.

Brain Stem

The brain stem is often referred to as the *"primitive brain,"* the *"reptilian brain,"* or the *"lizard brain"* and this is because it is the most primitive part of the brain. This part of the brain exists in frogs, fish, and reptiles. The brain stem controls arousal, or surges of energy that propel us to move to seek satisfaction from food or sex, and other reward center activity including safety. The brain stem also controls our ***fight, flight, freeze, or collapse and submit*** responses to high stress situations or traumatic events.

Although it is the most primitive part of the brain, some of its functions will override the more advanced brain functioning in situations where trauma or high stress activities are happening. In a situation where a high stress event takes place, you will most likely not be using reason or rationalizing your response. You will be catapulted into a *fight, flight, freeze, or collapse and submit response.* This all happens in the brain stem.

I will also be referring to the sympathetic nervous system that works in conjunction with the brain stem to provide the *fight or flight* response. When you are hungry or thirsty, or when you are seeking other types of pleasure (such as drugs or alcohol), the craving cycle takes place in the brain stem. This is a very primitive function of the reptilian brain.

Midbrain

The midbrain area is concealed beneath the cortex or the gray folded outer region of the brain and is sometimes referred to as the "old" mammalian brain. This mammalian brain is present in all mammals, large and small, and the limbic area is most significant in midbrain functioning. This is because the ***limbic region*** drives *emotion.* The limbic region is also responsible for the attachment bonds we form with one another. (The previous chapter spoke to human attachment bonds and the neural connections made from bonding with primary caregivers.) This limbic region allows us to connect with each other and motivates this process of connecting.

The limbic region also contains the hypothalamus, which is responsible for hormone releases throughout the body depending upon the situation a mammal experiences. The amygdala is also a part of the midbrain and is known to be involved in our response to ***fear*** and can motivate us to respond to a fear-based situation. The hippocampus is another part of the midbrain that links and connects our experiences to thoughts, emotions, and body sensations and puts these experiences into memory.

Neocortex

Neuroscience, with advanced methods of looking at the brain, has made substantial progress in demystifying brain functioning. Neuroscience has increased our knowledge of brain activity as it applies to human behavior and cognitions. The ***neocortex,*** or ***newer brain***, is the outer area of the brain with which we most likely associate visually when we see a human brain. It is the outer gray folded matter portion of the brain that separates humans from other animals. This complex system of neurons allows us to have thoughts, make decisions, and experience our lives in other complex, creative ways.

If you consider the difference of ability between a human and a mouse, you can understand some of the advanced brain capability we have. A mouse has the brain stem activity of fight, flight, freeze, or collapse. A mouse also has midbrain activity that allows it to connect and bond with other mice and with its young.

A mouse's cortex is very limited, however, and while it contains some vision ability and motor skill ability, the mouse does not have the ability to reason, be creative, or think in complex ways like a human. This is primarily due to various complex regions of the neocortex in humans, especially the frontal lobe and the prefrontal lobe.

The ***frontal lobe*** is the area that sits behind the forehead area, and this is the most advanced area of the brain. The lateral posterior parietal cortex is toward the back of the skull. Within the frontal lobe is the prefrontal cortex, and this in combination with the lateral posterior parietal cortex works to function as the **central executive network** or the **frontoparietal network**, which is most responsible for the ability to make decisions, problem solve, and pursue goal activity.

The central executive network of the brain also somewhat acts as an "external mind" and coordinates high level tasks as well as establishes working memory. The central executive network of the brain is activated when a person engages in a task that requires attention. Damage or disruption to the central executive network is present in most psychiatric and neurological disorders.

When Your Brain is Functioning Optimally

Consider what it takes for your brain to function at its highest level. Think about how complex and responsive your brain is to your day-to-day experiences. We often speak about heart health and how to maintain various organs in the body in a healthy state. Brain health is also very significant in terms of being able to perform, think, and act at our highest functioning level.

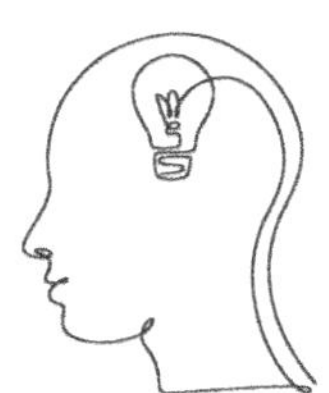

Brain Health Consciousness

Eating healthy will feed your brain and it will then be able to perform cognitive tasks that you need to do during the day. Decision making, interacting with others, planning, and other cognitive activities require the brain to be fed nutritious food to operate optimally.

Dr Sanjay Gupta (2021), a renowned neuroscientist and neurosurgeon, stated that the type of foods that are bad for high blood pressure, cholesterol, and diabetes are known to harm cardiovascular health, but also harm brain health—especially in the cognitive functioning area. Reducing high fat foods, sugars, and processed foods are your best bet to feeding your brain better. Eating fresh vegetables, lean meats, seafood, and berries can be part of feeding your brain optimally.

Hydrate your body and your brain. Water consumption is very significant to our brain health for optimal cognitive functioning. People will often mistake dehydration for being hungry, as the craving for either is similar. In addition to problems with cognitive functioning, mood can also be affected by dehydration.

It is best to intentionally drink plenty of water and stay hydrated rather than to wait until you feel thirsty. Stress levels are known to be reduced from simply drinking water and staying sufficiently hydrated. A good rule of thumb is to take your body weight in pounds and divide it by 2. This will provide you with a good baseline of the minimum number of ounces of water you should be drinking daily.

Sleep hygiene is becoming an area of concern to those who are experts in psychiatric disorders. The need for an adequate number of hours of sleep is important to our ability to function and it is equally important in brain health. The body replenishes itself and heals tissues during sleep. The brain is actively engaged in a process of discarding waste in brain cells during sleep.

"Stress levels are reduced from simply drinking water and staying sufficiently hydrated."

Additionally, memory is stored and strengthened when sleep hours are adequate. Research has shown that during sleep our brain is encoding, consolidating, and storing memory. Most recent research has found that everyone needs from 7 to 8 hours of sleep every night to maintain healthy brain functioning. I know that for myself, when I do not get adequate sleep on any night, the next day I am not functioning or performing at full capacity.

Lack of energy and physical exhaustion can be a result of not getting sufficient sleep. For optimal brain health, you must get 7 to 8 hours of sleep every night.

Physical exercise is especially significant to your brain's optimal functioning. Dr. Sanjay Gupta (2021) attributes a consistent physical exercise routine as the most important thing to enhance brain health. Consider the effect of exercise due to the brain's release of endorphins. Endorphins are a neurotransmitter, or brain chemical, called the "feel good" neurotransmitter. After intense exercise a person feels better because of some of the neurochemistry that occurs. Increased blood flow from activity delivers nutrients to the brain as well as oxygen. This in turn supports the development of new neurons.

Your ability to overcome mood disorders and cognitive decline can be enhanced by engaging in regular intense physical activity. It is also a coping strategy that can decrease anxiety and depression because of its effects on the brain.

It is important to consider that knowing about your brain and how you can keep it functioning well is a way of learning to be smarter than your brain. Understanding how to feed your brain and give it adequate rest and restoration can deter psychological problems and deterioration as you age. We will now move to looking at how your brain responds to unhealthy thoughts, trauma, and attachment.

When Your Brain is Not Functioning Optimally

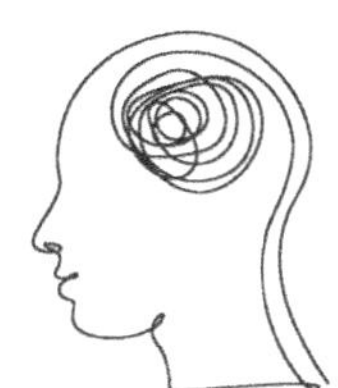

There are many reasons that your brain may not be serving you well. Brain malfunction comes from two primary sources: **genetic prewiring** and **environmental stressors**. Humans are born with genetics that may make them prone to a particular psychiatric problem. A person may be genetically prewired for the neurochemistry of depression, anxiety, schizophrenia, or other conditions.

A person may also be subjected to situations in the environment that affect brain functioning such as trauma, insecure attachment, or relational trauma (abuse). A person may also be subjected to both genetic prewiring of psychiatric disorders and environmental stressors that compound brain functioning problems. I will begin with speaking to the neurobiology of brain disease.

There is some knowledge and much speculation about causes of various disorders and I will speak with limitation to what is known about a few common psychiatric conditions and brain functioning. Some abnormalities in the brain and neurotransmitter levels are present for various conditions. It becomes the "*Which came first, the chicken or the egg?*" question.

In some situations where there is a genetic predisposition for a disorder, the neurobiology came first. In some situations, life challenges were present that created the brain chemistry for various disorders. Then there exists the individual differences between people. ***Individual differences are an important consideration because what we do with our genetic prewiring and the conditions that occur from the environment will differ from person to person.*** Following is some of what we know about common psychiatric disorders.

Depression

Depression is a disorder that is widespread throughout our world population. Some depression is associated with a difficult situation that a person is dealing with, and some depression is a result of trauma or difficult past life experiences. Some depression is genetically "predisposed" and is known to be passed down from generations. The core elements of depression include a pervasively sad, empty, or irritable mood that is accompanied by changes in a person's ability to function. Other symptoms in conjunction with the *sad and empty feelings* are:

- loss of energy
- loss of motivation
- hopelessness
- sleep problems (oversleeping or inability to sleep)
- loss of interest in things that were at one time of interest
- appetite disturbance (overeating or having no appetite)
- an overall feeling of lethargy

Neurotransmitters are the brain chemicals that cause action or inaction. They send signals from one neuron (nerve cell) to another.

Serotonin is a neurotransmitter that is known to be associated with sleep. Dopamine is a neurotransmitter that is associated with *"reward"* and reward-related learning processes. Dopamine is often referred to as the *"feel good"* neurotransmitter and is involved with mood, decision-making, and stress-response. Norepinephrine is a neurotransmitter that is known to be associated with forward motion. Serotonin, norepinephrine, and dopamine are known to be at lower levels for those with depression.

It is like your car being *"a quart low"* in oil. When your car is a quart low in oil, it will not run as well as when it is full. When your brain is not producing the proper amount of serotonin, norepinephrine, and dopamine, you are likely to be running a quart low in some of those neurotransmitters. This will cause some of the symptoms of depression. Antidepressant medications serve to regulate some of those neurotransmitters to a level that will produce feelings of normalcy and motivation.

In addition to the brain chemistry being altered during a depressive episode, there are also areas of the brain that are affected. The prefrontal cortex area is known to have lower volume, or actually decrease is size, which affects the ability to think and make decisions. The reward center of the brain (basal ganglia) is also affected with decreased stimulation and responsiveness. Depression that is caused by trauma has most likely affected other areas of the brain which will be discussed later in this chapter.

Anxiety

Some people are genetically prewired for anxiety and can trace the symptoms to past generations. Some of the symptoms of anxiety are excessive fear and the anticipation of a future threat. There is also a great deal of worry that a person is unable to control. Other symptoms of anxiety in conjunction with ***excessive fear and worry*** are:

- restlessness
- fatigue
- difficulty concentrating
- irritability
- muscle tension
- sleep disturbance

Anxiety that is associated with post-traumatic stress disorder (PTSD) is interrelated with a ***sympathetic nervous system*** response that will be discussed further in the chapter.

The amygdala and parts of the limbic system are known to play a role in anxiety disorders. The origin of anxiety may be biological or environmental. Neurotransmitters, or brain chemicals, are known to affect anxiety. Some of the same neurotransmitters such as serotonin and norepinephrine play a role in anxiety. However, others such as GABA and glutamate may also play a role. Altering levels of serotonin through antidepressants can provide relief from depression and can also have a positive effect on anxiety.

Schizophrenia

Schizophrenia is known to be characterized by progressive clinical and cognitive (thought) changes. People who suffer from this disorder often lose touch with reality, engage in paranoid or delusional thinking, and have difficulty overall with the ability to attend to daily functioning. Additionally, a person with schizophrenia may display social withdrawal, difficulty sustaining tasks, lack of pleasure or enjoyment in life, and difficulty with emotions.

There are many structural brain changes that occur over time with someone with this disorder. There are lower volumes, or shrinkage in the neocortex frontal lobes and temporal lobes, which are areas that regulate thinking and judgment. As stated earlier, dopamine, associated with the reward center of the brain, runs at a deficit for those with depression. However, with schizophrenia, individuals are especially sensitive to dopamine and there may be a surplus which causes hallucinations and delusions.

Medications used to treat schizophrenia are antipsychotics which block the dopamine activity in the brain. This helps to lower the frequency and intensity of hallucinations and delusional thinking. There is evidence that schizophrenia is a genetically predisposed disorder.

Neurocognitive Disorders

Neurocognitive disorders are most often associated with aging and are neurodegenerative conditions. Dementia is often used to describe the symptoms a person experiences with neurocognitive decline. Dementia, Alzheimer's, vascular disease, brain injury, Parkinson's, and Huntington's disease are categorized as neurocognitive disorders.

They usually involve:

- memory loss
- confusion
- trouble concentrating
- trouble performing tasks
- struggles with communication
- poor judgment
- poor decision-making
- struggles with finding words
- wandering
- personality and behavior changes

The various types of neurocognitive disorders may be caused by different factors. However, there is neuron damage in the various disorders.

Alzheimer's is known to be associated with "amyloid plaques" that create tangles of neurons in the brains of those affected. Traumatic brain injury is caused by physical injury to the brain which impairs functioning. Vascular disease can cause damage to the blood vessels within the brain. Lewy body forms of dementia, which includes Alzheimer's and Parkinson's, are known to be associated with clumps of protein that block normal functioning of the brain. Infections and endocrine problems may also lead to changes in the brain where damage occurs, and the result is dementia-type symptoms.

Addiction

The past twenty years of addiction and brain research has brought extensive new knowledge and understanding of addictive processes in the brain. I will provide a minimal amount of information on how substances and addictions affect the brain. Various drugs of abuse interfere with signals that process the action of release or suppression of neurotransmitters. Some drugs serve to mimic neurotransmitters in the brain, and some activate the actual neurons to release more of the neurotransmitters. Substances serve to alter the brain chemistry to provide a desired effect for the user.

The part of the brain that is significantly involved with addiction to drugs is the "***reward center***" of the brain, or the basal ganglia. If you recall in the section on depression, the reward center has a decrease in activity with depression, and a person has very low motivation to be active. Many recreational drugs, however, over-activate this reward center, producing a high or euphoric feeling.

This reward center is key to feeling pleasure associated with sex, food, and socialization in a healthy brain. Drugs have the potential to flood this area with a sense of pleasure that causes a craving cycle demanding more and more of the associated good feelings from the drugs. After time, the feeling of pleasure diminishes and there is a need for increased amounts in more frequent intervals of time.

The amygdala is responsible for feeling discomfort, irritability, and anxiety when there is lack of the drug being taken. This is when a person will also try to get more of the substance to alleviate the feeling of withdrawal from the drug. The basal ganglia and the amygdala are in the midbrain region, and the compulsion to use drugs associated with addiction overrides the ability to think clearly.

The compulsion also overrides the ability to rationally consider how these drugs may be causing bad consequences. So higher levels of the brain's executive network functioning are bypassed, and a person will succumb instead to seeking pleasure.

The ***pleasure or euphoria*** from substance use is not fully understood. However, surges of the body's natural chemicals (such as endorphins) are released, along with neurotransmitters in the basal ganglia, and surges of dopamine to cause feelings associated with extreme pleasure (Cohen & Inaba, 2004).

In most recent studies of the brain and addiction, it was found that some people are more susceptible to the craving cycle in the reward system of the brain. These are individuals who likely have a genetic predisposition to addictive disorders. Similarly, a depressed or anxious person who is looking for a shift in mood may attempt to use substances to create feelings of pleasure that have been absent for them. This is also known as "self-medicating" where a person will attempt to alter their mood through use of drugs to alleviate the pain of depression.

Rounding It All Up

Understanding the brain and how it functions can provide a better understanding of trauma responses, attachment responses, and ways we respond to stress. It can also offer promise in how we can practice activities that will facilitate creating new neural pathways toward healing our brain. I have stated in the subtitle to this chapter that the "brain is your friend." It is especially true when you have knowledge of how it works and how you can create greater brain health.

The following chapter will look at loss and Chapter 10 will speak to changes in the brain associated with trauma.

8.a Reflection

- If you brain is like a computer that gathers data from external sources, what type of misinformation do you think your brain has received?

- In what ways do you provide yourself a brain health consciousness?

Eating healthy? / Hydrating? / Sleep? / Exercise?

- In what ways did you relate to the various malfunctions of the brain due to mental and emotional health issues?

____

____

____

____

____

____

8.a

Chapter 9

My Loss and High Stress Event Recap

Moving Beyond Those Barriers

"After all, when a stone is dropped into a pond, the water continues quivering even after the stone has sunk to the bottom."

— *Arthur Golden, Memoirs of a Geisha*

It is somewhat alarming to consider that much of our personal canvas is formed from a chain reaction to events that cause ripples in our existence. Some of the biggest ripples come from loss. We are prone to adopting a fantasy mentality that the things that are precious to us will always be with us.

Yet when we experience a loss, we are struck with the reality that things change, and that fate will sometimes claim what we hold so dear. When we experience pain, heartache, disappointment, or loss, we must learn to embrace, accept, and then let go. Are you ready to identify the stones and the ripples? Comfort will come from the release.

The introductory quote by Arthur Golden indicates an important concept relative to our personal well-being. That is the reality of how some life experiences can cause a ripple effect and be present in the wound that we carry throughout our lifetime. The wounds that we carry then cause a ripple effect throughout our lives until we examine and explore them. We can alter the intensity of the wounds we carry as we face them rather than run from them.

One universal aspect of the human experience is that we will experience loss, high stress events, and sometimes traumatic experiences that become a part of our wound. Our experiences can cause ongoing discomfort and may surface randomly. We often become good at hiding the feelings and emotions that surge. This chapter will explore some types of loss and traumatic experiences that we want to bring out into the light of day. Burying these events will only create a huge shadow over our lives.

If you have experienced severe trauma that has never been addressed, I ask that you consider working with a therapist while reading this chapter and the next chapter on trauma. There are many skilled psychotherapists that are capable and able to support you through a journey of working through your trauma.

There are also many types of trauma therapy that can be extremely helpful. Trauma Processing Therapy (CPT), Trauma Resilience Model (TRM), and Eye Movement Desensitization and Reprocessing (EMDR) therapy are some of the therapy methods that can be used to effectively treat trauma.

This chapter is intended to have you consider the impact of the losses and high stress events that potentially block you from living and experiencing your life to the fullest. These events may also block you from experiencing a full range of feelings or may heighten your emotional experiences. These events lose their power when exposed to the light of day and when they are validated as real things that affect you. Minimizing or disregarding these events only increases the size of the wound that you carry.

You may be reading this chapter thinking that you have not experienced much loss in your lifetime. However, there are many events that can take place that are now regarded as traumatic loss due to the emotional consequences. I have had many individuals who have come to receive psychotherapy from me that initially minimize their life experiences of loss and highly stressful events. They have not considered these events to be traumatic for them. It is important to put things into perspective and shine the light onto the things that may be weighing on you in various ways.

As stated earlier, *a part of the human experience is that we will experience loss, high stress events, and sometimes traumatic experiences that become a part of our wound.* The "wound" that I speak of is the emotional pain of our life experiences that lies just beneath the surface of our day-to-day interactions with the world around us. We all carry a wound. Our emotional injuries, big or small, are a part of life.

The only way to avoid injuries is to be bound in bubble wrap throughout your lifetime and never experience hurt, loss, or pain. However, that would not be truly living and experiencing life to the fullest. And that would also be injurious to the human soul. Let's look at the types of life events, loss, and traumatic experiences that may be a part of your experience.

Loss

People experience various types of loss. The greatest type of loss is usually the death of a loved one. However, other types of loss may have significant emotional consequences and should not be denied. Loss of a loved one through estrangement and distancing can provoke grief and emotional responses. Death of a pet can be significant to many. Loss of employment can also provoke a grief process.

"Any loss has the potential to open the doors to the memory of all our past losses."

Our attachment to people and things can create a sense of emptiness when they are no longer present for us. This is a natural human experience that can provide perspective or cause significant pain. Despite our response to loss, we are always just on the "other side" of all our losses. Any loss has the potential to open the doors to the memory of all our past losses.

Natural disasters such as fires, earthquakes, hurricanes, and pandemics can cause a feeling of loss of the order of life and a decrease of a sense of stability. The Covid-19 pandemic changed many people's sense of freedom and safety. The loss of lives that follows disasters also brings up mortality and the grief process.

Because we experience life and love and moments of joy with others, it is difficult when we need to experience the antithesis of happiness. The sadness that accompanies loss is often painful and disturbing. The end of a life of a loved one or the end of a situation that was comfortable and brought pleasure is hard to comprehend. We want the previous way of life to return. We want the anguish of loss to end, and yet it does not.

We must grieve that which was lost so that we can seemingly return to what life was like before the loss. And yet our lives will always be altered by those things once cherished that are now absent from our experience.

Western cultures do not prepare us for losing things, people, loved ones, and security. Western cultures prepare us for acquiring things and getting more new things such as the relationship, the job, the income, the house, the toys, the car, and other material things. We are not prepared, however, for losing these things.

Grief is the experience we have when we lose things that are sacred to us. Elisabeth Kubler Ross (1970) wrote extensively about loss and identified stages of grief. She identified the stages as:

- **Shock and disbelief:** The initial feeling of numbness and difficulty believing the loss really happened.
- **Anger:** Feeling angry about the loss or redirecting anger toward other people or things that you associate with the loss.
- **Bargaining:** Thinking about how you might have done things differently to prevent the loss or to alter the loss.
- **Depression:** The sadness that accompanies losing someone or something.
- **Acceptance:** Embracing the reality of what has happened and no longer wanting to change the memory of what happened.

Most experiences of loss go through these stages in various order. I have found that a person may feel stuck in one of the stages before coming to acceptance. Each person's journey through loss is their own, and ***there is no time limit*** in walking through the stages of loss. So many of the people I have worked with in therapy have indicated that they have been told by well-meaning friends and family that "*they need to move on.*"

Each person's journey is their own and sometimes people need time to "*wear the shroud*" of loss for extended periods of time. I refer to the ***"shroud"*** as that comfortable place of non-movement in the grief process. Where there is death of a close loved one, the shroud may become a ***"cocoon"*** that a person encases themselves in to hold onto the feelings and memories of the person they lost.

> *In my experience of the loss of my mother, I entered a cocoon of a sort. I was much less able to be socially available to friends, and I stopped my daily workout routines. My mother carried me in her womb and loved me and bonded with me, and my attachment was disrupted upon her death. She had many years of decline with strokes and loss of her physical abilities, and I had a lot of time to say my final important words to her.*
>
> *However, her death still had a profound effect on me. I allowed myself the comfort of my isolation and staying within my cocoon for almost a year. Thanks to talking to a close friend who I felt safe with, I was able to identify that I was essentially "holding in" all the feelings and all the memories of my mother by non-movement. I became ready to emerge from the cocoon and reclaim my active life.*
>
> *I do not regret the opportunity to stay in this safe place. This was a part of my journey in the loss of my mother. I now can love her, appreciate her life, and I still have memories of her gentle touch, her encouraging words, and her loving spirit. Being stuck in any life process can alter the ability to move through the process.*

Irrational Narratives and Grief

Sometimes, being stuck in a stage of grief involves irrational personalized narratives about a situation. Feeling ***irrational guilt*** about a loss is often a part of the process. Irrational guilt is when we experience thoughts about a loss that implies that we are the reason for the loss. It is sometimes an attempt to explain the loss. Irrational guilt is not based on fact and implies that we have a huge part in the loss. It is often a part of the ***bargaining*** stage of loss. Examples may include:

- A person feels irrational guilt about losing a job when their position was cut due to budget finances.
- A person blames themselves for a friend's car accident because *"they should have called them that day."*
- A person feels responsible for their parent's death because they *"should have been more involved in their life."*

Quite often the ***irrational guilt*** is preceded by the ***shoulds***: "*I should have done this, or I should have done that.*" We have the capacity to torture ourselves with false narratives that would not have prevented the loss, but that we feel to be true anyway. Irrational guilt is often a part of the grief process, and it is helpful to explore or identify. It is important to examine and process these things with a close friend or a professional if possible.

Your Personal Journey of Loss

Let's take a walk through your life and identify any of your major losses in life by placing a star next to them. Consider:

- ***death of loved ones***
- ***death of pets***
- ***estrangement of close friends or family***
- ***loss of trust***
- ***major moves***
- ***loss of friends***
- ***unwanted loss of jobs***
- ***loss of health or well-being***
- ***other losses***

Having a concrete representation of your life losses can help you to put the cumulative effect of your losses into perspective. Keep in mind that each event influenced you and more than likely you experienced the various stages of grief. Are there losses that are difficult for you to think about still? Is there unresolved internal conflict that you feel?

9.a Your Personal Journey of Loss

Let's take a walk through your life and identify any of your major losses in life. Consider:

- death of loved ones
- death of pets
- estrangement of close others or family
- loss of trust
- major moves
- loss of friends
- unwanted loss of jobs
- loss of health or well-being

Example: Year or Age: Age 5 **Loss:** Grandmother (maternal)

I was very close with my grandmother. She lived with our family. My mother was so very upset that her mother died, that I don't remember being comforted or helped through my sadness. I felt frozen at her funeral.

Year or Age: Loss:

Year or Age: Loss:

Year or Age: Loss: ______________________________

____

____

____

Year or Age: Loss: ______________________________

____

____

____

Year or Age: Loss: ______________________________

____

____

____

You may need additional journal pages to thoroughly inventory your losses. Continue to use this format in your journaling. Having a concrete representation of your life losses can help you to put the cumulative effect of your losses into perspective. Keep in mind that each event influenced you and more than likely you experienced the various stages of grief. Are there losses on the list that are difficult for you to think about still? Is there unresolved internal conflict that you feel with things on the list?

9.a

Place a star next to your list of losses with which you feel you still have unfinished business.

Being Stuck in Grief

Now with each of the starred loss items, let's look at the stages of grief and identify if there is a stuck stage for you.

- Are you still in **shock and disbelief** about the loss? *(Example: "I still feel numb, and I can't accept the truth about my dog's death. I can't cry and I still think he's home.")*
- Are you still **angry** for the loss? (*Example: "I'm still mad that my sister did not seem to care about my dog's death. I'm angry at the vet, too."*)
- Do you feel that this loss was unjustified (**bargaining**)? (*Example: "I can't believe that the veterinarian didn't do more to save my dog."*)
- Are you still **bargaining** about the loss? *(Example: "Maybe if I just would have taken my dog to the vet sooner, he wouldn't have died. If the vet would have done more, or performed surgery, maybe my dog would have had a chance.")*
- Are you feeling **depressed** or extreme sadness over the loss? (*Example: "I carry a feeling of emptiness and deep sadness all day because my dog is gone."*)
- Are you feeling **irrational guilt** about the loss? (*Example: "I feel guilty that I was never home for my dog because I was working every day the whole year before he died."*)

9.b Your Personal Inventory of Unfinished Business

Recall the Stages of Grief: Shock and disbelief / Anger / Irrational Guilt / Bargaining / Depression / Acceptance

Look for Losses with Unfinished Business. For each of the starred items on your list of losses, fill in the form below.

- Identify from your list of losses, areas of unfinished business.
- Identify the stage of grief that you think you are stuck in.
- List the FALSE narrative associated with your grief process that has blocked you.
- Write how you would prefer to alter your narrative about the loss.
- You have permission to indicate, "I am not ready to move on just yet."

Loss With Unfinished Business: Death of My Grandmother.

Stage of Grief: I feel stuck in shock and disbelief. I don't think I ever processed my feelings about losing my grandmother.

False Narrative: "My mother's pain is so much worse than mine, so I don't really want to add to the emotions. I need to hide my anger and sadness because it will only add to everyone else's discomfort"

9.b

I would prefer to alter my narrative to: "I am ready to move through this sadness. I know my feelings are important despite everyone else's emotions. I deserve to experience the loss of my Grandmother now and find a place of acceptance."
or "I'm not ready to move on yet."

Loss With
Unfinished Business: ______________________

Stage of Grief: ______________________

False Narrative: ______________________

____

Alternative Narrative: ______________________

____

____

or "I'm not ready to move on yet."

Loss With
Unfinished Business: ______________________

Stage of Grief: ______________________

False Narrative: ______________________

____

Alternative Narrative: ______________________

____

____

or "I'm not ready to move on yet."

If you marked ***"I'm not ready to move on yet"*** in any of your losses, know that there is no timeline that you need to adhere to.

Loss With
Unfinished Business: ____________________

Stage of Grief: ____________________

False Narrative: ____________________

____

Alternative Narrative: ____________________

____

____

or "I'm not ready to move on yet."

Loss With
Unfinished Business: ____________________

Stage of Grief: ____________________

False Narrative: ____________________

____

Alternative Narrative: ____________________

____

9.b ____________________

or "I'm not ready to move on yet."

If you marked ***"I'm not ready to move on yet"*** in any of your losses, know that there is no timeline that you need to adhere to.

"I'm not ready to move on yet."

If you feel you are not ready to move from your loss, know that there is no timeline that you need to adhere to. You may be immersed in the grief process and are in a plateau regarding movement. I spoke earlier about the *"shroud"* of loss or the cocoon we sometimes experience that feels like a safe place even though there is little movement or change in the grief process. If the loss is something that you experienced years ago, and you feel stuck, the inventory of the stages of grief may provide some good clues about stuck points.

You always have the option of seeking help professionally or from a close friend with whom you can confide. Your first step toward change, however, is to list the losses and inventory the stages of grief that you experience. Shining light on the stages of grief can take the mystery out of why you are still feeling immersed in suffering.

The road toward acceptance can be winding and long and may be very uncomfortable at times. You may find yourself sitting along the side of road toward acceptance and feeling depression or sadness or anger. Sometimes the experience is emotionally painful. ***Embrace each moment and identify what you are feeling.*** Attempt to be authentically where you are along the road toward acceptance.

Finding acceptance of the loss of a loved one

Loss can have a life-long effect on you. Some will stay with you in your memory with little or no associated emotional surges. Some memories may come up when you experience a new loss. Some may be like a dream-like floating recall of a person or an event. Embracing the memory of loved ones lost is significant to the process of letting go. You are not letting go of the memory or of the impact the person had on your life, but finding your way toward acceptance of the loss.

The process of walking on the road toward acceptance can include expression of your feelings and having at least one person you can feel safe with to talk about the emotions that come up.

- Be patient and do not set up a "timeline" that you believe should be the end of your grief process.
- Be gentle with yourself and know that time will pass, feelings will change, and thoughts and memories of your loved one will still be there.
- Sometimes the road toward acceptance means experiencing unwanted feelings or survivor's guilt.
- This is part of the grief process.

Sometimes the path toward finding acceptance of a loss can ***narrow***. The path narrows when you don't feel you have as many options as you had in the beginning of a loss. In the beginning, people are understanding and are compassionate and give you support. A few months later, however, the support often dwindles, and this is when grieving people often hide that they are still in emotional pain.

The path narrows when you are influenced by the "should" of emotional response. Examples are, "*I should be over this by now.*" "*I shouldn't be so upset by this.*" "*I should have been able to let go by now.*" These false narratives can narrow your path and you can be faced with feeling no exit from the pain. ***Be willing to seek professional help*** if you are feeling that your path has narrowed, and you have no escape.

Be sure to take care of yourself during the most severe part of your grief process. Remember that all your past losses may surface. New loss triggers memories of all past losses. Allow yourself time to heal. Some days you just may want to be alone. Some days you may not feel like talking to others. Give yourself permission to experience all your feelings and needs for comfort. ***Trust yourself.*** If you are feeling excessively depressed, seek help.

Traumatic Loss

Some of your losses include intense emotional responses and, possibly, intrusive memories of the event. These losses are potentially traumatic losses. ***With any losses that include trauma, it is best to consider getting help in therapy with a trusted psychotherapist who can lead you through the processing of these memories.*** Trauma will be discussed further in the following chapter.

9.c Reflection

- Are there any losses that continue to cause ripples in your day-to-day life?

- Do you have losses with unfinished business or losses with which you have unresolved internal conflict? If so, what are they and what is the conflict?

- Has your timeline of losses provided you with new insight? If so, what have you learned?

9.c

Chapter 10

Traumatic Events

Ruptures in our Life Experiences

"The paradox of trauma is that it has both the power to destroy and the power to transform and resurrect"

— Peter A. Levine, *In an Unspoken Voice: How the Body releases Trauma and Restores Goodness*

The brain and the body work overtime to change and heal. Old cells die and new ones emerge. The departing of the old and the welcoming of the new is a part of life. Life is flowing and changing. As youth, we become accustomed to the new teacher each year at school. We acquire new clothes, homes, cars, furniture, and we let go of the old. Friends come into our life, and we let them go. Jobs and schools may change, and we are flowing with life in acquiring and releasing.

A disruption in the process can occur when we experience the unexpected, the unthinkable, or the unacceptable. The accompanying hurt, pain, intrusive thoughts, or distrust of people on our journey can be the rupture that suddenly stops the flow of our existence. Are you willing to move toward transformation and get back on the path of healing?

The beginning quote to this chapter by Peter A. Levine indicates that trauma is a powerful life experience that can cause personal devastation and destruction, and it can be a turning point for us to seek help and transform ourselves.

Unresolved trauma can have life-long consequences and cause suffering for an individual. Whether an experience is the traumatic loss of a loved one, loss of status, loss of a sense of safety, a natural disaster, or loss of a long-term relationship, the emotional consequences are significant if they remain unresolved or unprocessed.

"Trauma for the individual carries emotional, psychological, somatic, and often long-term consequences."

Trauma can be the story of undue cruelty experienced by a Holocaust survivor, or it can be the story of the constant and more subtle disregard and ignoring of early childhood needs by a parent (relational trauma). It can be the story of a person experiencing an unexpected natural disaster such as fire, flood, earthquake, or tornado. It may be the story of a lifetime love lost to betrayal or a loved one lost to sudden death.

Trauma extends to the first responder law enforcement officer or firefighter who experiences persistent exposure to the unthinkable or unimaginable visuals of human suffering and death. Emergency room physicians and nurses also face multiple traumatic scenarios hourly and daily. Trauma can be the story of a person who diligently enlists in the military and eventually finds themselves in a war zone, seeing or committing the atrocities of war.

It can be the story of a woman carrying a baby during pregnancy for 9 months, and then losing that child within months to sudden infant death. It can be the childhood experience of neglect, physical abuse, emotional abuse, sexual abuse, or the childhood experience of bullying and cruelty by other children. Trauma may be the story of a person who suddenly learns that they have a major medical condition that alters their lifestyle.

Or it may be the story as seen through the eyes of the victim of domestic violence or sexual assault. It may be the story of a small child who suddenly finds themselves separated from their parent and placed in a foster home with strangers. Trauma may be a physical injury suffered through accidents, negligence, lack of accountability, or being at the wrong place at the wrong time.

The stories of trauma are extensive. The stories are sometimes brutal and involve a human's inhumanity to another human. The stories sometimes involve the unexpected and shocking reality of earth's volatility. The experience of trauma for the individual carries emotional, psychological, somatic, and often long-term consequences. As a psychotherapist, I have heard the many stories of pain and suffering and know that the individual response to trauma can vary.

Traumatic and High Stress-Related Loss: Individual responses to life experiences

The individual response to life situations has to do with many factors. Some are biological and some are environmental. Trauma and traumatic loss can be very different for various individuals, as the response and psychological distress over a loss can vary significantly. Two people can experience the same event and have very different emotional responses to the event. Two people can experience the same situation and one might have a trauma response and the other will not.

The resulting trauma or non-trauma can be measured by the amount of time it takes to no longer have emotional surges or intrusive thoughts about the event. Emotional surges, flashbacks, and intrusive thoughts that last beyond 30 days are usually indicative of post-traumatic stress.

Cumulative Trauma

Different responses can be attributed to the cumulative effect of loss. A person who has had many significant losses can have a stressful event "push them over the edge" emotionally. Loss is stored in the same area of the brain in memory networks, so an event can trigger the memory and emotional/somatic memory of all past losses. The cumulative effect of loss can create the sudden feeling of desperation and emotional overwhelm.

I have worked with individuals who have had many significant losses, and then one smaller "fender bender" car accident will push them over the edge into a severe trauma response. They become suddenly flooded with emotion and memories of past traumatic experiences. Or they may become suddenly flooded with emotions and find it difficult to comprehend why a smaller incident has created such emotional distress.

The Biology of Trauma

Everyone has a different ability to handle stress dependent upon their genetic predisposition to deal with stressors. The combination of genetic tolerance to stress and the cumulative effect of loss can determine why some people experience a greater emotional and psychological response to a loss than others.

Additionally, the genetics associated with being emotionally attuned versus being logically or rationally oriented can affect a person's response to loss. This may also be why two people experiencing the same event might have two very different responses.

Another reason that two people experiencing the same event can respond in very different ways is due to the attachment of the situation to the individual. Two people seeing a stray dog get hit by a car can have very different emotional responses because of the feelings they may have about dogs. A "dog lover" will more than likely feel a more intense emotional response than someone who is disconnected from feelings about pets and dogs.

Additionally, two people may be genetically prewired to handle seeing a traumatic event differently. There are many factors that can influence a human trauma response.

Your Brain

Our brains are wired to adapt to trauma at some level. Some of us are genetically "prewired" to be able to withstand high levels of stress or traumatic memory. Some of us have a lower ability to withstand high levels of stress. Additionally, repeated traumatic events can cause an expansion of capacity for high stress or a narrowing of capacity to withstand stress. Dr. Daniel Siegel (2010) refers to this as a "window of tolerance".

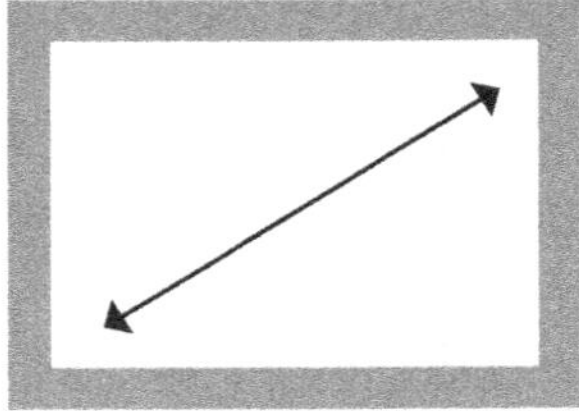

Imagine that this square represents a person's ability to tolerate high stress or traumatic events. People are born with a level of tolerance. Some of us are born with a calmer disposition and can tolerate a high level of stressful events. Some have a shallower or narrower capacity to withstand high stress or trauma. A traumatic event may allow a person to tolerate the event, or it may change a person's capacity for tolerating future stressful events.

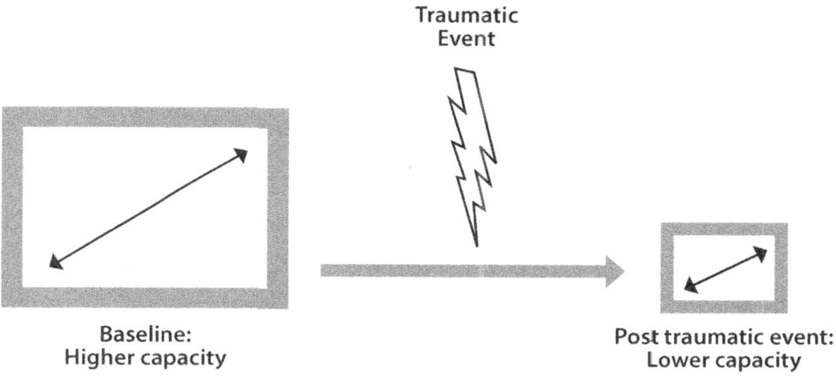

Trauma may affect a person's capacity for tolerating stress and it may result in a lower threshold for pain. The preceding diagram shows that a person's tolerance can change following high stress events. Post traumatic effects may cause a lower capacity to deal with future stressors. People who have experienced trauma will sometimes say that they can no longer handle minor stressors. They are more anxious and have difficulty with things that used to be easy for them. Their capacity to handle stress has changed.

Hypo-arousal or Hypervigilance

A person may find themselves outside of their area of tolerance and stuck in a *hyper-vigilant (anxious)* state or *hypo-arousal (depressed)* state. I refer to this as being either "***stuck on a highwire***" or "***stuck in the basement***." This is what occurs when a traumatic event causes a person to move beyond their capacity for stress. The next section will continue to address the "*stuck on the highwire*" or "*in the basement*" phenomenon.

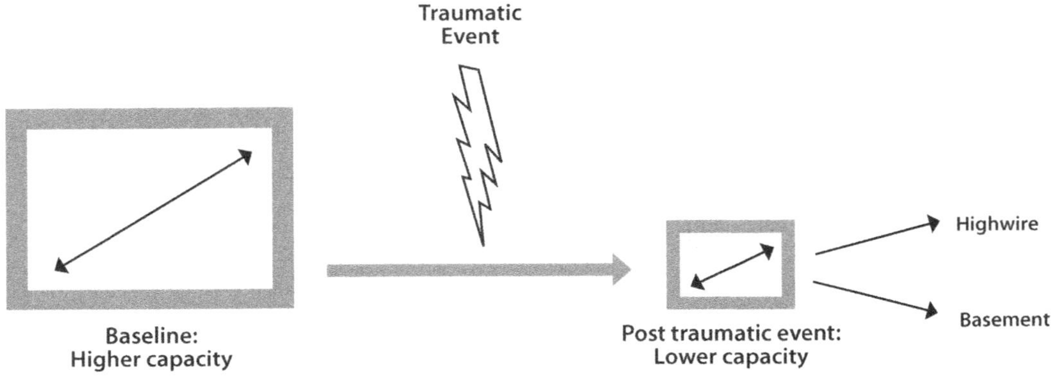

Trauma and the Brain

> *"Nothing ever goes away until it has taught us what we need to know."*
>
> — *Pema Chodron*

Emotional trauma or highly stressful life experiences affect the brain and its functioning. As the quote by Pema Chodron indicates, ***we can learn from trauma*** as we are in the healing process. The psychological distress that a person experiences from an extremely stressful event affects different people in different ways.

High anxiety, extreme depression, or dissociation from the memories of the aversive event are some of the results. Inadequate caregiving during childhood is a *relational stressor* that can lead to long-term alterations in the central nervous system response. It is important to understand aspects of the central nervous system when discussing trauma.

Central Nervous System

This is your biology 101 lesson on the central nervous system (CNS). The central nervous system is comprised of the brain and the spinal cord, and all the nerve endings that extend from the spinal cord. The central nervous system can receive data from the brain and transmit that information to various parts of the body to initiate activity based upon the information it receives.

Because of its significance to trauma response and healing responses, I am going to provide information on the autonomic nervous system. Within the central nervous system is the somatic nervous system and the autonomic nervous system. The autonomic nervous system is comprised of the ***sympathetic*** and ***parasympathetic*** nervous systems.

Parasympathetic Nervous System (resting state)

The parasympathetic nervous system goes into action when you are in a resting or relaxed state. The parasympathetic nervous system can activate heart rate decrease, blood pressure decrease, and digestion increase. This is sometimes referred to as the "rest and digest" response. In this state, we are relaxed and can find greater healing ability or recovery from stress or illness. Our bodies function optimally when the parasympathetic nervous system is in action.

Mindfulness and meditation techniques can create a parasympathetic nervous system response in your body. Mindfulness and meditation can also expand a person's ability to regulate emotions. The main nerves within the parasympathetic nervous system are the ***vagal nerves***, which regulate mood, immunity, digestion, and heart rate. The vagal nerve functions get disrupted when you experience a high stress situation.

Parasympathetic Nervous System – Rest and Digest; Breed and Feed State

- Heart rate decreases
- Blood pressure decreases
- Breathing rate decreases
- Pupils contract
- Digestion accelerates
- Sexual arousal, tearing, and salivating increase

Sympathetic Nervous System (fight, flight, freeze)

The sympathetic nervous system prepares you for action. This part of your nervous system allows you to respond to dangerous, stressful, or traumatic situations. The sympathetic nervous system will trigger the ***fight or flight*** response during a traumatic event. For example, if a lion were to walk into your room right now, the sympathetic nervous system would activate, and you would either want to run from the lion or fight the lion. I would personally run. But we all have a different response to a high stress event.

I will also be speaking to the *dorsal vagal* response which is the ***collapse and submit*** response to a traumatic event. When the sympathetic nervous system goes into action, heart rate increases, blood pressure increases, digestion stops, and stress hormones are released. Your body is designed to help you in situations by providing you with automatic responses to protect you.

The sympathetic nervous system functioning is designed to activate only when needed. But if you are working a very high stress job, or if your environment creates high stress events throughout the day, you are in sympathetic nervous system mode and your body is preparing you for action. The consistent release of stress hormones and consistent elevated heart rate, breathing rate, and blood pressure can be hard on your body.

The greatest difficulty with the sympathetic nervous system response is that your body cannot sustain this type of stress to your nervous system and will eventually create physical harm to you. That is why moving to a parasympathetic response through meditation or relaxation techniques can be a healthy way of countering continuous high stress situations.

Sympathetic Nervous System – Fight or Flight State

- Heart rate increases
- Blood pressure increases
- Breathing rate increases
- Sweating increases
- Pupils dilate
- Digestion stops
- Stress hormones release to boost alertness and heart rate

Vagal Nerve Response

The previous chapter on attachment began to speak about the vagal nerve development in infancy, as a baby responds to the stress of seeking food, comfort, and emotional regulation through their primary caregiver. Dr. Stephen Porges (2017) identified how trauma affects the nervous system as it is associated with a polyvagal system. The *vagus nerve* is comprised of the dorsal (reference to the back of the nerve) and the ventral (reference to the front of the nerve). It is located at the lowest part of the old brain or primitive brain, at the base of the skull.

The Dorsal Vagal is responsible for the "***collapse and submit***" response that comes when a human or animal experiences a threat or dangerous situation. In this state, a person or animal will experience a desperate and hopeless response of shutting down and submitting to the threat or danger. The Dorsal Vagal response is evident in wildlife when you see a predator chasing prey.

> *Imagine that a coyote is chasing a rabbit. The rabbit (prey) will run from the coyote (predator) for some time until the rabbit deems that they are no longer able to escape the coyote. At this time, the rabbit will collapse and submit to the predator's desire to consume the rabbit for dinner. The rabbit will look suddenly immobilized, and the Dorsal Vagal nerve will have been activated.*

This primitive brain response can also be seen in humans when they ***collapse and submit*** to a predator or a traumatic event in which they feel they cannot escape. You may initially see a sympathetic nervous system response where the person attempts to fight or flee from the situation. Then when hopelessness enters, the Dorsal Vagal response will kick in, and the person will collapse and submit to the predator or situation.

I have worked with so many victims of sexual assault who have felt such shame and guilt because of their Dorsal Vagal response to their predator. When they learn about the primitive Dorsal Vagal response, they are comforted by the fact that they did not willingly give in to a situation. They were unable to respond and became immobilized.

Stuck on the high wire – Mobilized from the fear

When a person has a history of trauma, they often become very stress sensitive. Due to this sensitivity, relationships or life experience can trigger a *sympathetic nervous system response* of fight or flight, and feelings of anxiety, panic, or rage. This is a feeling of tension that can be very difficult to dislodge from and a person can feel "stuck" in this elevated state. It is like being *stuck on a high wire* gripped with fear of falling. In this state, the sympathetic nervous system has been activated.

Stuck on the basement floor – Immobilized from the fear

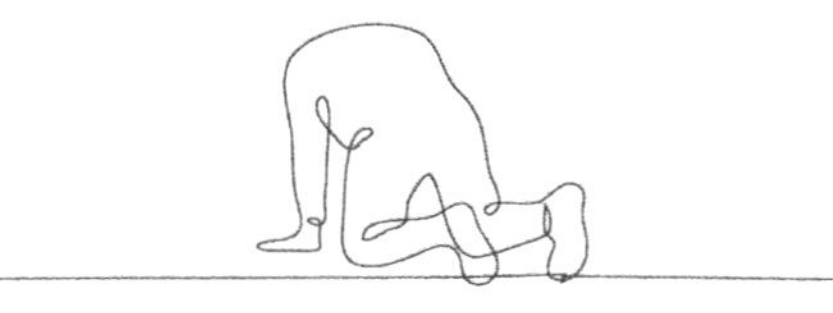

There is another response that some people may feel when they have a history of trauma that involves stress sensitivity. A person may utilize a different defensive mode when they experience relational or life experience stressors that induce fear. While this stress sensitivity can cause an elevated fear response, it can also create a depressed state.

This is when the *Dorsal Vagal nerve is activated*, and the person is immobilized. The result is a "collapse and submit" response. A person may feel depressed, disconnected, numb, a loss of energy, or unable to move. It is like being stuck on the *basement floor of emotions* and this experience may feel quite hopeless to the individual.

From the high wire to the basement floor and back

Many people describe their post traumatic experience as going back and forth between the high wire and the basement floor. At times, they describe feeling high anxiety and panic and at other times they may feel very emotionally low and depressed.

This is the central nervous system looking for ways to deal with attempts to feel safe when they do not have the ability to use relationships to calm themselves. At times, the sympathetic nervous system (*stuck on the high wire*) will be activated and at other times, the dorsal vagal nerve (*stuck on the basement floor*) will be activated. Some people report feeling both at the same time.

Dissociation

Trauma may cause a *dissociation* from the emotional memory of an event. This is your body's attempt to protect yourself from the emotionally devastating effects of trauma. Your brain may also *dissociate* from the memory of a traumatic event and block the event from your conscious access.

Some people who experience a traumatic or stressful event have long-term effects that include flashbacks (sudden memory intrusions of the event), emotional surges (feelings that seem to come randomly), nightmares of the event, dissociation from the memory of the event (a feeling of emotional disconnect and numbness about the event), and overall long-term effects. When the effects of a traumatic or stressful event last longer than one month, it is considered a trauma response.

There are many other criteria that a professional will look for to identify trauma responses. It is important to consider how various losses may create such an intense state of emotional/psychological/somatic response that can be categorized as a traumatic loss.

Journaling Activity

Review your list of losses from Chapter 9 (Exercise 9.a). Look at your list of losses or think about the losses that you experienced throughout your lifetime. Are there any losses that you would categorize as a traumatic loss? Remember that it is different for everyone, and people respond differently to that which they are exposed.

Place a check mark next to the losses on your list that may qualify as a traumatic loss. Complete the following inventory on each area of loss that you have checked and consider to be traumatic. Consider the effects this traumatic event has had on your beliefs about yourself, others, and the world in the areas of ***safety, trust, power/control, esteem, and intimacy.*** Journal on this and for each traumatic loss write a paragraph. Share this with your therapist if you are working with one. Bring your journaling to them.

- Identify any areas of your traumatic loss that are limiting your ability to interact socially with others.
- Identify any areas of your traumatic loss that affect your close or romantic relationships.
- Identify how this situation may have affected your ability to trust others.
- Identify any situations or specific types of people around whom you do not feel safe.
- Identify if you feel a need to exert control over others or situations due to the fear of loss of control.
- Identify any aspects of your self-worth that have been affected by the traumatic loss.

Keep in mind that if you have experienced traumatic loss and have not addressed it with a therapist, it is important that you seek therapy. Trauma is best worked through with a professional. Review your list of losses again from Chapter 9 (Exercise 9.a). Your inventory of losses and traumatic experiences can provide a good roadmap into what issues are unresolved or in need of work.

There are many trauma therapies that can be effective in releasing you from the shackles that bind you to blockages of personal happiness and well-being. Your relationships are significantly important to your happiness in life. It is time to break the chains that bind you to past experiences that still haunt you. ***Find a therapist that you can trust, feel safe with, and work with.***

Trauma is a complex and sometimes misunderstood condition. The intent of this chapter was to provide you with a better understanding of the ways trauma can affect your present day life. The following chapters will look at some healing strategies.

10.a Reflection

- Are you aware of your traumatic experiences in life? If so, have you identified anything that continues to be a disruption to your present-day life experiences?

____

____

____

____

____

____

____

- Can you relate to being either stuck on the highwire, or stuck in the basement, or a combination of both? Elaborate about what that is like for you.

- How have your traumatic life experiences affected relationships? Trust?

Chapter 11

Healing Your Wounds

The Path From Brokenness Toward Wholeness

"Don't turn away. Keep your gaze on the bandaged place. That's where the light enters you."

— Rumi, Rumi Poetry: 100 Quotes on Life, Love and Happiness

There is a path from brokenness toward wholeness that welcomes us and is open to all who dare to risk moving from the wound to healing. The path may have detours and moments of doubt. It may bring moments of clarity or new insights. Each person's individual journey is unique and designed to beckon or challenge. Every moment is sacred and deserves attention and mindful presence.

Sometimes, during the most difficult parts of our journey, we simultaneously find purpose and meaning. Standing still and staying in the brokenness is optional. When we are moving along the path, we are moving out of the suffering and into possibility. The wound is beginning to heal. We have been released from the bondage of the past and are moving toward freedom. Are you ready to sort through it all and walk the courageous journey?

Turning away or disregarding our painful past is not the solution to the process of healing. If you have read the previous chapters and have examined your life up until now, you have identified some of the things that have caused you pain or suffering. We as human beings all carry a wound. We may have multiple life experiences that have caused pain. We may have just one or two major painful moments in life.

As Rumi describes in the introductory quote to this chapter, we must look at the places of hurt if we want to transform them to light. Wounds and healing are like two sides of the same coin. You may be experiencing the wound or the healing of the wound, and sometimes they may both cause pain. But the pain of suffering without being on the path toward healing can swallow you and create a self-imposed victimization of your life experiences.

Following is an example of a physical wound and the healing process from my personal history:

> *I recall when I was seven years old, I fell on my knee on my friend's cinder rock driveway. I cried because of the pain, and I remember that I was terrified when my friend's mother said that she needed to clean out the wound. The scrape on my knee was so painful and the tiny pieces of black cinder were visible throughout the wound.*
>
> *My friend's mom took me to the sink and cleaned the wound with soap and water and I was crying because it hurt so bad. A part of me wanted to avoid cleaning the wound to avoid the pain I would feel. Fortunately, she was committed to preventing an infection in my wound and although I wanted to resist in order to avoid more pain, I complied. This was followed by a disinfectant that stung even more.*
>
> *Today I am grateful for my friend's mom who cleaned my wound, and although it hurt, it allowed the healing to begin on my knee.*

The story of the wound on my knee is a memory of physical pain. You may find yourself avoiding looking at the painful life experiences that are a part of your emotional wound. Like my experience as a 7-year-old, if you do not clean out the wound it will fester and eventually become infected and magnified in your subconscious mind. The previous chapters and exercises have provided many opportunities to inventory aspects of your personal pain and suffering.

Whether you relate to aspects of unhealthy attachment styles, losses that have remained unhealed, or traumatic memories of life experiences where emotions and thought intrusions linger, you may consider these a part of your wound. Your wound may consist of parental neglect or a well-meaning parent saying things that have made you self-conscious about your appearance or capability. The wounds from your parents are often the most significant and have the greatest effect on who you are today.

You may have wounds from your 4th grade teacher who embarrassed you in front of the classroom. You may have experienced racial trauma or name-calling from the school bully on the playground in elementary school. Your wound may stem from a coach on a high school sports team that belittled you in front of the team. Your wound may include losses such as the death your dog, family members, or friends. The situations are endless, and if you have walked the planet as a human being, you will have a wound.

"Healing begins with the ability to embrace the life experiences that have contributed to your wound."

This wound lays just beneath the surface of your day-to-day experiences, and ***the emotional responses to life situations often are reflective of the wound you carry, rather than the situation itself.*** This is why it is important to clean the wound that you carry by first acknowledging it is there.

Healing begins with the ability to acknowledge and embrace the life experiences that have contributed to your wound. Looking honestly and openly at your emotionally painful events is the beginning. When we embrace our pain, we can transcend the wound. It is important to remove the bandage and allow for the healing to take place by recognizing the hurt and pain that you have had. Minimizing or attempting to control the pain is not the solution.

When a patient that I am working with in psychotherapy emotes and begins to weep, I encourage the expression of feeling. When you are embracing the depth of your hurtful experience, you are tapping into your authentic self that experiences the associated emotions fully. Allowing for the feelings to surface is important. We all experience the emotions of an event differently.

Be gentle with yourself and know that your human experience will include emotional hurt as well as joy and love. Most of us like the good feelings and have a negative view of emotions that represent pain. All emotions are necessary to create a whole and complete life. Appreciate your full range of emotions as they are all a necessary part of who you are.

Suffering

As you have probably discovered in the previous chapters, life can present us with situations that are difficult and that bring us pain. This is a part of the human experience. We will experience pain. The experience of hurt, heartbreak, abandonment, loss, or a human's inhumanity to other humans can bring pain. Pain is not optional in this human lifetime. The idea of suffering, however, may be considered an option in many situations.

Some situations that are painful can be taken to therapy or "worked through" by talking with others. Some situations are painful, and people learn of a way to find acceptance in their experience through embracing what happened and walking their path toward healing. Some people may believe they have resolved their painful experiences when in reality they have buried them. In these situations where a painful past is swept under the carpet and disregarded, a person may find emotions or memories coming back throughout their lifetime.

Recall the story of my physical pain as a child with cinder particles in my knee. The painful wound needed to be cleaned or it would not heal. Most areas of pain in our emotional wounds need to be addressed. Our experiences often give us a feeling of devastation as we question the "why" of them. Pain needs to be addressed and your thoughts and emotions must be embraced. ***Transcending pain begins with embracing the entirety of the situation that caused it.***

Finding Meaning and Purpose

Suffering, however, is not necessarily optional in some of the most severe situations. The experience of a Ukrainian national living in a war zone where lives are lost, homes are crushed, and dreams are shattered brings both pain and suffering. The Holocaust survivor also has experienced pain and suffering. Viktor Frankl (1946) describes in *Man's Search for Meaning* his experience in a Nazi concentration camp during World War II.

The idea of suffering in a situation as devastating as being a Jew in the Holocaust is unavoidable. The unthinkable stories of a person's inhumanity to other humans are many. Some people survive and thrive, and some are destroyed by their experiences.

Frankl experienced extreme suffering and he was firmly committed to the idea that finding meaning in the suffering is key to transcending the pain. He affirmed that even in the concentration camps, he observed the people who thrived and those who succumbed to the torturous experiences. He contended that freedom came from finding meaning or maintaining a meaningful attitude.

In the camps, Frankl thought of his wife and imagined her waiting for him upon his release. This brought him comfort. He found that his imprisoned companions who had generous attitudes and shared their last crust of bread with others fared better. These individuals had found a tremendous sense of purpose, and this drove their benevolent behaviors.

We can be bound by a memory of being held hostage to an actual imprisoned situation. Or we may be held hostage to our past. There is hope in the inner freedom that we can potentially find in responsibility, meaning, and purpose.

An example of finding the treasure trove of freedom through responsibility and purpose is the 12-step fellowship of Alcoholics Anonymous or Narcotics Anonymous. Some individuals experience the "incomprehensible demoralization" of addiction or alcoholism and find their way to the groups of a 12-step fellowship. There they may find sobriety, and then go on to find meaning and purpose in their shame-based memories of being devastated by addictive disease.

These members usually find that there is tremendous purpose in being able to share their experience, strength, and hope with others who are newer to the fellowship. Their stories are many and most all end in a state of desperation and being held hostage to their disease of addiction.

In the program they take on responsibility when they commit to sponsorship of a newcomer to the program. They adopt a principle of giving back the things that were so freely given to them upon entry to the program. They find meaning and shared purpose in their efforts to help others recover.

It is through these responsible actions that members of the 12-step fellowship can find a new freedom. This includes freedom from active addiction and freedom from the self-hatred that comes from living as they did in addiction.

The Prisoner You Have Become

Finding meaning and purpose through personal responsibility is something that you can do as you identify the prisoner you have become to your past or to a memory. I am not suggesting that this is a simple process. I think, however, in the process of healing it is important to identify the walls in which you have imprisoned yourself because of life's painful experiences.

Finding a "silver lining" is difficult considering the brutal or debilitating experiences some of us have experienced. Some of our experiences include the element of "unavoidable" suffering such as Viktor Frankl's experience in the concentration camps. Some of our experiences as children that include suffering at the hands of our caregivers were unavoidable. Natural disasters, floods, famines, fires, and hurricanes can be unavoidable situations that have created pain and suffering. Death of a loved one is an unavoidable fate.

Sometimes a traumatic situation is one where a person feels an extra burden because they believe that their actions caused the trauma. For example, a person that was driving under the influence gets into a car accident where injury or death of another person occurs. This can cause an extra feeling of responsibility over what happened. Some people carry a great deal of shame associated with a traumatic event that they perceive as something that could have been avoided.

Holding yourself hostage to these feelings of shame and guilt can intensify a traumatic response. You are dealing with the trauma of the accident as well as feeling responsible for causing the event. Common "shame-based" narratives are: "*I am a bad person,*" "*I am worthless,*" and "*I deserve bad things to happen to me*". These narratives suggest that your actions are unforgivable.

Sometimes people will use self-blame in situations where they believe that their traumatic event could have been avoided, like a person who becomes the victim of a robbery while on vacation, and then blames themselves for going on the trip. This is the type of situation where people feel **over-responsible** for a situation that happened.

Typical false narratives are the use of "*should*". "*I shouldn't have booked that vacation.*" "*I should have not left the hotel room.*" "*I should have known better.*" These narratives reflect responsibility of something that was beyond your control.

Sexual assault trauma can often bring about irrational feelings of responsibility. I have worked with so many women and men who were assaulted or raped and felt responsible because they did not fight or flee from the situation. Quite often the false narratives associated with sexual assault are: "*I should have fought them.*" "*I allowed it to happen.*" "*I was drinking and deserved what happened to me.*" "*I shouldn't have let them come home with me.*"

In looking at the biology of sexual assault trauma as described in the previous chapter, there is often a dorsal vagal nerve response in a situation like this. A person will collapse and submit to the situation because our nervous system is prewired to do this in what feels like an inescapable situation.

Understanding the biology of situations such as these is significant to healing from the trauma. When people have learned that they could not escape and their body submitted to the assault by default, it helps to alleviate the self-blame and shame-based beliefs about what happened.

Three Stepping-Stones Toward Freedom

First: Embrace the reality and entirety of the situation

The first step toward healing is to embrace the reality and the entirety of the situation. If you can think of meaning and purpose for the situation, that is optimal. This may not happen initially. As you are walking along the path from brokenness to healing, you may have many stops along the way. Some of the stops may include strong emotions such as anger, fear, sadness, or shame. This is normal and a part of the healing process.

You may want to run from these emotions. Keep in mind, however, that your authentic self is experiencing emotions. To move toward your authentic self, you must feel all emotions and embrace them. You are not alone. There are many travelers along this same path who are in different stages of healing. If your personal freedom is your goal, it is important to stay on the path and continue your journey toward transformational change.

Second: Sorting through it all

Sorting through your experiences allows for the identification of any mistaken beliefs or private logic that you have established regarding the event. Finding a safe person or place to explore further with you is a part of this step. The story of my experience at age 7 with the wound on my knee gave the example of my friend's mother who prevented infection to my wound. Sometimes we need a guide to help us face the pain, especially when we want to turn and run from the pain.

This is where a trained professional can assist you in sorting through the pain and getting you onto the path toward healing. Moving from the wound to the process of healing is a transformational process. Keep in mind that the scar of the wound and the scab on the wound are evidence of the healing process. You are in motion.

If you have been reading this book and doing the work of the previous chapters and exercises, you are on the path toward transformational change. If you can see your scar, it is evidence of your healing. Find someone to talk to with whom you can share this journey. ***Find a professional*** if you feel stuck along the way or if the pain has turned to "suffering."

Once you have made the decision to face the pain and to engage in the process of sorting through it all, the intensity of feelings may begin to emerge. It is important to embrace the emotions that surface. It may also help to move away from the pain temporarily. Engage your creative self to find an area of focus outside of the processing of your wound.

When I was 7 years old and my friend's mother was cleaning the wound on my knee, she first washed it which was very painful, and I cried. She waited awhile prior to putting on the antiseptic which was again very painful. Then the gauze bandage was another step that she waited to do prior to ending what felt torturous to me. The intervals between the painful experience of cleaning the wound and administering the antiseptic and putting on the bandage were necessary. I needed the breaks between engaging in each of the painful steps.

Similarly, you may need to step away from your process and do the work in intervals so that you have periods of relief in between the stings of your hurtful past. Give yourself permission to disengage at times and remove yourself from the recall of painful experiences.

Third: What have you learned?

You will also want to learn as much as possible about yourself from that painful place when you engage in the healing process. Answer the following questions and ***place a "check mark"*** next to any that apply. ***For each item that applies, journal a paragraph*** on your discovery. Keep in mind that self-discovery and new awareness is key to personal growth and transformation.

- What do you now see in yourself that you didn't see previously?
- Are you protective of yourself?
- Have you put yourself in high-risk situations through reckless behavior?
- Do you tend to deny your pain?
- Have you developed a rigidity that blocks you from your emotions?
- Do you divert from pain?
- If you divert from your pain, what methods do you use?
- Do you dissociate ("cut off") from your emotions when you face your losses?
- Do you "busy" yourself to move away from your pain?
- Do your emotions overwhelm you and block you from looking deeper?
- Are there attachment issues associated with what your deepest experiences are reflecting?
- Are there mistaken beliefs that are driving false narratives that cause you to suffer or attempt to deny your experience?
- Have family members or primary caregivers given you false narratives about yourself?
- Have various influencers created false ideas about yourself that perpetuate your present-day behaviors or thoughts about yourself?
- Have your experiences caused you to lose trust in yourself or others?
- How has your sense of safety and security been affected by your painful life experiences?
- Have you become aware of neurochemistry that is driving your highs and lows?

"The sun shall always rise upon a new day and there shall always be a rose garden within me. Yes, there is a part of me that is broken, but my broken soil gives way to my wild roses."

—C. Joy Bell C.

11.a Reflection

- What does your wound consist of and what are some of the primary people who are a part of your wound?

____

____

____

____

____

____

____

11.a

- Have you found yourself being either over responsible for life circumstances or under responsible for the choices you have made? Explore this further.

- In what ways do you deny or divert from your pain?

Chapter 12

The Brain, Mind/Body Attunement, and Energy-Shifting Solutions

Strategies for Healing

"Do not dwell in the past, Do not dream of the future, Concentrate the mind on the present moment."
— *Buddha, The Teaching of Buddha*

Staying in the present frees us from rumination over the past and obsessive fears of the future. The past may hold painful memories, errors in judgment, embarrassing moments, or regrets. The past is history and cannot be changed...only accepted and embraced as "what was." The future may hold anxiety, fear of things to come, focus on outcomes and attempts to predict the unpredictable.

The future will unfold despite our concern over "what's next." The present moment is all that is real. It is a powerful place to stand in. The present moment allows for attunement to others and to what is happening now. Are you prepared to release yesterday and tomorrow? Are you ready to focus with intention on the now?

Understanding the brain and its amazing ability to defend you in times of high stress or trauma is significant to also understanding ways to be on the journey toward healing. There are many paths toward healing your stressed or traumatized nervous system. Some of these paths are geared toward reversing your central nervous system response. Considering that the problem associated with high stress or traumatic events exists within the nervous system, we will now move to the solution.

The Solution

Creating parasympathetic nervous system response and increased vagal tone

It is important to not feel overwhelmed or helpless when discovering that you may have a *sympathetic nervous system* response or *dorsal vagal* response to stress from trauma. Chapters 9 and 10 looked at these nervous system responses that are your body's defenses to trauma or high stress situations.

I have worked in psychotherapy with many people who do not see themselves as having experienced trauma. Many situations, however, are traumatic for any individual to endure. Major disruptions of childhood stability, relational trauma, and situational stressors can create high levels of stress and the brain will work to protect you from it through the central nervous system responses.

I believe that as human beings, we can endure the most horrific and traumatic life experiences. As human beings, we are also extremely sensitive to the subtle difficulties experienced. Despite the high or low level of distress you have experienced over a lifetime, your body and brain may have adapted to the disruption. There are strategies for coping with this and managing your responses to life experiences that trigger the high wire or basement floor emotions.

First and foremost, it is important to understand that you can be *smarter than your brain* by knowing how it operates and looking for ways to change the way your brain works to defend you during stressful situations. The concept of *neuroplasticity* is significant to not losing hope.

Neuroplasticity

Your brain is continuing to grow and develop throughout your lifetime. When your brain is injured in any way, or when neural repair is needed, your brain engages in developing new *neurons* (brain cells). This is called ***neuroplasticity*** (Siegel, 2010). I used to think that my brain stopped developing new neurons during early adulthood. However, the truth is that your brain continues to work for you *throughout your lifetime.*

Your brain is changing depending upon the neural firing that happens due to your life experiences. This neural firing creates the development of new neurons. Your brain is growing and developing in the direction of your focus. ***Learning to direct your brain's neural pathways toward healing is where neuroplasticity will work for you.***

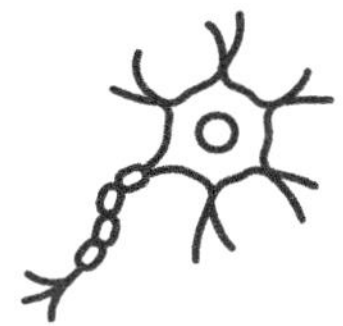

When you understand that you can engage in practices that encourage development of new neurons in the brain area that affects emotional regulation, you gain an "edge" on your brain.

Mindfulness

Research has demonstrated that ***mindfulness*** practices can change the way the brain functions. The area of the brain that controls emotion regulation is especially susceptible to development through mindfulness practices. Examples of being emotionally dysregulated are when you feel your mood changing toward anxiety or depression, when you are unable to control a surge of anger, when you burst into tears, when you engage in road rage, or when you yell at a family member and later regret your loss of control.

Emotional dysregulation is about your inability to feel grounded enough to have some control over your emotional response to life experiences. Experiencing your emotions is a healthy response to life situations. Our emotions are our barometer for determining if something is bothering us, or if someone has crossed our boundaries. However, being emotionally dysregulated is about having over-reactions or mis-directed emotional responses that are problematic.

If you recall in Chapter 7 on Attachment, we learn to regulate our emotions early in life during the bonding and attachment processes and in early childhood. The neural connections that our brains develop are geared toward regulating emotions when the environment is safe and secure. In an unstable or insecure environment, our brains are wired to prepare for action and emotional regulation is difficult. Some of us are genetically prewired to have difficulty regulating emotions.

There are two routes to learning to regulate emotions. One is through "co-regulation" where we find safe, stable people who help us to feel more regulated. The other route is through internally strengthening our ability to regulate. ***Mindfulness*** practices can be one of the antidotes to dysregulated emotions through an internalized process. Let's begin by defining and understanding what mindfulness is.

Roots of mindfulness: Originating from the Eastern religious practice of Buddhism, and based on Zen and Tibetan meditation styles, *mindfulness* has become popularized in western cultures. You may consider mindfulness as a *practice* or a *state of mind*. It is the ability to be focused on the present moment, with intended concentration, and without judgment.

Some people practice mindfulness through meditation, and some ascribe it to maintaining a mindful presence in all relationships. Our minds, our bodies, our emotions, and our environment are areas of attunement that lead to seeing our lives with greater clarity. Ancient Buddhist practices of mindfulness imply that greater presence, awareness, insight, and alertness are byproducts of mindful meditation practices. In addition to mindful presence is a calmness and peace or tranquility that a person develops.

The original intent of practices of mindful meditation by Buddhist devotees is to be on the path toward *enlightenment*. *Enlightenment* is close to meaning "awakening" or the awakening of one's intellect, which includes freedom from the bondage of one's negative thinking. To be asleep is to be unaware and "un-awakened" to one's illuminated consciousness.

In today's world, mindfulness is being studied for its effect on regulation of emotions and managing stress, anxiety, depression, and medical conditions. Mindfulness is about having a moment-to-moment presence and focus on thoughts, feelings, and body sensations. It is about being aware of your internal experience as well as the external environment. This is to be done in a very relaxed state or closed eye meditative state. The process brings clarity, insight, and calm to the individual practicing it.

Mindfulness can also be accomplished through open-eyed focusing on an object without judgment. Or it can be accomplished by paying attention to the breath or the heartbeat. When being mindful, you are intensely aware of your body sensations and feelings in the present moment without evaluating or judging the situation.

Mindfulness and Stress Reduction

Jon Kabat-Zinn (2005) began a stress reduction program called Mindfulness-Based Stress Reduction (MBSR), which is taught globally. It involves teaching mindfulness for the purpose of stress reduction as well as for the elimination of pain and illness. He describes the mindfulness process as:

- Paying attention
- On Purpose (with intention)
- In the Present Moment
- Without Judgment

Paying attention. Today's busy world with multiple electronic distractions can promote the idea of multi-tasking. Life is full of distractions and the electronic world of cell phones, computers, televisions, and social media can complicate and distract us further. Is the idea of multi-tasking an advantage or is it a myth? Perhaps some people credit themselves with the ability to focus on several things at once. However, does divided attention to several things at once only "water down" the ability to focus on the present?

Mindfulness gives credit to the ability to give full attention and attune to the present reality whether it involves a closed-eye meditation or whether it is being attentive to a person or situation at hand. Mindfulness teaches us the power of paying attention and focusing on less, rather than more.

The executive networks of our human brains are more complex than other animals (as discussed in Chapter 8). The neocortex allows for us to "*busy our minds*" with multiple things and to jump from one thought to another. This ability can be useful for some situations that require our ability to do complex tasks. However, the inability to think of one thing at a time, focus, and give full attention can be difficult.

Our human mind wants to jump around and think of other things when someone is talking to us. The power that comes from being able to pay attention to the situation in front of us is what allows us to have connection to others and undivided focus on things that matter. Mindfulness gives us the opportunity to "practice" paying attention and attuning to matters at hand.

Consider how you feel when you are talking to someone who is looking at their phone or gazing away from you as if they are not listening to you. You probably feel that you are not important or that your presence is discounted. You may also feel disregarded when someone's computer screen takes priority over you. Giving your full attention to the person in front of you is practicing relational mindfulness.

Our fast-paced world today is critically in need of people to pay attention to each other. Your relationships can and will improve when you give your full attention to those close to you. You can create sacred moments through giving your full attention to others. Do not miss out on the opportunity to be present and pay attention to your loved ones.

On purpose. *Intention* is a conscious choice to be or do something. It begins as an idea about something that you plan to do. When you clearly state a goal or plan, you are likely to bring it to completion. You will presumably be purposeful in following through with the task.

An intention is much like a promise to yourself to be purposeful in your plan to do something. When you purposefully plan to be mindfully present, you are promising yourself that you will not miss opportunities to engage with others or be in the present moment. Everything we do in life begins with intention. When you wake up in the morning, get out of bed, say good morning to family or pet the dog, it begins with your intention to act.

As you begin your day, you can purposefully state your claim to being mindfully present. This can provide you with the pledge to yourself that you will not miss opportunities to fully engage in the present.

Plan your action and not the outcome of your intent. You may divert from your desire to be mindfully present, but you can find your way back to the promise you made to yourself. It is easy to get lost in the busy-ness of your life. You can redirect yourself to the present at any moment. Attempt to maintain your awareness of your environment and purposefully be in the present.

"Plan your action and not the outcome of your intent."

In the present moment. Essentially, being focused on the present moment is powerful because that's all there really is. What happened 5 minutes ago, yesterday, or 10 years ago is all in the past. The past has value in exploration for determining how we experience the present.

However, ruminating over the past can be a distraction from the *now*. Tomorrow has not happened yet, and although we may plan or set goals, there is no guarantee that it will happen. The present moment is powerfully alive and when in the present, you are developing greater capacity for awareness in the here and now.

Without judgment. Judgment is something that we all have and is intended to be a skill we can use to make decisions in a situation where our safety and survival are at stake. For example, you need to utilize judgment when you cross a street. If there are no cars in the street, you are safe to cross. However, if there is traffic, you would need to judge when it is safe to cross.

You need to use judgment within your environment. Your environment consists of where you are (home, school, office, store, or country) and who is present (family, friends, strangers, classmates, or professionals). You need to determine if a person or a place is safe within your environment. Other types of functional judgment can include more complex decision-making processes. Having the ability to make sound judgments is critical to our survival and advancement as a species.

When we speak to judgment in relation to mindfulness, we are speaking to an internalized critical commentary that is potentially harmful. Harsh judgments may taint the ability to see something objectively for what it is. Harsh judgments can take away from being in the moment and looking honestly and clearly at a person, situation, or place.

It is difficult to be mindfully present to another person if your internal conversation is looking for things with which to criticize them. If I am judging your character, I am blocked from clearly hearing your message. It can take practice to stay out of judgment while practicing mindfulness.

Our advanced mammalian brains like to work overtime in comparing, contrasting, and making judgments. There is a time and a place for critical thinking skills and for judgment to be used in situations. However, the goal is to be "without judgment" while practicing mindfulness.

How do I stay out of judgment? It can help to switch gears to "describing" rather than judging a situation or a person. If I am truly describing something objectively, I am out of judgment. Be aware of emotionally laden terms, emotional bias, and personalized opinions. For example, practice describing and judging the following image:

Judge	Describe
Icky bug	Black insect
Ugly black beetle	Six legs
Bug with creepy legs	Two feelers
Disgusting crawly thing	Beetle

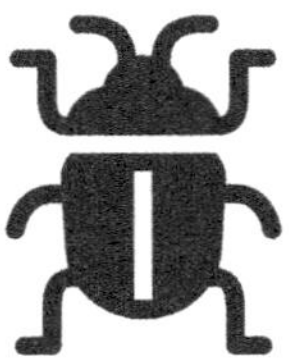

In the beetle example, the judgment of the object is very different from the description. The judgments are emotionally laden with critical commentary. The description is objective and is not personalized. In mindfulness, we are looking to be without judgment, to be fully present and to be uninfluenced by the critical mind.

Mindfulness Activities

Mindfulness activities can include a variety of things to put into practice. These tasks are intended to create an increased presence, focus, and awareness of yourself and your immediate surroundings. Mindfulness practice begins with the assumption that ***multi-tasking is a myth***.

When we believe we are effectively doing many tasks at once, we are falling short of being fully attuned to one task or another. Your day may get busy and require you to drive and talk on the phone at the same time, talk to someone at your door while directing your child away from snacks, or be on your computer at work while talking to a coworker.

Become aware of how directing your attention to one thing at a time provides you with the ability to be more effective in each task. Your undivided attention is more effective than multi-tasking. The "timesaving" element of dividing your attention is minimal compared to when you are mindfully present to each event.

Mindfulness activities allow you to pay attention, on purpose, to stay in the present moment, without judgment. It is about practicing staying focused on just one thing.

The following are some activities that you can use to practice mindfulness. ***The activities suggest journaling a few sentences about your experience. This is optional.*** It can, however, be affirming to briefly jot down your experience. You may want to use a new journal to record your experiences with mindfulness practices and to identify which were most useful to you.

Mindfulness Grounding Activities

There are many types of mindful grounding activities that require focusing on an object. These activities can be very calming in a moment of chaos or emotional turmoil. Sometimes our emotions get "triggered" and it is difficult to be present to what is in front of us because we are in fear or worry. Our busy minds have taken us to the past or future. Try these grounding activities to practice mindfulness.

These activities can be done in a quiet place but can also be done amidst the turmoil of an office setting, classroom, or waiting room. I will provide many suggestions, and perhaps you can come up with some grounding activities of your own.

Pen or Pencil Focus Grounding Activity

- Pick up a pen or pencil and focus your gaze on it.
- Notice the color, the shape, the writing, and other aspects of it.
- Look for things you have not noticed before about the item.
- Continue to affix your gaze on the pencil or pen.
- Become aware of the unique qualities of this item.
- When outside thoughts or incoming intrusions happen, just refocus and attempt to put all your attention on your pen/pencil.
- Continue to look at the pen/pencil for 2 minutes.

When you are done with this mindfulness exercise, notice any new awareness you have about the pen or pencil. Think about the value of the item and appreciate that it allows you to write, doodle, or create art. Journal a few sentences about your experience. Find something to be grateful about for the pen or pencil.

Hand Focus Grounding Activity

- Lift one hand and place it within 1 foot to 6 inches of your eye gaze.
- Look at the outer side of your hand and notice the folds, crevices, colorations, bumps, veins, and other specifics of your hand.
- Look at the palm of your hand and notice the creases, the coloration, the specifics of your palm and underside of your fingers.
- Think about your fingers and affix your gaze on your fingers and how they are attached to your hand.
- Look at your fingernails and the various shapes and coloration of your nails.
- Notice any bone structures that are visible in your fingers or hand.
- Continue to affix your gaze on your hand for 2 minutes.

When you have completed this activity for 2 minutes, just sit and notice if you feel different, less stressed, or less fearful or worried than prior to focusing. Think about any new awareness you have about your hand. What are things you noticed about your hand that you did not think about previously?

Think about how much your hands do for you throughout the day and what you appreciate about your hand. Journal a few sentences about your experience. Then identify at least one aspect of gratitude that you have about your hand.

"Scan the Room" Grounding Activity

- Sit or lay in a comfortable position. If you are sitting, put feet flat on the ground. If you are lying down, be on your back. (It is preferred that this is in a quiet place, but this can be valuable also in a crowded waiting room, a classroom, or at work.)
- Scan the room for anything within your visual scope without turning your head.
- Find something in the room to fix your gaze on (e.g., a clock, a light, light switch, a blind, a curtain, a vent, a shoe, etc.).
- Affix your gaze on the item and just notice.
- Notice the shape, the colors, the shadows, the imperfections, and focus on the item.
- Notice anything you were not aware of in the past about this item.
- Consider how this item affects your life in a positive way.
- Affix your gaze on this item for at least 2 minutes.

Notice how you feel upon completing this activity. Notice if your stress level is lowered or if your busy mind has temporarily been suspended from thinking intrusive thoughts. Notice if you feel calmer. Think about anything you saw about this item that you didn't notice previously. Think about this item and appreciate the positive things about this item.

Journal a few sentences about your experience. A clock provides you with the time. The curtain provides shade from the sun. Your shoes protect your feet. These are aspects of appreciation that are often forgotten. Find one aspect of gratitude that you feel about the item of your focus.

Falling Feather Grounding Activity

- Sit comfortably in your chair with feet flat on the ground.
- Look at the top of your wall, where the wall meets the ceiling.
- Imagine there is a feather where the wall meets the ceiling.
- Create a feather of your choice in your imagination… it can be colorful, brown, gray, or glittery.
- Now watch your feather fall from where the wall meets the ceiling to where the wall meets your floor.
- Count very slowly backwards from 10 to 1.
- As you are counting slowly from 10 to 1, imagine that the feather is slowly falling from the ceiling to the floor.
- The activity is completed when the feather reaches the floor. You can repeat this if needed.

This mindful activity has a self-hypnotic effect on you. When you have completed this activity, notice if you feel calmer upon completion of watching the feather fall to the ground. Notice if you feel a lower level of stress upon completion.

Think about your feather and why you picked the feather of your imagination. Think about your ability to find calm and to ground yourself no matter where you are sitting. Think about how effective you are at being able to regulate your emotional state. Think of an aspect of gratitude that you have about yourself.

Outdoor Tree Grounding Activity

- Step outside and find a comfortable place to stand or sit in front of the tree of your choice.
- Affix your gaze on the tree and become aware of its beauty.
- Notice the colors of the tree, the imperfections of the tree, and anything you have not noticed previously.
- Notice the leaves (if there are leaves) and the variations of shape and color on the leaves.
- Notice if there is a breeze or wind and how the tree gently bends to accommodate the wind.
- Find one leaf or one branch to focus upon.
- Think about how that leaf or branch is clinging to maintain its life before dropping.
- If outside thoughts enter your mind, just notice, and let them go. Then return your focus.
- Maintain your focus on the tree for 2 to 5 minutes.

When you have completed this task, notice if you feel calmer and more grounded than prior to the activity. Think about any new awareness you have about the tree and about the tree's majestic presence.

Journal a few sentences about your experience. Think about anything that you didn't notice previously about the tree. Think about how trees provide shade and in what ways they provide you with comfort. Does the tree provide a home to small animals? Find an aspect of gratitude you have about that tree and other trees.

Your personal mindful grounding activity

Now it is your turn to use your creative thinking. You can now think of your own grounding activity that you want to focus upon. Find something that you can affix your gaze to that you can easily use for grounding. Perhaps it is a picture on your computer screen. Or maybe something outdoors that you have identified to practice focusing and grounding upon.

There are unlimited possibilities that can provide vast opportunities for relaxation and reflection. These are "mini meditations" that can furnish you with relief throughout your day. These activities can take you away from worry, fear, and unwanted negative thought intrusions.

As you continue these practices, you are slowly but surely gaining power over your dysregulated emotional states. You are slowly gaining power over your negative and false narratives that can sometimes occupy your thinking and cause discomfort or "bad days." You are increasingly being able to fight the fear and worrisome thoughts that bring you down. The process is slow, but you can conquer your negative private conversations.

Research has proven that mindfulness activities work to grow new neural connections that allow you to increase your ability to emotionally regulate. Trust and believe that you are increasing your personal power.

Mindfulness and Your Senses Activities

Your ability to hear, smell, taste, touch, and see are areas that can provide you with mindfulness and attunement. We often take our senses of taste, smell, sight, touch, and hearing for granted. Our senses provide us with the ability to take in our environment and function according to what we are aware of. Most animals that walk the planet have the need for use of the senses for survival purposes. All animals utilize their senses to help them navigate their environment and protect themselves, including humans.

The practice of focusing on any of the senses will expand and enhance your ability to hear, smell, taste, touch, and see. This can be seen throughout the animal kingdom. We are aware that a dog's ability to smell is exceptional. When dogs are provided time on walks to stop and smell grass and foliage, the neural connections in their brains are growing and developing to eventually have an even greater sense of smell.

Dr. Daniel Siegel (2010) did research on dogs before doing research on the effectiveness of mindfulness practices on humans. Dr. Siegel began by doing MRI's (neural imaging) on the brain of a given dog. In his research, he had the dogs respond to visual cues and rewarded them over and over again.

Then he did an MRI after these sessions of rewarding the visual responses, and their brain had developed new neural connections in vision. Dr. Siegel then did the same thing with dogs and had them respond to auditory cues. The MRIs proved that the dogs had developed new neural connections associated with their hearing.

This is the concept of *neuroplasticity* that I described earlier in this chapter. ***Neuroplasticity*** is the ability for new neural connections in our brain to grow throughout our lifetime depending upon where we focus our attention.

I mentioned earlier in this chapter that mindfulness practices will provide growth and development of your brain in terms of emotion regulation. Dr. Siegel did research on this, and his findings confirmed that the areas of the brain that regulate emotions grew and developed with the practice of mindfulness, meditation, or deep relaxation techniques. Specifically, the prefrontal cortex control of limbic regions and the anterior cingulate cortex work to regulate emotion in humans.

We have a gift in knowing that we can create a climate for growth in emotion regulation as well as in enhancing the senses. I have listed some activities that will establish focus on various senses.

Listening – mindfulness of your auditory senses

The following mindfulness activities focus on the auditory senses. We so often take for granted the experience we have in listening and hearing. These activities require attuning to sounds and things we often do not notice about the sounds around us.

If you are hearing impaired and hard of hearing, you can still do these activities and attune yourself to sound. If you are hearing impaired and deaf, you can mindfully practice your internal sounds.

Activity 1 – Listening Mindfulness Practice (Outdoors)

- Step outside your house, work, or indoor environment.
- Find a comfortable place to stand or sit where you won't be interrupted, if possible.
- Close your eyes (you may also keep them open) and take a deep breath.
- Attune yourself to the sounds around you.
- Listen for sounds around you.
- First notice the loudest sounds—sometimes they are the sounds of cars, trucks, planes, or man-made machinery.
- Next listen for the sounds of nature beneath the louder noises.
- Can you hear the wind? Can you hear the birds? Can you hear insects?
- Embrace the sounds that you hear and focus on one sound of nature if possible.
- Take another deep breath.
- Maintain the listening for 2 to 5 minutes.

When you are done with this activity, notice if you feel any different in your body after the activity as compared to before completing the activity. Do you feel less tension? What did you notice as you listened to the sounds?

Journal a few sentences about your experience. What sounds of nature were you able to hear (if available)? Think about the gift of sound and the gift of the sounds you heard. Identify something that you are grateful about regarding the natural sounds around you.

Activity 2 – Listening Mindfulness Practice (Indoors)

- Sit or lay down in your home or office without television or radio playing.
- Get comfortable. If you are in your chair, be sure to have your feet flat on the ground. If you are lying down, it is preferable to be on your back.
- Close your eyes and take a deep breath.
- Now just listen. What does silence sound like?
- Do you hear ringing?
- Notice any background noises. Do you hear water running, heat or air conditioning, a fan, a clock, or other sounds?
- Notice any sounds coming from outdoors.
- Can you faintly hear wind, rain, birds, insects, or other sounds of nature?
- Focus on one sound either indoors or outdoors.
- Attempt to stay with that sound for 2 to 5 minutes.

When you have completed this activity, notice if there is a difference in how your body feels. Is there less tension? How is your breathing? Think about anything you noticed about what you heard during this mindfulness practice.

Do your best to stay judgment free about the sounds you heard. What stood out to you about what you heard? Have you considered the sound of silence? You may want to journal a few sentences about your experience. Think about an aspect of appreciation you have for the sounds that you heard. Identify a thought about gratitude for your ability to listen.

Activity 3 – Listening Mindfulness Practice (Bedtime)

- After you have gone to bed and the house is quiet, position yourself on your back with your eyes closed.
- Take three deep breaths. Breathe in through your nose and out through your mouth. Breathe from your belly to your lungs and fill yourself with air.
- Now just listen. What do you hear?
- If others are still awake and making noise in other parts of the house, just notice it. If you can hear people chatting outdoors or in other parts of your building, just notice it.
- Attempt to focus on other sounds outside the house. What do you hear?
- If you can hear any sounds of nature, what are they? Do you hear the wind?
- Focus on one sound of nature or man-made sound.
- Stay with this sound for 2 to 5 minutes.

Notice if there are changes in your body because of this activity. Notice if you feel less stress and less mental activity. Were you able to let go of unwanted intrusive thoughts? Remember that it takes practice to master mindfulness activities. What did you notice about the evening sounds? What sound did you focus on? You may want to journal the next morning about your experience. Think about something that you appreciate about what you were listening to without judgment or sarcasm. Think about something for which you are grateful about your ability to listen.

The Chinese character for the verb "to listen" provides a comprehensive way of truly hearing another person. It translates that truly listening is with your ears, your eyes, your heart, and your undivided attention. To give that attention to another, captures what we strive to do in mindfulness. In the next activity, ***listen with your ears, your eyes, your heart, and your undivided attention.*** *You can then practice this throughout the day when interacting with another.*

Activity 4 – Listening Practice (With Another Person)

"The ear is only a petal,
That grows from the heart.
When we hear each other,
It all becomes a garden."

— *Mark Nepo*

- Use this activity with any one-on-one conversation you are having with another person.
- Sit facing the person without distractions of electronics.
- Have your feet flat on the ground and position your body leaning toward the other person.
- Make eye-to-eye contact with the person.
- Listen to what they are saying and stay out of judgment. Just hear their message to you.
- Notice their voice inflections, and the sounds and tone of their voice without judgment.
- Hear beyond their message and listen with your ears, your eyes, and your heart.
- Respond when called upon to respond, but mostly listen to the other person.
- After they have spoken, repeat back to the other person what you heard them say.
- If they clarify back to you, repeat back to them what you heard them say. This validates that you have heard them.
- Summarize what you heard from the other person and thank them for the talk.

After you have completed this activity, notice how you feel. Do you feel that you listened effectively to the other person and reflected what they were wanting to say? Do you feel you were distracted and failed to hear them? Did you find other intrusive thoughts interrupted your ability to listen to the other person? What insight or awareness did you gain from actively listening to the other person? Did you want to burst into commentary about what they said? Did you gain insight about their tone and voice inflections? Was it difficult to just listen and allow the other person to talk? You may want to journal a few sentences about what your experience was. Identify something you appreciate about the other person. Find an item of gratitude that you feel about your ability to actively listen.

Taste – Mindfulness practices of your sense of taste

The following activities focus on your sense of taste. There may be some suggestions to taste something that you do not want to eat or put in your mouth. You can substitute suggested items for taste. If you lack the ability to taste or if you are limited, you can do this activity with an attempt to taste to the best of your ability and focus on texture.

Remember that as you practice these mindfulness activities you are growing new neural connections in taste. Sometimes compulsive eating habits stem from gobbling food and not taking the time to taste or chew. These activities require you to slow down and really notice taste, flavor, texture, and other aspects of your sense of taste.

Activity 1 – Taste: A Burst of Flavor

- Find an item to use for this activity that is like hard candy that you are able to eat. It may be a "Skittles", a "Starburst", a lozenge (may be sugar free), a lifesaver, or any piece of hard candy.
- Close your eyes and take a deep breath.
- Keep your eyes closed (if possible) during this activity.
- Place the candy on your tongue without closing your mouth if possible.
- Notice the flavor on your tongue and the sensations you feel where the candy lies.
- Now close your mouth but refrain from sucking or chewing the candy.
- Just notice how the candy feels inside your mouth and what sensations or flavors you can taste.
- Continue to notice how perhaps your saliva begins to flow also.
- Notice anything about the taste that you had not noticed previously. Are there different flavors present?
- Continue to hold the candy in your mouth until it has dissolved.

What did you notice about your body after completing this activity of focusing on taste? What do you notice about how your mouth feels following this activity? Are you more focused after the activity and are you less stressed? Were you able to let go of any intrusive thoughts that came up while focusing on taste? Did you notice the heightened sense of the burst of flavor in your mouth when you mindfully focused on taste?

You may want to journal a few sentences about your experience. What appreciation do you now have about your sense of taste? Identify some aspect of gratitude that you feel because of your ability to taste.

Activity 2 – Taste: Mindful Chewing Activity

- This activity can be done when you sit down for a meal. It is easier to do initially if you are eating alone and without distractions. Later you may want to practice this when others are present to strengthen this skill.
- Sit at your table with your food/meal and take a deep breath before taking a bite.
- Initially just notice the food on your plate and the various colors and shapes.
- Take a deep breath and take your first bite.
- Take the time to chew the food at least 50 times before swallowing, and up to 60 times if it is meat, fish, or poultry protein.
- Notice any flavors in your mouth that you may not have noticed previously.
- Notice the texture of the food you are chewing.
- Notice how the texture of the food changes as you chew.
- Notice the influx of saliva that also is intended to break down the food before swallowing.
- Keep your focus on the taste and the chewing of the food throughout the meal.
- If you have intrusive thoughts or judgments, just notice these thoughts, and let them go.

What do you notice about your body after completing this activity? Did the focusing on taste and chewing allow you to divert from other intrusive thoughts? Did your hunger feel more satisfied by the activity? Do you now feel more relaxed? What did you notice about the taste sensations in your mouth as you took time to chew and fully break down the food in your mouth?

You may want to journal a few sentences about this activity. What insight and awareness do you now have about your sense of taste? What do you appreciate about your ability to taste and chew? Identify one aspect of gratitude that you have about your ability to chew and taste food.

Activity 3 – Taste: A Liquid

- Take your beverage of choice (coffee, tea, soft drink, juice, etc.) and place it in front of you.
- Take a deep breath and close your eyes if possible.
- Take a sip of the beverage, and just hold it in your mouth for 60 seconds.
- Notice how the flavor and taste change as you hold it in your mouth.
- Notice any sensations on the roof of your mouth with the beverage.
- Swallow the beverage after one minute. Notice any after-taste in your mouth now.
- Notice any sensations in your mouth that feel different.

After you have completed this activity, what do you notice about your focus and concentration? Did you have difficulty letting go of intrusive thoughts or judgments coming in as you were focusing on taste? Did you notice any shift in the tension within your body after completing the activity? What did you notice about the taste sensation in your mouth when doing this activity?

You may want to journal a few sentences about your experience. Do you have any new awareness or new appreciation for your sense of taste? Identify one aspect of gratitude that you feel about your sense of taste.

Smell – Mindfulness practices of your olfactory sense

Your sense of smell can provide you with the ability to identify things in the environment that are pleasant (such as flowers) or unpleasant (such as smoke or chemicals). While all your senses are intended to give you awareness of your environment, your olfactory senses are in alignment with what you taste. The olfactory sensory neurons are found high inside the nose and transmit information to the brain.

Many people have had temporary or long-term conditions of inability to smell or smelling "phantom" smells following episodes of Covid-19 or other viruses. Despite your ability or inability to smell, practicing mindfulness olfactory activities can be useful. The following are some mindfulness activities associated with focus and concentration on smell.

Activity 1 – Smell: A Lavender Oil or Soap

- Find either a lavender oil, another aroma therapy oil, or a soap.
- Sit in a quiet place with the item.
- Take a deep breath and close your eyes.
- Take time to smell the item first at arms-length with your eyes closed.
- With the oil or soap at arms-length, attempt to smell the fragrance.
- Gradually bring the oil or soap closer to your nose.
- Notice the change in intensity of the smell as you bring it closer to you.
- Notice any changes in your mouth as you practice this for 1-2 minutes.
- Notice any taste you experience resulting from the smell activity.

After you have completed this activity, notice any changes in your body as you have been focusing on your olfactory sense. Notice if your stress level has decreased because of the mindfulness activity of paying attention with intention. Think about any new awareness you have regarding your sense of smell. You may want to journal a few sentences about your experience. Think about your appreciation for your sense of smell and how it enhances your life. Identify an aspect of gratitude you have for your olfactory sense.

Activity 2 – Smell: A Food Exercise

- Find a quiet moment in your home environment, preferably with nobody around.
- Find an item of food. It may be a piece of fruit, a vegetable, or another food item.
- Close your eyes and take a deep breath.
- Put the item at arms-length and attempt to smell it from a distance.
- Notice the faint smell as your olfactory senses attempt to identify the smell.
- Strive to smell the item at arms-length for at least 10 seconds.
- Gradually bring the item of food closer to your nose.
- Notice the changes of intensity of smell as you draw the food closer to your nose.
- Notice any taste that comes up in association with the food item.
- Continue to smell the item for 2 minutes and just notice the smell.

When you complete this activity just take some time to notice how different your body feels from focusing. Notice if you feel less stress following a mindfulness activity. Think about anything that you were thinking about as you were focusing on the smell and associated taste. You may want to journal a few sentences about the experience. Think about any appreciation you now have for your olfactory sense. Identify one aspect of gratitude you have regarding your ability to smell.

Activity 3 – Smell: Outdoor Activity

- Step outside of your home or workplace and find a quiet area if possible.
- Close your eyes and take a deep breath.
- Focus on your ability to smell and activate your olfactory senses.
- Attempt to smell the outdoor smells.
- If there is a tree or flower that you smell, walk closer to it, and notice if the intensity of the smell changes.
- If there are unpleasant chemical smells or smoke odor, just notice how you feel from that.
- Notice any sensations in your body in association with what you can smell.
- Stay in this practice of exercising your olfactory sense for 2 minutes.

When you have completed this activity, notice any changes in your body as a result of focusing for the past 2 minutes or more. Notice any changes in your level of stress or anxiety. Think about any awareness or insight you gained as you practiced exercising your olfactory sense. Think about what you noticed that perhaps you did not notice previously about the smell outdoors.

You may want to journal a few sentences about your experience. Think about what you now appreciate about your ability to smell your surroundings. Identify an aspect of gratitude that you have for your olfactory sense.

Touch – Mindfulness practices of your tactile sense

Our ability to touch or exercise our tactile sense is the ability to feel anything that touches our skin. Our hands are most often utilized to feel and experience the environment. The sense of touch is controlled by networks of nerve endings and touch receptors throughout our body.

Through touch you can feel textures, temperatures, vibration, pain, and other tactile sensory experiences. Touch may signal danger or may be a pathway toward physical intimacy when it is in relation to other people. The following activities will allow you to experience and focus on your tactile sense mindfully. Consider the miracle of your ability to touch.

Activity 1 – Touch: Soft or Furry

- Find an item that brings you comfort. It may be a furry throw, a soft blanket, a silky pillowcase, or a small furry animal (if they are able to stay still).
- Find a comfortable place to sit, preferably without distractions.
- Take a deep breath and close your eyes.
- Keeping your eyes closed, hold the item that brings you comfort.
- Experience the soft or furry item through touch.
- Rub your fingers over the item and notice what you feel.
- Notice any new sensations you feel in your body as you touch this item of comfort.
- Keeping your eyes closed, experience the item to the fullest and make the connection between how touch affects your emotional state.
- Maintain this mindfulness activity for at least 2 minutes with your eyes closed.

When you have completed this activity, notice any changes in your body resulting from focusing and being mindfully present to your tactile senses. Notice your level of calm resulting from focusing on touch of a comforting sensation. Think about any new awareness you have about the ability to touch and feel and how the tactile sense connects to your emotional well-being. Think about how touch provides you with information about your immediate environment.

You may want to journal a few sentences about your experience. Think about any aspect of appreciation you now have for your tactile ability. Identify one aspect of gratitude that you feel because of your ability to touch.

Activity 2 – Touch: An Office Item

- Find an item that is usually associated with an office supply. It may be a stapler, a pen, a tablet of paper, or a book. You can even use this book.
- Find a quiet place to sit comfortably.
- Take a deep breath and keep your eyes closed.
- Hold the object in your hands and experience all aspects of it using your tactile senses.
- Rub your fingers and hands over the item and notice anything that you may not have noticed about the texture, temperature, edges, etc.
- Notice if there is any area that is sharp and could be painful to touch.
- Just sit with eyes closed with this item and experience it completely by using your tactile senses.
- Continue this for 2 minutes.

When you have completed this activity, notice any changes you feel in your body resulting from focusing. Notice if mindfulness has allowed you to feel calmer than prior to the activity. What did you notice about the item on which you were using your tactile senses?

You may want to journal about the experience. What can you think about regarding your appreciation for this item as it makes your life easier or more efficient? Identify one aspect of gratitude that you have for the item.

Activity 3 – Touch: Another's Hand

- This activity requires using another person. Find someone that will engage with you.
- This is a closed eyes, silent activity.
- Sit facing the other person on a comfortable chair in a preferably quiet place.
- Place your hands palm to palm and fingers to fingers.
- Take a deep breath and close your eyes in silence.
- Notice any temperature differences in your hands and fingers.
- Notice any textures you feel in the other's hands and fingers.
- Notice the sensations on your hands and fingertips as they are touching the other person.
- Focus on any sensations or energy you feel from the touch of the other.
- Continue to focus on the energy you feel from the other person for 2 minutes.

After completing this activity, take a few moments to just notice any changes you feel in your body. Are you less stressed and do you feel more relaxed? Do you feel any energy shifts or changes from touching another? What new awareness do you have about touch with another following the activity?

You may want to journal a few sentences about your experience. What do you appreciate about your tactile sense? Identify one aspect of gratitude that you now have for your sense of touch.

Vision – Mindfulness practices of your visual sense

The previous grounding activities were some examples of mindfulness practices of your senses associated with listening, taste, smell and touch. The following activities will be focused on vision.

The biology of our ability to see is complex and amazing. Things that are within our scope of sight are picked up by visual receptors located in our eyes, which is the primary organ involved in sight.

Your ability to see provides you with information about your surrounding environment. The eye transmits information to the brain through neural circuitry and the brain utilizes a significant amount of space for vision. The brain utilizes more area for vision than any other of the senses. Most of the neural activity for vision is present in the occipital lobe of the brain.

Our ability to see and perceive what is in our environment is a complex and fascinating process. Whether you have good or limited visual ability, I invite you to engage in the mindfulness practices focused on what you see.

The following activities will focus on your sense of vision.

Activity 1 – Vision: Color

- Find a comfortable place to sit in any room, in preferably a quiet environment.
- Close your eyes and take a deep breath.
- Open your eyes and with your head still, look all around the room within your vision and look for color in the room.
- Without moving your head, look as far as you can to the left and then move your eyes to the right.
- Look up and then down without moving your head, scanning the room for color.
- Identify five colors that you see within your scope of sight.
- Fixate on one color for two minutes.

Upon completion of this activity, notice any changes you feel in your body due to the mindfulness exercise. Are you less stressed and are you feeling calmer? What did you notice about the colors you found in the room and what colors did you not notice previously?

You may want to write a few sentences in your journal about the activity. Think about your ability to see color and what you appreciate about your vision. Identify one area of gratitude you have today for your sense of sight.

Activity 2 – Vision: Outdoors

- Step outside and find a preferably quiet and comfortable place to either sit or stand.
- Close your eyes and take a deep breath.
- Open your eyes and look around you at the colors and formations of nature.
- Notice the shades and pigments of trees, flowers, soil, grass, rocks, or other natural items.
- Fixate on one item and take in the colors, the tones, the shading, the textures, and the whole of nature's item.
- Notice in detail all the things you did not pay attention to in the past.
- Maintain this fixation on an item for at least 2 minutes.

When you have completed this activity, notice any changes in your body now that contrast to how you felt prior to the mindfulness exercise. Notice any changes in your emotional state. Think about what you became aware of during the activity.

You may want to journal a few sentences about what you noticed. Think about some aspect of appreciation you have for nature. Identify at least one aspect of gratitude you have for your sight.

Yoga, Deep Relaxation Techniques, Deep Breathing, and Meditation

Yoga

The practice of yoga incorporates deep breathing and stretching into body movements that can effectively create ***vagal nerve*** soothing and ***parasympathetic nervous system*** responsiveness. Increasing your "vagal tone" means enhancing your ability to emotionally regulate rather than be caught in the high wire or the emotional basement. Yoga is established as a practice that increases flexibility in the body and muscles. There is also a nervous system benefit.

Yoga is also known to include deep breathing techniques which also activate the *parasympathetic nervous system* and increase vagal tone. Various positions help to reduce stress in the body and decrease trauma responses.

Keep in mind that much of trauma is stored in the body and muscles which is called "***somatic memory***". Your body remembers trauma and stores the memory of high stress and trauma. Releasing or dislodging the traumatic somatic memory can happen from the positions and stretching that are included in yoga practices. Quite often your body may remember the trauma in addition to the stored memory in your executive network.

I have had many of my patients describe a very calm and peaceful feeling following yoga practices. I have also had patients who describe a sudden release of emotions and becoming tearful after an intense session of yoga. This is more than likely a result of somatic memory being dislodged in the body following the deep breathing and yoga positions.

Find a yoga class close to you or find an online yoga site where you can put into practice the various positions and deep breathing techniques. The stretching alone can create the release of tension and somatic memory. The positions can help you with flexibility. Flexibility is something that decreases with age, and yoga can slow down the loss of movement for older adults. Balance is also known to improve through yoga.

There is also evidence of various health advantages in practicing yoga. It is known to improve cardiovascular health as well as improve overall immunity. Reduction of inflammation can be another advantage of yoga. Improved mental health is also something that can be the result of regular practice of yoga. Stress levels decrease and anxiety reduction is also a common response to incorporation of yoga into a regular practice.

I think most people want to improve their quality of life and putting this into practice can be effective in your overall well-being. Yoga has its origin in ancient Eastern practices. Modern yoga is used world-wide and many research projects have concluded that the benefits are significant to overall emotional well-being and physical health.

Mindfulness Breathing Activity

This mindfulness activity can be done in just a few minutes. The following are steps toward the practice of mindful breathing:

- Find a preferably quiet and comfortable place to sit or lie down. (*Although it is preferred for you to be in a quiet place, this can be done in a crowded waiting room, your office chair, or anywhere. You can find peace amongst the chaos around you.*)
- Close your eyes and just focus on your breathing.
- Become aware of this automatic process that happens all day long.
- Pay attention to your lungs as they expand and retreat.
- Pay attention to the breath. The sound of your breath. The feeling of how your breath expands your lungs and then retreats.
- Keep it simple and just continue to focus on the breath.
- Continue this for 2 to 5 minutes. If your busy mind wants to distract you, return your focus to your breath.

When you are done, open your eyes and take a few moments to consider how your breathing is your life source and brings oxygen to your cells throughout your body. Journal a few sentences about your experience. Name something you are grateful for about your breath.

Meditation

Meditation is another practice that originated from Eastern religions. It has been utilized for thousands of years as a sacred practice to develop deep awareness. Meditation has most recently been adopted world-wide for individuals to find a sense of peace, calm, relaxation, and for health benefits. Establishing a balanced mind and body connection is significant to wanting to improve your emotional health and well-being. Putting into practice the activities in all the previous chapters requires establishing a more balanced mind and body relationship. It is all connected.

Your thoughts, feelings, behaviors, and physiology as well as your brain functioning require you to have a greater connection between mind and body. Meditation can assist you in increasing self-awareness and personal insight. It can reduce negative emotional states and decrease anxiety and depression. Physical wellness is affected with the regular practice of meditation, and you may reduce blood pressure rate, heart rate, stress, and tension. The practice of yoga can bring you to a meditative state and assist you in finding calm and peace through the stretching and optimal positioning of your body.

Keep in mind that all the "mindfulness" activities associated with the five senses are forms of meditation. There are other various types of meditative practice that can assist you on your journey of personal growth.

Quiet Time and Reading Meditation

One type of meditation that you may already be practicing is taking time to sit quietly and read something that feeds your spirit. You may find that a daily meditation reading can help you to find comfort. You may want to practice this as a ritual first thing in the morning, sitting in a quiet place indoors or outdoors and reading a passage or a daily meditation. Be sure to select something that is thought provoking and has you feeling "spiritually connected." Then sit and ponder what you have read.

The next step would be to journal a few sentences about what you read and how it applies to your life. A daily ritual of this practice can be a way to start your day in peace and grounded thoughts. You may find that you are more "centered" for the rest of your day.

Traditional Breathing and Closed Eye Meditation

Another type of traditional meditation is the closed eye meditation, and it begins with deep breathing techniques.

- Find a comfortable place to sit with your back straight or lie down flat on your back.
- Close your eyes and engage in deep breathing for at least 5 deep belly breaths.
- Breathe slowly in through your nose and out through your mouth.
- Beginning with your feet, visualize the muscles in your feet fully relaxing.

- Moving up your calves, tense and relax. Visualize your calf muscles fully relaxing,
- Visualize your thighs. Relax them.
- Visualize your back and relax any muscles that feel tense.
- Shrug your shoulders and then relax them. Make sure that all muscles in your neck and shoulders are relaxed.
- Notice your arms and hands and relax any tense muscles in them.
- Tense all the muscles in your face, and then relax the face.
- Continue to notice the breath.
- When you hear any intrusive thoughts or visuals, just notice them, and let them go.
- Do your best to sit still and quietly, and just quiet your mind.
- Pay attention to the breath.
- Notice if there is still any tension throughout your body. Relax those muscles.
- Try your best to find the peace within you.
- Find the peace in the quiet and the sound of silence.
- Notice any visual you have of light. What color do you see?
- Continue to be in touch with your peace within you.
- Stay in this state for as long as you are able or as long as time permits.
- Stay in this place of peace and calm for anywhere from 5 to 30 minutes.
- When you are ready, come back to the room where you are sitting, and notice your body.
- Notice if you feel different because of the practice of meditation.

Keep in mind that it is called "practicing meditation" because it takes practice, and it takes time to get used to doing it. Notice how different your body feels and how different your emotional state is because of the meditative practice. You will likely be better prepared for whatever your day holds ahead of you. You will likely be more balanced and grounded throughout the day. Take notice of how differently you can respond to your daily stressors and how much better you are able to respond to others after the practice of meditation.

Guided Imagery Meditation – "Safe Place"

Guided imagery is a way of meditating while using a narrative or while listening to a narration that guides you through the process of deep relaxation and then has you visualize a calm and peaceful image. Along with finding a peaceful and calm place within you, it also engages you in a visual that allows you to creatively see the picture of something or somewhere that is calming and relaxing. You can find guided imagery narratives online, in podcasts, or on recordings made by people to assist you with visualizations.

The following is a narrative for you to follow that can be recorded or memorized. It requires you to imagine a "safe place." That place can be anywhere that you find relaxing and calming and peaceful. It may be on a beach, a mountaintop, a wooded area, a place in your home, or your back yard, just to name a few options. ***You will need to think of a place that you can identify as your "safe place."***

- Find a comfortable place to sit or lie, preferably where it is quiet. If you are sitting, place your feet flat on the ground.
- Take five deep and cleansing breaths, in through the nose and out through the mouth.
- Scan your legs and arms for any tension or tensing of the muscles. Notice them and attempt to relax them.
- Scan your torso, your back, and your chest for any tension. Notice and attempt to relax those areas.
- Scan your shoulders and neck for tension. Relax.
- Scan your facial muscles for any tension or tense muscles. Relax those.
- Visualize yourself on a warm summer day walking along a path through a meadow. Visualize any flowers or colors that you see.
- You feel wonderful and you know that you are headed toward your "safe place."
- You feel a gentle breeze on your face and the sun is warm on your face and body.
- You are so safe.
- You continue to stroll along the path and can see your "safe place" just beyond the meadow.
- You are relaxed and warm and safe.

- Visualize that you arrive at your "safe place." (It may be a beach, a mountaintop, a wooded area, a place in your house or outside your house, etc.)
- Visualize that you find a comfortable place to sit or lie in your "safe place."
- Now visualize and notice everything that surrounds you in your "safe place."
- What colors and what object do you visualize?
- What are the sounds that you would hear?
- What are the sensations you would feel (the breeze, the sun)?
- What are you hearing? Can you hear the wind, the breeze, the birds, or waves?
- What smells do you smell in your safe place?
- Embrace the moment and the feeling of safety and security that you feel. Embrace the whole of what you are feeling as you visualize this place.
- Stay here for anywhere from 5 to 30 minutes.
- You are calm. You are safe.
- When you are ready you can get up and leave your "safe place," knowing that you can return at any time.
- Visualize that you are walking away from your "safe place" and headed toward the path through the meadow that brought you here.
- You are now feeling calmer than ever and feeling safe and grounded.
- You head back on the path toward where you currently sit or lie.
- When you are back in your room notice the feeling of your back that is supported by your chair or the ground. Begin to wiggle your toes and fingers and become aware of being back in the room where you began. Become aware of your actual surroundings. When you are ready, you can open your eyes. Return to where you are presently.

Notice how you are feeling now that you have journeyed to your safe place and back. You have essentially "tricked" your brain into assuming that you are in your safe place. As a result, you are feeling more relaxed and grounded. Notice your heart rate and your sense of peace following the meditation and guided imagery.

Remember that you can return to your safe place at any time. When you feel unsafe or stressed, you can use this imagery to temporarily take you away from your unwanted thoughts or misperceptions.

Walking Meditation

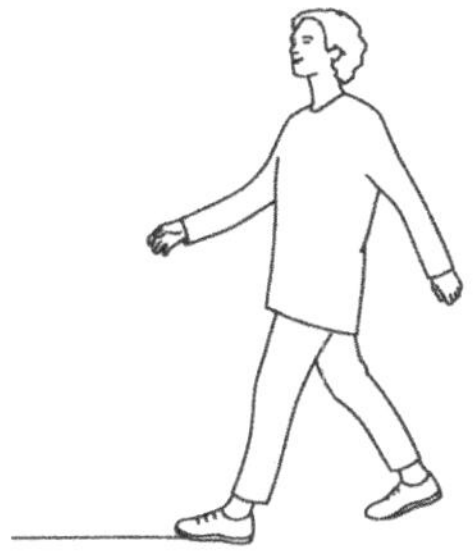

This type of meditation is a mindful experience of looking around you, seeing nature, and looking for the amazing gift that surrounds you. If you live in a city or concrete area, you can still observe the trees, birds, the sky, or whatever aspect of nature you can see. This is a quiet walk and mindful experience of looking around you and just noticing.

- Step outside in a preferably quiet area and take a deep and cleansing breath.
- Begin a very slow walk.
- Look around you at nature…tress, flowers, buds, plants, birds, the sky, or rain.
- Continue an open-eyed mindfulness walk, just noticing any aspect of nature that surrounds you.
- You can stop if it feels right and gaze at a tree, a flower, a bird, or any other thing that captures your attention.
- Continue your slow walk and take in the whole of what you see.
- Notice your breath.
- Notice smells, sensations, sounds, and feel the peace.
- Continue the walk for 5 to 30 minutes.

This meditation practice is different as it calls for a walking experience and an open-eyed meditation experience. This practice allows you to get in touch with yourself and your surrounding environment and the experience that surrounds you. This often goes unnoticed in our day-to-day busy routines.

Upon completion of the walking meditation, sit for a moment and think about what stood out to you. You may want to journal a few sentences about your experience. Think about something that you appreciate about your surroundings and about anything you noticed on your walk. Identify one aspect of gratitude associated with what you saw, experienced, and observed.

Meditation: Using a Mantra

A mantra is a word or phrase that you can repeat over and over to help you to feel calmer and to help you to avoid distracting thoughts during a meditation. The word "mantra" stems from Sanskrit: *"man"* means mind, and *"tra"* can be translated to mean release.

Mantras are essentially used to release the overwhelming thoughts that can be distracting when attempting to meditate. Mantras were originally considered to be a sacred group of words used in ancient Eastern cultures to inspire truth, reality, peace, and love. Mantras continue to be a spiritually meaningful experience.

Finding Your Mantra and Putting It into Practice

You may use a single word such as "peace, love, freedom, release," or other words that reflect your inner desires. You may also find a phrase to use such as, "I am safe," or "I am free," or "I am love," or other short phrases that speak to your inner longing. You repeat the word or phrase repeatedly. It will help you to tune out unwanted thoughts or distractions when you are practicing meditation. Follow these steps to practice meditation using a mantra:

- ***First think of a personal mantra. Think of a word or a phrase that speaks to your inner longing or desire.*** Words such as *"freedom," "love," "release," "God," "trust,"* or other words can be used. Or find a phrase such as, *"I am safe,"* or *"I am love,"* or *"I am one with God,"* or *"I am free."*
- Find a preferably quiet place with minimal distractions.
- Sit or lie comfortably with a straight back. If you are lying down, lie on your back. If you are sitting in a chair, place your feet flat on the ground. If you are sitting on the floor, sit cross-legged if possible.
- Close your eyes and take five deep and cleansing breaths.
- Sit or lie with the intention of focusing on your mantra.
- Begin to repeat your mantra over and over, developing a rhythm.
- Continue your mantra meditation for 5 to 15 minutes.
- When you are ready, notice where you are sitting and return to the room you are in.
- Open your eyes and notice any changes in your stress level.

When you have completed your mantra meditation, notice how you are feeling and notice any changes in your emotional state. Feel the difference in your breathing and heart rate. Notice if you were able to successfully decrease intrusive thoughts and negative thoughts because of the mantra meditation. Think of something that you appreciate about your life. You may want to journal a few sentences about your experience. Think of one aspect of gratitude that you have for your life.

Mantras and the effects on your brain functioning

Although ***mantras*** have been used in religions and as a sacred or spiritually meaningful experiences, it is also interesting to note what happens in the brain when repeating a word or phrase "over and over" again. Although we can recognize that there are physical, emotional, and spiritual benefits, it is interesting to also acknowledge what neuroscience can teach us about the use of a repetitive word or phrase.

Research has found that repeating mantras can block the release of the stress hormones adrenaline and cortisol. They also stimulate the vagus nerve, and this activates your parasympathetic nervous system. As you recall from Chapter 10, the parasympathetic nervous system is what goes into effect when you are in a resting state or preparing for sleep. Heart rate decreases, blood pressure decreases, breathing slows, and digestion is activated. This is the optimal response for your health and well-being.

Mantras and meditation are also known to decrease the levels of GABA receptors, which are neurotransmitters that are associated with higher levels of anxiety (Krishnakumar, Hamblin, & Lakhmanan, 2015). Serotonin, a neurotransmitter that is stimulated through many types of SSRI (selective serotonin reuptake inhibitor) anti-depressants, is also released when using mantras and meditation. Norepinephrine is another neurotransmitter that is associated with anxiety. This brain chemical has an association also with fear. Mantras and meditation have been found in research to lower the amount of norepinephrine in the brain, increasing calmness.

A neurotransmitter that is associated with social anxiety is dopamine. People with social anxiety often have lower levels of dopamine in their neurochemistry make-up. Mantras have been found to increase the dopamine levels in the brain.

People who have obsessive-compulsive disorder (OCD) often use repetitive behaviors such as handwashing or door checking to relieve their anxiety. Perhaps they are doing this repetitive behavior to get the release of dopamine that they feel when engaging in their OCD behaviors.

Through the use of ***mantras***, you can feel a decrease in anxiety and a decrease in social anxiety. You will feel more relaxed and be more alert. Try it and see if you experience these calming benefits from mantras that are scientifically proven.

Chapter Summary

All the chapter's practices are "mind and body" solutions to decrease stress, anxiety, depression, and other worry-oriented thinking. Many activities are mindfulness-based practices, and some teach basic meditation skills. Consider the science behind the effectiveness and practical value of doing these activities on a regular basis. Try doing any of these activities every day for two weeks and see if you feel better. You will more than likely begin to notice the difference in how you feel throughout the day and in how you are able to interact with others more effectively.

Some of the changes may be more subtle. It is important to notice how you respond differently to situations that may have triggered you in the past. Notice the contrast of how you may have dealt with a life stressor prior to practicing mindfulness and meditation and how you are able to respond now.

There is so much to learn about our bodies and our brains and how we can train ourselves to feel better through the use of some daily practices. These practices are free and only require your self-discipline. These practices are so simple you may doubt their effectiveness.

The medical community is now suggesting the use of mindfulness and deep relaxation techniques to cardiac patients, cancer patients, and other individuals who have stress-related conditions. Doctors and practicioners of primary care medicine are recognizing how lowering stress levels can be valuable to anyone with a stress-related illness or a condition where stress antagonizes their problem. Consider the state of a "fight or flight" response of your body and the adrenaline and oxytocin that are released that do long-term harm. These are just some of the undesirable physiological responses to high levels of stress.

Your emotional and mental health are at stake also. If you are looking to improve your ability to be resilient and respond effectively to life situations, you will want to put these practices into a daily routine. You will think more clearly, feel less tension, and your overall sense of well-being will be enhanced. It is clearly worth the few minutes of time spent daily.

You may want to begin with just some of the deep breathing exercises in the morning for 5 to 10 minutes. Notice if it improves your stress level and your outlook on life.

Many people I have met have rejected the idea of "meditation" or "mindfulness" because of the old ideas they have attached to those words. If that deters you, consider the need to discard old ideas that block you from personal freedom. (This is described in Chapters 3-6 about beliefs.)

If you are willing and able, do not hesitate to put these activities into practice. If you have hope for a better and more fulfilling life, engage in these practices. You will not regret it. What do you have to lose? You only have the potential to gain from giving it a try.

The next chapter will provide other types of coping skills that can help you to find freedom from your negative thinking and overwhelming emotions that may cause problems for you. Consider that all the previous chapters have identified the need for exploring your thinking, your life experiences, and your emotional pain from the past. We are now looking at solutions that will allow you to remove yourself from "stuck" places that only create barriers to feeling better.

12.a Reflection

12.a

- Which of the mindfulness activities were you willing to try? Write a little about your experience.

- Was there a mindfulness activity that challenged your ability to focus? If so, write about that and about the outcome.

- How has judgment become a part of your negative thinking? What is it like to attempt to eliminate judgment around the activities and the concept of mindfulness?

Chapter 13

Coping Strategies and Solutions

More Strategies for Overcoming the Past: Finding Strength from Pain

"Everything is either an opportunity to grow, or an obstacle to keep you from growing."

— *Dr. Wayne Dyer, The Power of Intention*

The ability to find strength from pain is a paradox. Movement away from the pain is available when we embrace what we perceive to be a barrier and move toward a solution. The right perspective can shift us from suffering to riding the wild wave of life in the direction of opportunity. When we have clarity, we can see that pain and strength are not polarized or contradictory states of being.

They complement each other. Pain invites us to use our strength to overcome barriers and blockages. In the absence of pain, we are unlikely to see that there are areas of our life that need to change. Basking in complacency may seem to be a refuge from stress, but it does not allow for growth or for the demonstration of our courage and strength. Are you willing to explore your strength?

The introductory quote to this chapter by Dr. Wayne Dyer is accurate in that we have an opportunity for growth with every obstacle that we encounter. We sometimes see the barriers as stumbling blocks and do not accept our ability to take action to move beyond those deterrents. The obstacles are often self-imposed and are a part of our false narrative that keeps us stuck.

The first 11 chapters of this book may have brought up your tendencies to have intrusive negative thoughts, overwhelming emotions, over reactions to life stressors, or need for social involvement. Chapter 12 provided many types of coping strategies (mindfulness, awareness, meditation, and mind-body connectedness) that can assist you in developing a stronger spiritual connection and a more meaningful life. This chapter will look at other practical coping strategies.

Adaptive Coping Versus Maladaptive Coping

When it comes to dealing with life stressors, we can engage in adaptive coping or maladaptive coping. Adaptive coping involves strategies that will enhance our lives. Maladaptive coping includes behaviors that are not in our best interest or behaviors that are unhealthy responses to situations. Examples of ***maladaptive coping*** are:

- Isolation
- Addictions (drugs, alcohol, sex, gambling, excessive money spending, etc.)
- Non-suicidal self-injury (cutting, burning, scratching, or rubbing)
- Anger outbursts or raging
- Property destruction (punching walls or breaking things)
- Excessive and out-of-control displays of emotion
- Excessive binge-watching of television or video games
- Attempts to control others close to you
- Dissociating (cutting off from emotions or situations) or "spacing out"
- Bullying
- Irritability

These are just some of the ***maladaptive coping strategies*** that are used to deal with uncomfortable emotions, intrusive or negative thoughts, discomfort with social situations, or anxiety and depression. We tend to turn to things that temporarily take us away from the discomforts of life through an internal or external "fix".

As you review this list, you can see that some of the maladaptive coping strategies are things we do to ourselves, and some are things that we impose upon others. Either type is harmful and will interfere with our ability to live a happy and fulfilling life.

You may want to now think about any maladaptive coping methods that you use and jot them down in your journal. Through this, you can look for alternative adaptive coping strategies to apply to your life.

Let's look at some other potential coping strategies that can improve your personal well-being and move you through your emotional state. You can identify some skills that will decrease your negative thinking and intrusive thought patterns. I have divided the adaptive coping strategies into four categories. You may want to try all of them to see what is most practically useful to you. The four categories for adaptive coping are: **1) Problems and Solutions, 2) Stress, 3) Emotions, and 4) Existential Solutions.**

Coping: Problems and Solutions

As a part of our human experience, we encounter problems. Our response to the problems is sometimes to avoid it through procrastination or by looking the other way. We also may respond to problems that arise by blaming others and staying stuck or by having angry outbursts that do not solve the problem. Learning to face problems through some practical methods can be a healthy coping strategy.

Step One: Identify the problem

The first step in finding solutions to problems is to identify the problems. Your problem may fall into different categories. I have created four basic areas that problems fall under:

- Relationship problems: spouse, partner, family, friends, etc.
- Work, school, or lack of employment problems
- Emotional issues: fear, anger, hate, sadness, etc.
- Physical problems: illness, weight issues, energy level, etc.

Now let's identify where you may need problem-solving. Complete your inventory, and leave areas blank if there are no problems to report:

Relationship Problem(s): ______________________________

____

____

Work-School Problem(s): ______________________________

____

____

Emotional Issue(s): ______________________________

____

____

Physical Problem(s): ______________________________

____

____

Step Two: What has been your part?

The preceding chart may have many problems that you are aware of. ***Identify your top 3 problems and we will be working on them as a priority.*** Pick which problems are causing you the most distress.

As you define the problem it will be important to look at the specifics about your problem. For example, let's say you have a problem with a family member. What are some bullet points on the specifics of the problem? What part have you played in the problem? How have you tried to solve the problem that didn't work?

> *"It is important to trust that you potentially have many of the answers to your problems within you."*

If you have a problem with a coworker or supervisor at work, ask yourself what your part has been in the problem. What are the specifics? If you have an emotional problem, for example with anger, what are the specifics? What part do you play in the problem? If you have a physical problem such as being overweight, what are the specifics? What has been your part in the problem?

Looking for how you have contributed to the problem:
Looking at your part you play in the problem is often uncomfortable and difficult to see. This is probably the most important part of the process in problem solving. If you are having difficulty in seeing your part, you may want to ask a few friends, family, or a professional about what they see as elements of the part you're playing in the situation.

However, if you are honest with yourself, you can probably identify your role in having created the problem. If you have a problem in a relationship, what were some of the things that you did that may have contributed to the problem? What are some of the underlying issues that have been in your hands?

- For relationships: Have you lacked communication or trust?
- For relationships: Have you been argumentative, critical, or accusatory?
- For relationships: Have you ignored this person or been avoidant?
- For work or school: Have you lacked accountability?
- For work or school: Have you been over-responsible and taken on too much?

- For work or unemployment: Have you looked for jobs or career changes?
- For emotions: Are you fearful of things that you imagine?
- For emotions: Do you deal with irrational anger?
- For emotions: Do you find yourself crying and sad all the time without cause?
- For physical problems: Are you taking care of your health?
- For physical problems: Are you eating healthy and maintaining a healthy lifestyle?
- For physical problems: Despite your condition are you doing something to improve your health?

Complete the following inventory for your top 3 problems:

PROBLEM 1 SPECIFICS

What are the bullet point specifics about the problem ?

What has been your part and how have you contributed ?

PROBLEM 2 SPECIFICS

What are the bullet point specifics about the problem ?

What has been your part and how have you contributed ?

PROBLEM 3 SPECIFICS

What are the bullet point specifics about the problem ?

What has been your part and how have you contributed ?

Step Three: What have you tried so far?

This step asks you to identify what you have already tried that has not worked. The reason that this is important is because you don't want to continue trying the same thing that didn't work and get the same result. This is the definition of insanity. Problem solving requires that you identify what you tried that did not work and identify the unsuccessful strategies you have used.

It is said that Thomas Edison made 10,000 failed attempts before successfully creating a light bulb. Not sure who was counting, but it is important to consider that often our unsuccessful attempts can guide us to finding the solution. Edison is said to have stated that he did not fail 10,000 times, but successfully found 10,000 ways that don't work.

In assessing what has not worked, you are looking to not repeat the errors you have already made. It is also important to not give up on new attempts to resolve the problem. Your next step is to identify the things you have tried that have not worked.

Use the following chart to list the things that didn't work:

PROBLEM 1 SPECIFICS

What you tried that didn't work ...

____

____

____

PROBLEM 2 SPECIFICS

What you tried that didn't work ...

____

____

____

PROBLEM 3 SPECIFICS

What you tried that didn't work ...

____

____

____

Step Four: Finding other adaptive solutions

Looking for options to solving your problem is inherent in your ability as a human being. You have ideas within you that you can tap into that can help to solve your problem. You have options, and the next step will require that you begin to explore your options. The neocortex in your brain, or the executive functioning area of your brain, is equipped to look for solutions. Your human brain is prewired to work for you if you believe that there is a possibility of a solution.

It is important to trust that you potentially have many of the answers to your problems within you. Trust that you are capable. Trust that you have ideas. Trust your competence. Look for healthy and adaptive solutions to the problem. Stay away from any unhealthy ideas, negativity, addictive ideas, or things that can hurt someone else. Some examples are:

- Relationship problems: *Find an opportunity to communicate with the person you are in conflict with. Make an appointment for coffee or lunch with the person you are in conflict with. Find a way to communicate your part in the problem.*
- Work or school problems: *Schedule a time to speak with your boss. Make an appointment to talk with your teacher. Look to improve your grades through scheduling dedicated times for study.*
- Emotional problems: *Find coping skills to use to decrease emotional reactivity. Implement anger management techniques.*
- Physical problems: *Engage in daily workouts at the gym. Begin a healthy eating program. Find a system for managing medications and sleep.*

These are just some examples of techniques that you can use to resolve your problems. The specifics of your problems and the specifics of your ideas are unique to you. If you are unable to find some new options to explore and feel that you have exhausted all of your own ideas, then turn to someone else that you trust for their thoughts.

Now it is your turn to identify what problem-solving strategies you will be using. ***In the following chart, list your ideas about how to better resolve your challenges:***

PROBLEM 1 SPECIFICS

What is a new strategy? __________

____

____

What are other ideas of coping? __________

____

____

PROBLEM 2 SPECIFICS

What is a new strategy? __________

____

____

What are other ideas of coping? __________

____

____

PROBLEM 3 SPECIFICS

What is a new strategy? ______________________________

____

____

What are other ideas of coping? ______________________________

____

____

Step Five: Your action plan

Now it is time to put your plan into action. For every problem, you have strategized solutions. Continue doing this until you are living in the solution. Again, if you are having a difficult time thinking of new ideas, ask others. You will feel free when you have resolved your problem. Otherwise, it is as if you are carrying your problems around with you everywhere you go.

You carry the weight of the things that are bothering you and things that occupy your mind every day. Consider a grudge you have against a family member. You carry the weight of the emotions that surround your anger toward them. You also feel uncomfortable around them. It is important to do your best to put these issues to rest.

Coping Skill: Release—Finding Acceptance in the Unacceptable and the Unresolvable

Some problems may stay unresolved. There may be a friendship that never heals. There may be a health issue that is unresolvable. There may be an emotion that is difficult to alter. There may be a coworker relationship that is not able to heal. Knowing that you have made every effort to resolve these things is important. Knowing that you have done your best to find a solution may lighten your load.

Now it is time to "let go." Let go of the burden you carry regarding the situation that is a problem. This means finding acceptance in what may feel unacceptable. This means embracing the unresolvable and letting go of it. Ruminating and overthinking about your conflict will only bring you pain and stress. Letting go means accepting that the situation is what it is and that it is unchangeable by you.

Some situations from the past are unchangeable and even though you do not like that it happened, you can embrace that it "is what it is" and let go. Some relationship conflicts are with people who you cannot reach and since you cannot change others, you can embrace "they are who they are" and let go. Some internalized emotions are difficult to deal with and you can embrace your biochemistry and do your best to overcome your reactions. Some physical problems are going to persist despite all efforts. You can embrace this fact and find acceptance in the reality. Then let go of the struggle.

Visualization on Letting Go:

- Find a comfortable place to sit or lie.
- Take a deep breath.
- Visualize that your problem is in object form and that you are holding it in the palm of your hand.
- Accept that this issue "is what it is" and is unchangeable by you despite your efforts.
- Visualize letting the object fly off your hand into space.
- Visualize feeling a ***release*** of the object.
- Visualize letting go and finding acceptance in the unacceptable.
- You are free.

You may need to do this activity daily for several days until you feel a ***release.*** Finding a release means no longer carrying the weight of the problem. Finding a release means feeling free from the stress associated with the problem. Finding a release means no longer over-thinking the problem and being preoccupied with what feels unacceptable to you. *You are free.*

Coping: Stress

Coping Strategies for Stress-Related Problems

Stress is something that we all experience. In fact, to get out of bed in the morning, we experience a certain level of stress. This type of "normal stress" is a part of our physical motivation to get things done. Stress in larger doses can be very unhealthy and can sometimes cause health problems. The medical community is beginning to suggest that heart disease, cancer, and pulmonary issues are escalated or caused by high levels of stress.

In Chapter 10, the sympathetic nervous system was addressed as well as the associated ways our body responds to stressful situations. Some of these responses are:

- heart rate increases
- pupils dilate
- breathing becomes rapid (sometimes hyperventilation occurs)
- blood pressure increases
- digestion stops
- stress hormones release

All of these symptoms are ways that our bodies put us into "action mode" when we experience high levels of stress or an extremely stressful event. Our bodies are preparing us for the need to flee or fight the incoming potential danger. The "fight or flight" response is something that can help you if a lion walks into your room, or if you need to act fast in any critical situation. However, to stay in "fight or flight" mode for long hours is very dangerous to the body. ***This is why most cardiologists now teach calming techniques to their patients.***

Stress Hormone Release

The most damaging sympathetic nervous system response is the release of ***stress hormones***. Some of these stress hormones are cortisol, adrenaline (epinephrine), and norepinephrine. These hormones are released by the adrenal glands and help you when you are dealing with stress.

However, when the cortisol levels remain high for long periods of time, a person may begin to experience weight gain, headaches, inflammation of the stomach area, irritability and anger outbursts, high blood pressure, sleep problems, digestive problems, muscle tension and pain, and other symptoms.

A condition called "adrenal fatigue" occurs when a person is exposed to high levels of stress for enduring periods of time. The body is unable to sustain production of cortisol and a person will feel the effects of this. Adrenal fatigue is said to cause long-term emotional and mental health problems, such as depression and anxiety.

The solution: There is tremendous value in finding ways to calm yourself and transfer from sympathetic nervous system mode to the parasympathetic nervous system mode, which prepares you for rest and relaxation. The parasympathetic nervous system goes into effect when you are preparing for sleep or when you are in a very relaxed state from meditation. The body experiences the following in parasympathetic nervous system mode:

- heart rate slows
- pulse slows
- breathing slows
- blood pressure decreases
- digestion increases
- stress hormones recede

Putting yourself into a relaxed state using the meditation techniques and relaxation techniques described in Chapters 11 and 12 is advantageous and can prevent the release of excessive amounts of cortisol. Some other coping strategies for stress are taking intermittent breaks through the day, getting exercise, eating healthy foods, getting sufficient sleep, maintaining friendships, journaling, establishing hobbies, and prioritizing your list of things to do.

Intermittent Breaks

Today's world brings higher demands from the workplace and family life. We are in the "age of information," where new information is at our fingertips consistently through electronic devices and various forms of communication. People will often tell me in therapy about how busy their lives are and how their stress levels are very high throughout the workday or parenting day.

Everyone can dedicate time for self-care throughout the day through establishing a pattern of intermittent breaks. It is a matter of writing those breaks into your schedule and making those breaks as important as the call to that "important person." Morning and afternoon breaks as well as a lunch hour are considered mandatory according to employee labor laws in most states. Many people will disregard the need for taking breaks because they are convinced that they are "too busy" for that.

This is not true. Your work will still be there when you return from your mini timeout. This can be a life saver for you. This can be a break from the stress hormone release as well. Your body needs a timeout or a time away from the "grind."

Perhaps you are in the category of worker that does not believe you deserve to take a mini timeout throughout the stressful day. If so, perhaps it would be a good idea to review Chapters 4-6 and their corresponding exercises and explore why you feel the need to push yourself beyond your body's capacity. Perhaps your false narrative is:

- "I need to work harder than everyone else because I must prove myself." (core belief of *not measuring up to others*)
- "I need to produce more and work harder than others because I feel I am not as good as they are." (core belief of *inadequacy*)
- "If I don't do my work perfectly, then I will lose my standing or lose my job." (core belief of needing to be perfect due to *inadequacy*)
- "If I don't work harder than others, then the bosses will see that I don't deserve my job and shouldn't be here." (core shame-based belief of being *defective*)

Perhaps you can relate to one of those false narratives or core beliefs. If so, it is time to re-examine your thoughts and beliefs and find a new adaptive belief that reflects:

- "I am deserving."
- "My work does not define me as a person."
- "I am competent at my job. People know that I am competent and capable."
- "I learn from my mistakes, and I am competent despite them."
- "I am as good as others at my job and do not need to prove myself."

Mini Timeout

One strategy is to dedicate the first or the last five minutes of every hour to moving away from your work, closing your eyes, doing deep breathing and visualizing a calm and peaceful place. This will give your body a chance to detox from the stress hormones and become emotionally regulated at intervals. Working perpetually and therefore pushing your sympathetic nervous system to work non-stop is unhealthy and does not lead to better work production.

I have had people tell me that they *"didn't have time to use the restroom"* throughout the workday. This is unacceptable. You deserve breaks and mini timeouts. In fact, if you are in an office situation, you can use the restroom break for your mini timeout. You are deserving. You are worthy.

Taking your mini timeouts and intermittent breaks from stress will alleviate your stress response at intervals and can prove to be a healthier way to perform. Your performance, in fact, may improve from giving yourself an opportunity to take breaks. This can also provide you with a more adaptive attitude toward your work. It is up to you to initiate these breaks. Nobody is coming to tell you that you need a self-imposed timeout. It is up to you. Love yourself enough to know that you are deserving of your mini timeouts.

The Four D's

This strategy is something I learned in management training, and it has proven to be a wonderful window into the thinking that often accompanies stress. It was made popular by Jack Canfield, a corporate trainer. I can "set myself up" for over-stressing when I feel the pressure of thinking that there is "*no way out*" of my many obligations and workload. I do not know who to give original credit to for this strategy; however, it is very useful.

The false narrative that can cause even more stress is when I say to myself, "*I have so much work and I have no option but to power through the work non-stop and work overtime.*" This mindset does not allow for options and does not allow for alternatives.

The Four D's give you the option of:

- Do
- Delay
- Delegate
- Drop

Let's review this concept. The pressure of work stress or family stress can be alleviated when we consider the alternatives to "*getting it all done, by myself, right now.*" There are some things that must be done and are a high priority on your list of things to do. Some things can be postponed and do not need to get done right away. Some can be delegated to others, and some can just be dropped or deleted.

- **Do:** These are the things on your workload that must get done. If you have a list of things needed to be done, you can prioritize things that are needed to be completed immediately. For example, in the workplace, you may need to respond right away to your boss's email. In the home, it may be that your baby is crying and needs to be responded to immediately.

  Items on your "do" list require your personal immediate attention.

- **Delay:** There are some things on your list that can be put off. Look for things on your list that do not require immediate attention. Perhaps there is a task at work that has a due date of next week. At home, your task to do the laundry may be okay to delay until tomorrow when you have more time. If you are swamped, you can put these things off until a time when you are not feeling the pressure of today.

- **Delegate:** This is something that is most significant to the busy person who often works hard to do it all by themselves. There is often the option of delegating or reassigning a task to someone else. If it is in the workplace, you can often ask another person to do something that is on your list that does not require you to do it. In the home, you can reassign job responsibilities to others in your household. Delegating is the option that is underused by those who often feel the pressure to do it all by themselves. Some people don't feel that others can do the task as well as they can.

  The reality is that whether it is making copies at work, or completing chores at home, there are others who are perfectly capable of doing these things. It is empowering to delegate to others and offers an opportunity to "let go" of the outcome of some of the things on your list. Delegating responsibilities provides others with a sense of ownership and proprietorship in the operation of your work or the household. It empowers others to assist and participate.

- **Drop:** There are some things on your list that you can drop. You can remove some of the unimportant things from your list and just drop them. In the workplace this may mean not reading ads and unimportant emails. In the home, it may mean not watching a soap opera or not engaging in social media for the day. Drop what is not necessary from your list.

Knowing that you have options can reduce your stress level and can also remove some items from your plate. A big stressor is feeling that there is no alternative or no work-around to the tasks at hand. You can reduce your task list by using the Four D's. This can provide you with more time for mindful presence and for mini timeout breaks. You are the master of your day. It is up to you to determine how you will spend your time. It is up to you to reduce your stress level by incorporating some new strategies.

Coping: Emotions

Emotional Overload

Emotional dysregulation and feelings of emotional overload can come from feeling physically depleted, overthinking things, or your neurochemistry. Your thoughts, behaviors, emotions, and neurochemistry are all interconnected (as explored in Chapter 2). One part of each of these can lead to feeling emotional overload. When this occurs, your ability to think clearly declines, and your behavior may become problematic.

Emotional dysregulation occurs when there is essentially an *"overload"* of thoughts, feelings, behavior, and physiology. Meditation and deep relaxation techniques are optimal to use when you feel dysregulated. You can also try a few of the following techniques.

P-A-U-S-E

I like to use the acronym PAUSE to stand for: ***"Postpone (your response)-And-U-Stop-Escalation."*** A "pause" in your daily activities can provide you with time for a "cool down" and an opportunity to rethink how you will respond to any situation. You can press your personal "P-A-U-S-E" button during many types of emotionally charged situations. You may be having a conflict with another person and feel yourself becoming escalated to the point of being emotionally dysregulated.

Keep in mind that when you are full of emotion, the emotions flood your brain and block your ability to think clearly. Your cognitive functioning stops or becomes blocked due to high levels of emotion. If thinking is blocked or distorted, you are not likely seeing things accurately or soundly. When your thoughts are not *"grounded in reality"* and are emotionally charged, there is a tendency for situations to be magnified.

Your decision-making ability will potentially be distorted, and this may lead to regretful choices. Poor decisions and unhealthy responses can lead to greater problems and increased emotional distress.

A remedy for feeling as though you are losing control of your emotional state is to implement "P-A-U-S-E." *If you postpone your response, you can stop escalation of the problem.* You can always "P-A-U-S-E" because you have the right to take time away from any problem, situation, conflict, or person that is causing you to feel emotionally dysregulated. With "P-A-U-S-E," you remove yourself from a situation and allow yourself to return to a regulated emotional state or *"baseline."*

Adrenaline is often the chemical that is released when you are escalated emotionally. Adrenaline will subside within 20 minutes for most people. You can always return to dealing with the problem at hand after you have had time to regulate your emotions. This will also provide you with time to think more clearly about what your next steps will be in resolution of your problem. If it involves conflict with someone else, you can now prepare for the best response to that person that will help you to feel ***effective*** rather than out of control.

False narratives associated with this coping tool are:

- *"I must address any situation immediately or I will look like I don't know what I am doing."*
- *"I don't have time to stop and cool down before proceeding with the argument."*
- *"I will lose power in the situation if I delay my response."*
- *"It won't be the same if I circle back and respond to the situation later."*

These are false narratives regarding the ability to P-A-U-S-E. In fact, you will likely respond much more effectively if you take the time to pause. You will not lose power in the situation. You will in fact look more intentional. Taking time to pause before proceeding in a dialogue is not a demonstration of incompetence. It provides a position of strength. All the false narratives are the opposite of the truth. Use P-A-U-S-E to take time to strategize and to cool down.

Name It and Claim It

Feelings can be confusing and difficult to understand. One of the first steps in managing emotions is to be able to label or name the feeling you have. Naming the feeling you have and then embracing that this is your emotional response to a situation can provide insight into the situation.

You may feel irritated by your partner, and then realize that the emotion behind your irritation is envy or jealousy. You may feel distressed about your child going to school and realize that the emotion behind your distress is fear. You may feel disturbed by a new company policy and realize that behind your disturbance is anger. Underlying the anger is a feeling of disregard or discontent.

The situations are many and the emotional responses are infinite. Identifying the major feelings behind your emotional responses to life situations helps to clarify why you are feeling the way you feel.

Stopping, pausing, and taking the time to sort through the situation is important if you want to move beyond your emotional state. Following is a *"mini inventory"* that you can use:

- What is the situation that is driving your emotional state?
- What is the primary feeling that you are experiencing right now?
- Are there underlying feelings or states of being?
- Does the emotion fit the situation, or is it exaggerated?
- Name the feeling and claim it.
- Embrace that your emotions are a barometer to your world of life experiences.
- Talk to someone if you are still feeling strong emotions.

Some of the emotions or states of being you may be experiencing include: anger, fear, love, jealousy, envy, distrust, rejection, abandonment, anxiety, sadness, hopelessness, resentment, helplessness, emptiness, rage, disregarded, dismissed, irritation, annoyance, confusion, bullied, targeted, betrayed, excluded, disappointment, or foolish. Your worksheet:

13.a

13.a Name It and Claim It Inventory

Primary Emotions: Anger, fear, guilt, shame, sadness, disgust
Secondary Emotions: Disappointed, lonely, rejected, insecure, anxious, dismissed, discounted, threatened, hurt, confused, frustrated, humiliated, regret, pride, jealousy

Situation driving the emotion: "I told my husband about how upset I was because my mother criticized me about my parenting on the phone. He said I always over-react and I am too emotional."
Primary emotion (pick from above): I felt anger
Secondary emotion: I felt hurt and discounted.
Does the emotion fit the situation? Yes
Name the feeling and claim it: I feel angry, hurt and discounted **because of** my mother's criticism and my husband's disregard of my feelings.

Affirmation: I embrace that my emotions matter and validate this emotion. My feeling is a demonstration of my humanity and I validate my experience.

A person I will talk to if I am unable to feel resolution about this matter: My sister Jill.

Situation driving the emotion: ______________________________

____

____

____

Primary emotion: ______________________________

Secondary emotions (if any): ______________________________

____

Does the emotion fit the situation? ______________________________

Name it and claim it: I feel ______________________________

because: ______________________________

____

____

____

I embrace that my emotions matter and validate this emotion. My feeling is a demonstration of my humanity and I validate my experience. **I will talk to:**

____

if I am unable to feel resolution about this matter:

13.a

Situation driving the emotion:

Primary emotion:

Secondary emotions (if any):

Does the emotion fit the situation?

Name it and claim it: I feel

because:

I embrace that my emotions matter and validate this emotion. My feeling is a demonstration of my humanity and I validate my experience. **I will talk to:**

if I am unable to feel resolution about this matter:

Situation driving the emotion: ____________________

____

____

____

Primary emotion: ____________________

Secondary emotions (if any): ____________________

____

Does the emotion fit the situation? ____________________

Name it and claim it: I feel ____________________

because: ____________________

____

____

____

I embrace that my emotions matter and validate this emotion. My feeling is a demonstration of my humanity and I validate my experience. **I will talk to:**

____

if I am unable to feel resolution about this matter:

13.a

Coping: Existential Solutions

Creating Meaning in the Face of Crisis

We most often only look at the negative aspects of a personal crisis, emotional crisis, or life crisis. The negativity of a situation is important to embrace, and it is significant to look honestly at the consequences of the crises in your life.

If you are dealing with an illness or sickness of a loved one, there are ramifications and consequential results of it. If you are dealing with the loss of a marriage, or of a loved one, there are many secondary losses you may experience. If you are dealing with a situation that is causing you emotional distress such as work overload, family problem overload, financial crisis, or conflict with a friend, there will also be emotional consequences of dealing with it effectively.

A visual would be to imagine a tornado has hit your house, and what you would be looking at after it was over. You would likely need to examine all the destruction and the damage and embrace that you are unable to change this. Various situations can bring significant stress to you. It can feel as though a tornado has blown through your life and disrupted it. Essentially, this is true.

It is important to embrace and look honestly at your crisis and the result of the tornado that hit. It is important not to minimize or catastrophize the situation. After assessing, dissecting, and autopsying the situation, you can take a turn in your focus. You can look hard to create meaning in the situation. Some situations may not apply; however, in most situations you can find meaning.

Consider Viktor Frankl (1959) in his book related to his experience during World War II in a Nazi concentration camp. He examined the mindset of various prisoners and found that it was significant to find meaning in the most extreme versions of suffering. Frankl believed that in every moment of living there is opportunity to find the meaning of life, even when the situation includes suffering and pain.

I challenge you to look for some aspect of meaning in any of your situations or life challenges. This can shift your focus and help you with looking at the larger picture of any crisis.

- First it is important to *embrace every aspect of your crisis* or emotional distress. If you have lost a loved one to a break-up or death, identify associated feelings of grief (shock/disbelief, anger, bargaining, depression, acceptance) and validate your experience.
- *Talk about the associated feelings of loss and thoughts* with a close friend or family member. Utilize a professional if you are experiencing deep feelings and feel stuck. Look at the secondary losses and the "what happens next" of the situation. Take time to hold on to each feeling and thought related to the loss.
- If it is a death of a loved one, *find ways to memorialize them* through pictures, writing letters, or putting together a collage of memories. This helps to process the feelings. If it is a relationship break-up or loss of another kind, you can decide when to remove some of the pictures and reminders.
- Then ***create meaning***. You can think of sacred moments you had or find meaning in the situation. You may find that the loss has provided new insight into the value of life or relationships. You may see the event as a turning point in your life. It may be difficult, but when you can move forward to thinking about what purpose it served, you can potentially see beyond the darkness of the situation.

If you can create meaning in even the smallest of stressors, you can shift your perspective on it.

- Let's say someone cuts you off on the freeway and is driving recklessly. You can feel a sense of gratitude that you did not feel the pressure that person feels. You can feel relief that you are not a part of that reckless behavior. You can feel happy that you have things in your life that are important to you and that you wouldn't want to endanger yourself.

Change your perspective on things, and you can change how you feel. Create meaning in situational stressors, and you can change your perception of the situation. Quite often, our perception guides our emotions and can create a new reality.

Gratitude

Maintaining a sense of gratitude in the small and big things in your life can also shift your perspective and make life more meaningful. If you find yourself in a state of negativity throughout the day, you may want to start your day with identifying something you are ***grateful*** for. Identifying ***appreciation*** allows you to focus again on the positive aspects of your life. Your ***intention*** is a commitment and promise to yourself about the day.

13.b In fact, starting your day with the following journal entries can start your day off in a more positive direction. The following is an example:

Gratitude: "I'm grateful for the blue sky today, the sounds of birds, the ability I have to trust others and create friendships."

Appreciation: "I appreciate those people in my life who are compassionate and listen to me, understand me, and love me despite my imperfections."

Intention: "My intention for the day is to stay focused and present and to be mindfully attuned to all of the people I encounter."

13.b Gratitude Exercise

Keep in mind that negativity feeds the darkest thoughts and emotions you may experience. A state of gratitude can shift your perspective. Identifying an intention for the day can provide you with a roadmap with how you want your day to look. ***Try doing 30 days in a row of a morning journal entry of writing an area of your gratitude, appreciation, and intention.*** You can also text this to a friend and have them text an entry back to you.

This can help you to adjust your perspective toward being more positive. Notice if after a week, two weeks, or 30 days, your perspective about life has improved.

Gratitude:

Appreciation:

Intention:

Gratitude:

Appreciation:

Intention:

Gratitude:

Appreciation:

13.b

Intention:

13.c Reflection

- What current problem stands out to you as the most outstanding barrier to being in the present moment?

- Have you been able to attribute meaning to any of your problems? If so, what meaning have you captured?

- In what ways do you believe gratitude and appreciation can influence your present state of mind?

- Why do you think that setting an intention for the day can be an important promise to yourself?

13.c

Chapter 14

Spirituality, Forgiveness, and Self-Forgiveness

Healing Through the Use of Spirituality: The Path toward Forgiveness of Self and Others

"Forgiveness is above all a ***personal choice****,*
A ***decision of the heart*** *to go against*
natural instincts to pay back ...."

— Pope John Paul II, from his message for the celebration of the World Day of Peace

Are we human beings that have spiritual experiences, or are we spiritual beings that are currently having a human experience? Or do we fall somewhere along a continuum of behavior where human being is on one end and spiritual being is on the other end? Certainly our "humanness" is characterized by our imperfections, our defectiveness, our flaws, and our challenges as we make our way through this material world dealing with difficulty in finding acceptance in people, places, and situations.

Conversely, our spiritual self is characterized by illumination, enlightenment, peacefulness, enthusiasm for life, and ease with finding forgiveness. Where do you find yourself along the continuum of behavior between humanness and spirituality? Are you willing to continue walking the journey toward becoming more spiritually attuned?

I liked this introductory quote by Pope John Paul II because it speaks to the ***personal decision*** we may or not make to forgive. It also brings up that finding forgiveness goes against our ***natural instinct*** for retribution. The full quote by Pope John Paul II ends by stating that there is a natural instinct to pay back evil with evil.

I left this out because I feel that wrongdoing is not always evil and a desire to pay someone back is not always an evil act. There is potentially a healing that can come from forgiveness and letting go of resentment. We will explore this further in this chapter.

First and foremost, I will be addressing the concept of God, a Higher Power, Higher Being, or what I like to call a "Higher Source." Some of you may already have a God that is a Divine Being that is associated with Christianity or other religions. Some of you may not necessarily have a God that is personified, as some see their Higher Source as the "Universe" or "nature" or the elements of nature such as earth, wind, water, and fire.

This is an opportunity to explore your thoughts and ideas about establishing a God Source that works for you and that you can find when you have the need for comfort and healing that only comes from a Higher Source. It is also an opportunity to look at aspects of forgiveness. Shame-based belief systems often prevent us from forgiveness of self and others. Shame-based beliefs often need the healing power of a Higher Source. Let's look deeper into the concept of spiritual healing.

Spiritual Coping Strategies

Many of the aforementioned ways of coping can be classified as spiritually oriented coping strategies. Looking at gratitude and finding meaning in life's stressors can be considered seeing life from a spiritual perspective. Mindfulness practices and meditation practices can also be spiritual coping strategies because they help to clear the mind and feel more connected to other people, to nature, and to your God.

A Higher Being...A Higher Source

Most of us have a construct of a "Higher Being," a "Higher Power," or "God." If you do not, you can develop your own idea of the "God of your understanding." Your ***Higher Source*** can help you if you have had a non-fulfilling religious experience. It can be your personal version of a Higher Source. Twelve-step fellowships such as AA, NA, CA, Alanon, etc., have historically given people the opportunity to establish their own concept of a "Higher Power."

This may rattle a reader who has a religion that does not allow them to give space to any alternative ideology of God. But the idea of an inclusive version of a Higher Power allows for people who do not have a God in their life to identify and find one. It may be a God of the Universe. It may be a God of Nature. It may be your very own version of the God of your understanding.

Everyone has the right and the freedom to identify their Higher Source that can provide them with a spiritual comfort that is different from human comfort. Human comfort is significant in times of stress, and your Higher Power can be present for you at any time. If you do not have one, I invite you to invent one now. Consider the characteristics and qualities you want your God to have. You have the right and the freedom to identify your personal Higher Power.

If this section is uncomfortable for you, or if you have experienced spiritual abuse in a religious setting, you can skip this section and go to the heading of meditation. But I hope you won't. I hope to have planted the seed for you to develop your own Higher Power if you don't already have a God of your understanding. I hope to have opened the door to consideration of having a Higher Power in your life that can provide comfort, relief, and perspective.

Reliance on a Higher Source can be different from reliance on self. It can also be healing and help to establish trust that a power greater than you is available when things are difficult.

Prayer

While meditation is often listening for messages from your Higher Source, prayer involves talking to that power. Talking to your God can be helpful especially when you have exhausted every possible human attempt to resolve a problem. Turning the problem over to your God can allow for the process of "letting go." This means ***releasing*** your concern and letting go of the outcome of the situation. Some things seem to be unable to be resolved by any human power, so turning to a Higher Source can be freeing.

Allow yourself the luxury of talking to your God regularly. The more you can release the unhealthy thinking and emotions, the better able you will see the presence of your Higher Source. When you are especially down from life circumstances, you may feel a need to be closer to your Higher Source. Utilize prayer regularly. This in combination with meditation in the morning can start your day in a positive direction.

Meditation

> *"Within you, there is stillness and a sanctuary to which you can retreat at any time and be yourself."*
>
> *— Hermann Hesse*

Mindfulness and meditation practices have been encouraged in chapters 10, 12, and 13. I have addressed the physiological benefits of meditation, and the benefits of feeling more emotionally regulated from meditation. There is also a ***spiritual benefit*** from the regular practice of meditation. *What does that mean*?

The concept of spirituality has expanded over time and may include religious content, but it also may mean one's individualized path toward personal growth and the seeking of purpose and meaning in life. *Spiritual individualism* is centered on a spirituality that is generated from "within" and involves a personal growth focus or a search for meaning and life purpose. *Spiritual collectivism* is related more to a religion or an institution of organized religion that is God-centered. When I refer to spiritual growth, both types of spirituality can be used or just one may be used.

The hope is that spiritual growth will help you to find greater hope and internal peace. If you do have a Higher Source or God, you may find yourself closer to that Power. It will involve sorting through feelings at times and seeing the value of interpersonal relationships as well as your relationship with a Higher Source. A spiritual path may involve looking more honestly at yourself and gaining personal insight into the things you need to change to feel a freedom from your self-centeredness and self-obsession. It also may involve moving away from materialistic focus and looking more at the value of life, relationships, and inner peace.

The preceding quote by Nobel Prize winning author and poet Hermann Hesse (1946) looks at the inner *"sanctuary"* that we have available at *any time* that can bring a *"stillness"* and peace through meditative practices. That sanctuary can be tapped into at any time during the day or at any time when we feel emotionally distressed. This sanctuary is a healing opportunity that we have available to ourselves when we have the willingness to practice it.

There is certainly a healing power that comes from meditation. Taking time to clear your mind, breathe deeply, and embrace the moment allows for finding the *sacred* in what is often disregarded as the *ordinary.* And there is the additional power of healing that can take place when your body is in an optimal state of relaxation and breath.

In past chapters I have discussed the nervous system's *parasympathetic response* to meditation and deep relaxation. Chapter 12 gives you many examples of meditation practices as well as mindfulness activities. Find what appeals to you and put them into practice. You may be amazed with the results in your ability to have greater clarity in thoughts and in emotional stability from meditation.

The Path of Forgiveness *(Five Steps)*

It would be difficult to speak to the concept of spirituality without mentioning forgiveness. Forgiveness, defined, is the letting go of past resentment, hurt, and associated anger. I speak to a *"path of forgiveness"* because it is a process. Many people think that forgiveness is merely stating the words, *"I forgive you."* But it is so much more and rarely that simplistic.

To clarify the meaning of forgiveness, I would like to begin with ***what forgiveness is not. Forgiveness does not necessarily mean that you endorse or agree*** with the wrongfulness of the situation that you have experienced. Most often when forgiveness is needed, there is opposition and there is the feeling of being wronged. *"I don't like what happened and I cannot believe that anyone would have done such a thing."* This is often the narrative that accompanies a state of non-forgiveness.

So, if you are engaging on the path toward forgiveness, you will not need to let go of your disagreement with what happened. You will ***not*** need to endorse the thing that happened to you as *"okay."*

Forgiveness is also not necessarily reconciliation. You can be on the path toward forgiveness and not necessarily reconcile with the person or entity that you feel resentment toward. Reconciliation may come inadvertently from being on the path toward forgiveness, as an added benefit.

If you feel an aversion toward forgiveness about a situation, be relieved that this is ***for you*** and not anyone else. Be relieved that you will not be required to offer up a friendship and reconcile with the person or entity that you still resent. Be relieved that you will not necessarily have to endorse or now like the situation that happened. This may happen from being on your path, but it is not required.

Another clarification is that ***forgiveness is not an event***. Forgiveness is more of a process and will not necessarily be the end result of your journey. You can consider that you are only on the "path" toward forgiveness, and you don't need to be at the end of the journey standing at the signpost that says, "*You are forgiven*."

Seeing forgiveness as an event can potentially create a barrier to beginning the journey for someone who is not yet ready to let go of the resentment and anger toward a situation or entity. You can enter the path and begin your journey toward forgiveness without fear of the last step of *actual forgiveness.*

Most organized religions address forgiveness because of the weight we carry when we feel we cannot forgive. Forgiveness can be stressed so much that people will often attempt to forgive before they have really worked through the issue that feels unforgiveable. The lingering feelings of resentment are still there, and people will attempt to sweep the feelings under the carpet.

Resentment can be toxic and can create emotional weight that is unhealthy. Clearing the way through honest assessment of the situation is a part of being on the path toward forgiveness. This can allow you to be "in process" of forgiving what has possibly felt unforgiveable. This process is for you if you want to lighten your load and no longer carry the dark feelings and thoughts that accompany the resentment. It is much like carrying weights or boulders on your back. Lighten your load and walk through the process of being *on the path toward forgiveness.*

1 – Identify the unforgiveable

Clearly identify the issue that you have not been able to forgive. Is it a person? Is it another entity? Is it a situation? Identify the specifics about the issue of forgiveness. If it is a person, is it about one situation that caused you to feel pain or hurt? Or has this person caused you to feel attacked or criticized for a duration of time? If it is an entity, what happened that caused you to not be able to find forgiveness? Get specific about the situation. In what way were you wronged by the person, entity, or situation?

2 – Assess for underlying feelings

Identify your resulting feelings that you have regarding the person or entity. Did you feel:

- disregarded
- targeted
- dismissed
- gaslit
- distrusted
- betrayed
- manipulated
- bullied
- admonished
- humiliated
- insulted
- assaulted
- blamed
- canceled

These are just some of the potential feelings that you may have because of the unforgiveable actions of a person. It helps to name the associated feeling you have so that you are clear about the issue. This is your emotional response which is significant to understanding the problem.

3 – Assess for anger

Assess the anger that you feel or have felt in the past. What are you most angry about? What aspect of this person or situation creates a surge of dark feelings? Are you disappointed in them? Did they not live up to your standards? Did they treat you in a way that you would never treat another person? Are you angry that they have no remorse for their behavior? Are you angry because you feel powerless?

4 – Acceptance

Find acceptance in the situation. This step is probably the most significant step toward forgiveness. Keep in mind that acceptance does not mean that you endorse the situation. It does not mean that you are okay with the situation or the person. It only means that the person and the situation are unchangeable and that you cannot change them. Therefore, you can only embrace that this person, entity, or situation cannot be changed, and you find acceptance in the idea that ***"this is the way it is."*** The Serenity Prayer can provide wisdom in this step:

"God, grant me the serenity
To accept the things I cannot change,
The courage to change the things I can,
And the wisdom to know the difference."

— *Unknown Author*

The things that have already happened are unchangeable. If you were in a situation where you felt humiliated and embarrassed, you cannot change history. You can only change the way you choose to look at the event.

If you are resentful and angry toward a person for something they said, you cannot change what they said, nor can you change that person. We sometimes get into a fantasy that if we can just say the right thing or do something to someone that they will change. But people are who they are for the most part. We may say something that helps us feel empowered or feel like we met the responsibility we have to ourselves. However, most often we are powerless over changing another person.

"*To accept the things I cannot change*" is a big part of this step. I can spend hours and days and inordinate amounts of time attempting to change what is unchangeable. Wisdom is reflected when I know the difference about what I can and cannot change. Finding acceptance in the situation, entity, or person is key in this step. This is a major step toward forgiveness. Even if you never reach forgiveness, acceptance can provide you with significant relief from the person or situation.

Finding acceptance in the unacceptable

Sometimes this step requires ***finding acceptance in the unacceptable***. There are things that happen and things that people say and do that are unacceptable. The following story is an example of that:

> *I worked with a woman who carried so much anger toward her recently deceased husband. He died suddenly and unexpectedly and left her with debt that she was unaware of. She also found that he had betrayed her in a long-term sexual relationship he had with another woman. He died from heart failure in the home of his lover.*

***Was this unacceptable? Yes.** Could she change what he did in terms of the betrayal of her marriage? No. Could she change the situation of being in debt and having to clean up his mess? No. Could she now express her anger to him, confront him, and divorce him? No. She had the choice of either staying angry, carrying the toxicity of the resentment, and being darkened by the situation, or finding acceptance in what she could not change.*

This required talking for several sessions about the betrayal, her feelings, and identifying underlying areas of pain. She shared about the painful loss and associated anger. She embraced the many feelings she had regarding him, her husband's mistress, and the situation. There was certainly a lot to process. Finding her way to acceptance was not easy. But ultimately, what happened was unchangeable.

Her healing task was to find acceptance in what was unacceptable. She needed to walk that path toward forgiveness of the unforgiveable. This was not for him. This was not for anyone but herself. She needed to be relieved from the bondage of the hurt and pain she felt. She needed to find freedom through acceptance, or she could not heal. After over a year of work on this traumatic and unforgiveable event, she was able to get to a place of acceptance and then emotionally let go of the betrayal and the negative aspects of the marriage.

She did arrive at acceptance. Somewhere on her journey between acceptance and forgiveness, she met a new man that was loving, kind, and loyal. They now travel and enjoy their lives together. Because she was able to let go of the resentment, she was able to find freedom and move on with her life. Staying stuck prevents us from letting go and moving on.

5 – Willingness and forgiveness

If you have reached acceptance in the person or situation that you found unforgiveable, you have conquered a large part of your journey toward forgiveness. If you have found acceptance, you are now experiencing a great deal of freedom from the bondage of resentment. You have hopefully found some peace associated with the person or situation.

This next step may take ***time and willingness.*** It may automatically just happen. It is the final step toward forgiveness. This step is ***to forgive.*** Some of your situations have probably felt unforgiveable, and therefore, this final step may be difficult. There are a few stuck points that may arise in your efforts to find forgiveness.

Stuck Points

After following all the steps toward forgiveness, you may still be unwilling to forgive the person or situation. These barriers are what we will refer to as "stuck points" in the process. I mentioned in the beginning of this forgiveness process that you could be "on the path" and not have to reach the place of forgiveness if you still feel resistant. Reaching the point where you have found acceptance in the person, entity, or situation is most important. If you want to get to the next level, however, and reach a place of forgiveness, you may want to explore stuck points.

1 – The unforgiveable, irreconcilable, and unamendable

There are those heinous crimes that a person or entity may have committed against you or a loved one that fall into this category. This is for you to decide. Perhaps there are things that others have done that you are not willing to forgive. ***In some situations, it may be good enough to find a place of acceptance and never move further forward into forgiveness.***

Some people have experienced a lifetime of trauma response and pain based upon assault or injury inflicted by another person. Perhaps someone has committed a heinous crime against a child or to you as a child. Perhaps someone has murdered a loved one and you have suffered from that loss. Perhaps someone has committed sexual or physical assault or molestation upon you and the associated trauma has affected your life. If you feel that you have reached a place of acceptance, and you have no willingness to forgive, you can stay in this place. Some things just feel unamendable.

Acceptance of the situation is accepting the unacceptable because you cannot change what happened or the person or entity. Forgiveness requires a "*personal pardon*" for their behavior. If you cannot and are not willing to forgive and have found acceptance in the unacceptable, then perhaps this is as far as you want to go. This is your journey and your path. Nobody has the right to tell you that you must forgive. You are the only person who can make this decision.

A patient named Judy told me the story of her childhood. At age 8, she experienced a home invasion where two strangers came to rob the household and murdered both of her parents and her 12-year-old brother in their beds. Her life was spared, and she hid from them, terrified. She lost her family and went to three foster homes before getting adopted. The home invaders were eventually caught and sentenced to life in prison.

Although they had to pay for their crime, Judy could not and did not desire to personally pardon them for what they did to her family. She could not shake the traumatic memory that plagued her every day of her life. She felt what they did was unforgiveable, unamendable, and irreconcilable. She reached a place of acceptance in what was unacceptable, knowing that she could not change what happened.

However, she chose not to forgive this horrific and traumatic life experience. That is her choice and that is understandable. She said that she would need to lie to herself about forgiving them. I validated her personal truth.

2 – "They" have not admitted their wrongdoing

One *stuck point* may be that the person or entity has not yet admitted their wrongdoing. This issue can be a barrier because you cannot forgive that person when they cannot see that they even did something that was hurtful or damaging.

For example, I had a male patient we will call "Chad" that had a hard time forgiving his brother for saying hurtful things to his wife. We processed the feelings, and Chad found his way to the place of acceptance of his brother's incapability of being sensitive and using a filter when he spoke. Chad's brother said some very demeaning things about his wife and although he accepted that his brother lacked insight into his hurtful words and behavior toward others, he could not find his way to forgive him.

Chad's reason was because his brother never admitted that he had done wrong in berating his wife and calling her names. In Chad's discussions on the topic, Chad's brother would continue to justify his reasons for disliking Chad's wife. Chad couldn't forgive his brother.

Chad confronted his brother and asked him to admit that his behavior and words were insulting to him and that he was sorry for insulting him and his wife with his judgments. Chad's brother finally apologized and said that he should not have been that judgmental of his wife. They have slowly been able to reconcile their relationship.

3 – Insufficient consequences for their behavior

Another barrier to forgiveness is when someone feels they cannot forgive a person who has not received consequences for their behavior. In this situation, the time or punishment does not fit the crime. In some situations, a person may take a stand about the lack of consequences for the unforgiven person or entity. Some actual examples of people I have treated in psychotherapy are:

- A date rape victim testifies about a rapist, and he is not charged.
- Abuse (sexual, physical, neglect) of children in a home where the adult perpetrators never get consequences or criminal charges for their crimes.
- An entity loses thousands of dollars of a person's finances, and they are not charged criminally because they were acting "within the law."
- A marriage where one partner has affairs, and the other person is hurt and damaged from the divorce. There is no legal consequence for betrayal. A spouse may feel unable to "personally pardon" their ex-spouse.
- A marriage where one partner loses all the family savings due to a gambling problem, and the other partner is left in debt. There is no legal consequence when one partner in a marriage spends or loses all their combined savings frivolously.

Emotional consequences: Whether or not a person has suffered consequences for their actions against you, it is still your personal choice about whether to forgive. I am of the belief that in most situations when concrete consequences have not happened in legal or financial form, ***the person will pay emotional consequences*** for their behavior. Some individuals, such as the sociopath who does not feel guilt or remorse, may not have an emotional consequence. Other people who arrogantly justify their crimes and inexcusable behavior also may not feel emotional consequences for what they have done.

However, many will carry the emotional baggage of having harmed another and will wear it as an enduring open wound. This emotional suffering can be worse than a legal consequence or financial restitution. The shame and narrative of *"being a bad person"* for having harmed you or another person can sometimes be very damaging and destructive. It is also a ***lifetime sentence***.

It still is your personal decision of whether to forgive or whether to remain on that path toward forgiveness. If you have been alleviated from the pain through finding acceptance, perhaps there is another level of feeling alleviated. Perhaps there is the opportunity to find a new strength in your personal pardon of that person.

4 – Haunting memories

Many people continue to experience the haunting memories of what a person or entity has done. When trauma is a part of the experience, the memories often return as a haunting reminder of the past that is very difficult to let go. If you have experienced a trauma, I will again suggest that you ***seek therapy from a professional*** to assist you with getting "unstuck" from re-experiencing the wrong done to you.

One definition of forgiveness is to reach a place where you no longer wish to change the memory of the past situation. When you are at a place where you can sit with the discomfort of the memory and transcend that emotional state, you are making progress on your path toward forgiveness. Sometimes finding the value or meaning of the haunting life event can bring you to a place of not wanting to change the memory.

Being at a place of not wanting to change the memory is a long journey, and it is possible to achieve. The process of doing work to alleviate thought intrusions, emotional surges, and memories of the person or situation can take time. The resulting autobiographical memory of the event that no longer causes emotional distress can allow you to experience that person or situation in a neutral way. A neutralized autobiographical memory can bring you greater peace and allow you to no longer feel the need to change the memory of the person, entity, or situation.

5 – Timing

Many have heard the expression *"time heals all wounds."* While this is not necessarily true in every situation, there is the element of time passage that can help to move you along the path toward forgiveness. Over time, you may see qualities of the person you resent in yourself. Over time, you may identify that person's incapability of being different. Over time, you may begin to see something in a different light with a different perspective.

Our perspective is everything. When you are closer to the situation, or when the wrongdoing is in your recent past, the sting and pain can still be intense and uncomfortable. Pain will often diminish with time along with a shift in your perspective. Remember that you are traveling along your path toward forgiveness ***in your own time frame*** and nobody can force change upon you.

Sometimes it takes feeling ready for the shift. Sometimes it takes feeling ready to let go and release the anger and other feelings. Only you can personally decide when you are ready. Although long-held resentments can be toxic for you, finding a place of acceptance can lower the toxicity. If you have reached acceptance and still cannot forgive, you may just need more time on that path to sort through things. Remember that it is your journey and your own time frame.

6 – Assumptions about intentions

Some people have a difficult time finding forgiveness or acceptance about another person because they make assumptions about what a person's intention was when they did something to them.

> ***Example 1***: *A woman we will call Beth came to me for therapy and stated that she was distressed over an encounter with her daughter-in-law. Beth's son, Mark, married Linda two years ago, and they now had an 8-month-old baby boy. Beth recounted a situation where her daughter-in-law, Linda, said to her that she could not come over and bring their baby because he was sick.*
>
> *This happened three times during the baby's first eight months of life. On those occasions, Beth was supposed to babysit while Linda went to a work meeting. Beth was disturbed because she believed that Linda's* ***intention*** *for canceling childcare was that she thought Beth incapable of caring for the infant when he was sick. Beth never spoke to Linda about the canceled baby-care situations and* ***made assumptions*** *that Linda did not trust her or think she was good with babies.*
>
> *After some therapy sessions, Beth was asked to contact Linda and ask her about those canceled visits and the reason behind it. Beth was made to recognize that she was guessing at Linda's intentions. When she spoke to Linda, Beth discovered that Linda canceled the babysitting sessions* ***not*** *because she did not feel Beth was good with babies, but because she was afraid that Beth would catch the baby's illness. Beth had an auto-immune disorder, and Linda was being thoughtful. Upon searching for Linda's intention, Beth discovered that her guess at Linda's intention was very wrong.*

> ***Example 2***: *Another example of making incorrect assumptions about the intentions of others is that of my friend, Sheila. She was angry with another friend of ours, Carla, because Carla canceled plans to go to a concert with Sheila and gave her the purchased ticket to use with anyone else. Sheila had not spoken to her since that time.*

Sheila came to me and told me that Carla did not like her, and that Carla would rather spend time with anyone else than her. Sheila painfully recounted the situation to me and felt it was proof that she didn't like her. Sheila also found selfies of Carla with another friend taken on the night they were supposed to attend the concert. I told Sheila that she needed to talk to Carla to see why she canceled plans and then went out with another friend.

Sheila contacted Carla and found out that Carla's other friend had just been told by her husband that he wanted a divorce, and she needed support after a very emotional week. She canceled the concert plans and went to help her friend in her time of need. Sheila had guessed at Carla's intention about the canceling of plans and could not find forgiveness until she learned the truth about Carla's intentions. Sheila made an incorrect assumption about Carla.

Example 3: *Another example of misperceptions and incorrect assumptions about the intentions of others involves one of my previous work situations. A previous supervisor came to me and began telling me that everyone on our team was falling behind and short of expected work productivity. She left my office quickly and appeared very angry. My assumption about her intention was that she was admonishing me for my work ethic and that she was angry with me.*

After a few hours, I checked with her, and I asked if I had fallen short of her expectations in terms of my performance. She looked at me with warmth and concern and stated that she was sorry for her outburst. She had just gotten in trouble from her supervisor about some reports and paperwork that had not been completed by some of my coworkers. She came to tell me because mine were up to date, and she needed to express her discontent to me because I was a responsible member of the team.

I had guessed about her intention and assumed that she was berating and scolding me. It was important that I found out the truth from her. My incorrect assumption about her intention could have resulted in my carrying a grudge and holding on to a resentment toward her.

The truth about intentions is that we do not really know what another person's intention is. We so often make assumptions about what "*we think they meant*" or why "*we think they did something.*" These assumptions also happen when you are very close to someone. In my experience with psychotherapy with couples, I have found that the longer a couple is together, the more assumptions they make about each other.

> *I worked with one couple in therapy, who had been married for 38 years and had three adult children. They found themselves in conflict consistently, arguing over many things throughout the day. They were considering divorce.*
>
> *In looking at some of their underlying themes to their arguments, the wife, Mindy, stated that she felt that her husband, Carlos, did not respect her opinion, discounted what she had to say, and did not feel what she said was important. This fueled her emotional responses to him. Carlos told her that he sometimes felt intimidated by her intellectual ability and perhaps only got angry when he felt he could not match her ability to articulate her point of view.*
>
> *Carlos and Mindy had argued incessantly over their incorrect assumptions about each other's intentions. It almost resulted in their divorce. Once they realized their mistaken assumptions, they no longer had the intense power struggle and began to enjoy each other again. There are many stories of couples that are like Mindy and Carlos. Learning to assume less and check in more with your partner is significant to having a healthy relationship with baggage-free communication.*

I repeat. The truth about intentions is that ***we do not really know what another person's intention is.*** We know our own intention, but often assume we know another's intention. This can put us into a place where we do not want to accept or forgive another. In the case of Mindy and Carlos, both knew their own intention, but they guessed at what the other's intention was.

Mindy guessed that Carlos was dismissive of her and thought she was stupid or unworthy of commentary. Carlos guessed that Mindy thought she was smarter than him and his defenses put him into an argumentative state. It became a power struggle. It became an issue of who was wrong and who was right. It became an obsession to be right. It became an ego struggle to win a fight rather than finding understanding with one another.

Think about when you have mistakenly assumed another's intention without checking first with them. Consider if you are at a stuck point in your desire to forgive because you are making assumptions about the intention of another. You are the one to suffer in these situations until you clear up the situation by talking to the other person.

7 – Expectations of change of the "other"

Another stuck point on the path toward forgiveness is that you have the expectation that the other person will change after they have committed unjust actions toward you. You may be in a situation where a person has admitted their wrongdoing, but they still are the same. Perhaps someone said some cruel things to you. Then this person apologized and admitted their wrong. You notice, however, that they continue to say and do cruel things to others. So, it appears that they have not changed.

Often times human beings need an external event or personal breaking point to commit to change. We only change when we recognize that we must change. Otherwise, there is little likelihood that change will happen. This is why acceptance is important. Acceptance allows you to find peace in what is unacceptable about situations and about others. Acceptance does not require you to condone a person's behavior. You only need to accept that they are who they are and there is no guarantee that change will happen for them.

It is likely that you will find greater comfort in lowering your expectations about others changing. On occasion it may happen. Embracing who the person or institution is can shift your focus of trying to change what feels unchangeable. Releasing and letting go of the expectation that others will change because of your relationship to them is significant. Remember that you are on your own personal path toward forgiveness. If you do not want to forgive their character, you can hold on to the grudge you feel. It is your choice. Forgiveness is your own personal pardon if you choose to release.

8 – Victim stance and unwillingness to see your part

I must begin by clarifying that there are some unforgiveable conditions where you do not play a part in the existence of the situation. In circumstances such as child abuse, molestation, sexual assault, murder of a loved one and other heinous criminal situations where you may have truly been victimized, let me be clear. You did not play a part. In childhood abuse, one is tethered to a tremendous imbalance of power between themselves and the perpetrator of abuse. **The child has not played a part. They are not at fault.**

In sexual assault situations, victims often blame themselves because they did not try to escape the assault. If this has been your experience, you must understand that **you did not play a part. You were not at fault**. If you are having a difficult time forgiving someone who has murdered a loved one, **you did not play a part. You are not at fault**. This is very important for you to see, as too many people carry self-blame or responsibility for the heinous crimes that others have committed upon them.

However, in other circumstances, such as ***conflict between two people and the inability to forgive the other person, you must be willing to look at your part in the situation.*** Looking at the role you played in the situation can be empowering. To ignore that you played a role in a conflict or disagreement is to ignore that there are contributions to the problem that you have made.

When we take that stance that this "wave of unforgiveable events" has hit us causing a drowning of our spirit, we are taking a victim stance that does not allow for movement in the problem. It also eliminates the ability for us to take responsibility for what is ours. It is important to consider that we may have played a role in the situation even when the other person's behavior feels unforgiveable. This is an example of a man who came to me for psychotherapy:

> *A man named Joel was in the process of getting a divorce and was at a place of inability to forgive his wife, who had betrayed the marriage with an affair with another man and was now asking for divorce. He reached a place of acceptance that the divorce was going to happen and was still furious that she betrayed him and broke her vows in the marriage. Joel burned with anger and rage when he thought about how he worked so hard and how during the time that he was away on business trips, she began seeing another man.*

As we processed Joel's emotions and his feelings about his wife, we moved into looking at what he would have done differently in the marriage. Joel recalled many occasions where his wife wanted to go to couples therapy and where she told him that she was unhappy. Joel ignored her requests and felt that his income and financial support were his contributions to the marriage.

He began to look deeper into the period of two years prior to her betrayal, and her expression of needs to him that he ignored. As he looked deeper, he began to see his role in the eventual break-up of the marriage. Joel's wife was wrong and had committed acts that felt unforgiveable to him.

When Joel looked at his role that contributed to the problem and was able to let go of some of the anger and rage that he felt, he began to walk further on his path toward forgiveness. She was wrong. Her behavior was unacceptable. But Joel could now release some of the toxicity that he felt by looking at his part and by realizing he played a role in the big picture of their problematic marriage.

We often play a role in a problem and refuse to look at the larger picture. A situation between two people can often demonstrate that the "two sides" of the story are often not seen. We tend to only look at our side and are more reluctant to see our part in the problem.

9 – Giving up too soon

This final stuck point in forgiveness is when a person gives up before the healing takes place and before the miracle of change of perspective happens. We may not want to see our part in a situation, or we may just give up prior to finding a forgiveness in our hearts. We may just categorize someone as a "never again" relationship and not take the time to autopsy the problems. We may close the door to looking thoroughly at a conflict or a set of circumstances.

Don't give up too soon. Quite often a stuck point happens when you give up prior to looking deeper into the situation. You carry the pain and misunderstanding with you everywhere. Be sure to process, journal, or seek therapy for any area of lack of forgiveness that you feel.

Self-Forgiveness *(in Seven Steps)*

The ability to forgive yourself is significant to your efforts toward personal growth. To not forgive yourself is to hold yourself hostage to your mistakes, your actions, and to your decisions. Not forgiving yourself can plague you with negative false narratives and can create barriers to living free of self-incrimination. If you are interested in growing and developing personally, you will need to look at steps that will help you to issue a *pardon* to yourself for past mistakes.

Your emotional health and your physical health are sure to suffer from lack of self-forgiveness. Lack of self-forgiveness for past errors may indicate a shame-based belief system that renders you feeling that you are permanently defective, damaged, or unworthy. This is not true, and we will look at steps to take to alleviate your difficulty in reconciling with yourself.

There is a path toward self-forgiveness that is like forgiveness of others. It is a process and can take more than the verbal statement "I forgive myself." It would be great if it were that easy. Often, however, there are deeper issues that foster our inability to self-forgive. We often have a difficult time forgiving ourselves because we feel we have done something we are ashamed of, and we punish ourselves through self-hatred or resentment.

This self-recrimination is often associated with blaming ourselves for a mistake or for a poor decision. Lack of self-forgiveness may stem from one incident of a mistake or bad decision. Inability to forgive the self may stem from a period where multiple mistakes and errors were made, and this can lead to a deeper wound that is more difficult to *self-pardon.*

Step 1 – Accountability

The first step in the process of forgiving yourself is taking accountability for what you have done. This may be about one incident that haunts you or that you replay in your memory. Each time you replay the memory it looks a little bit worse. An example is with a former patient I worked with in psychotherapy:

> *Bret was unable to forgive himself for betraying his wife with an affair he had with a coworker. He was married for 10 years and had two small*

children. He and his wife were busy with life, activities, social events for the kids, and they were often very tired and bickered with each other. Bret began an emotional relationship with a female at his work who was 12 years younger than him. Eventually, they became sexual while out of town together.

Bret decided he could not live with his betrayal and broke it off with his coworker. She became angry and texted his wife to let her know that she and Bret had a relationship. This caused a ripple effect of divorce, shared custody issues, and the loss of the valuable relationship he had with his wife. Because Bret was his coworker's supervisor, he also lost his job, as she reported him to human resources.

Bret could not forgive himself for his betrayal and for his actions. At times he replayed his mistake and the shame he felt in the workplace when others knew he was losing his job. At times he replayed how hurtful it was to lose his wife's respect and love. He replayed the idea of his children eventually learning of his infidelity. He tortured himself daily.

It was now important for Bret to take accountability for his actions. He needed to look honestly at his mistake and look only at his actions that lead to his error in judgment and indiscretions. In therapy, we looked at the facts of what happened, and Bret was able to clearly take responsibility for all his actions that lead to his betrayal.

Lack of the ability to forgive oneself may also include a series of events or things that you have done that your regret. There may have been several mistakes or events. There may have been an ongoing history of hurt toward another person. The following is an example of a woman who had a difficult time forgiving herself:

Martha was a 43-year-old woman who was estranged from her daughter, Barbara, who was now age 24. She sought help in therapy because she was in such pain that her daughter did not want to speak to her for the past year. Martha began looking at her mistakes as a single mother and had painful memories of how she sometimes became verbally aggressive with Barbara.

Martha was now sober, but recalled times when she used to drink and would say mean things to Barbara, such as calling her "stupid." Martha recalled times when she was drunk and had men over to party and Barbara had to retreat to her room as a child. Her worst memories were when she was not drinking but became verbally aggressive toward Barbara.

Martha had about 12 recurring memories that haunted her and that she was not able to forgive herself for. It was important for Martha to account for all the memories she had of things she had done that she regretted. She journaled and shared about them in therapy. She needed to list all the factual accounts of the events that haunted her. This was her first step toward self-forgiveness.

Accountability is important because you must identify all the primary things you have done that are difficult to accept. You cannot really move on until you take inventory of the things that you ruminate over. You must initially name all your regrets to be able to move the next stage of acceptance.

A police officer attempting to cite someone for a crime must be able to state exactly what the crime is that has been committed. An aspect of accountability is that it is best when you can name the things you cannot forgive about yourself as "facts." Like a ***police report***, you want to list the facts of your behavior without the emotion. That way you can clearly see what the things are that you want to forgive. In Bret's case, he would want to list:

- I engaged in an emotional relationship with someone at my work.
- I was this person's supervisor which was a breach of ethical responsibility.
- I hurt my wife and children.
- I violated my commitment to my marriage.
- I selfishly acted on my impulses.

In Martha's situation she would want to list the facts of what she did:

- I hurt my daughter by verbally abusing her.
- I drank and indiscriminately had men over when Barbara was a child.
- I put alcohol and drinking before my daughter.
- I hurt my daughter verbally when I was and was not drinking.
- I was selfish as a mother and did not consider my daughter's needs.

This is the beginning of change toward self-forgiveness. Being accountable for your actions and listing the facts of the things that you are having a hard time forgiving about yourself is the first step toward change.

Step 2 – Remorseful Reflection

It is natural to feel shame-based feelings about what you have done wrong. The examples of Bret and Martha demonstrate the self-incrimination and rumination over the dark things that they have done. Some people are so busy blaming the other person or letting themselves *"off the hook"* that they can see their wrong but justify their own behavior. These are two opposite ends of the spectrum of emotions that follow the acknowledgment of wrongdoing.

The inability to feel remorse can also impede the ability to forgive yourself. In Bret and Martha's story, they both are feeling quite remorseful about their behavior. They have surrendered to the dark emotions that accompany wrong-doing. They both cannot forgive themselves because they feel incredible remorse and are stuck. They are both becoming ***"dislodged"*** from their stuck point in self-forgiveness by factually accounting for their behavior. Consider the person who has not felt remorse for their behavior. This is potentially another stuck point.

> *Bobbie was a 23-year-old worker at a fast-food restaurant. He was employed at this organization for eight months when he was called before the store manager, who reprimanded him for arriving late three of his last five days of work. The manager warned him that this cannot continue or he will be let go. He told Bobbie that this was his first warning.*

Bobbie became angry and developed a poor attitude toward customers. Two customers wrote a complaint about Bobbie being inconsiderate and irritable when they asked him for condiments. He shouted at another customer because they told him that their order was incorrect.

The manager again pulled Bobbie aside and gave him a second warning. The manager showed the written complaints and said that this behavior was unacceptable. Bobbie then walked off the job site. The manager called Bobbie in the next day and terminated his employment.

Bobbie came to therapy for help with feelings of inadequacy because he lost his job. Though he could identify the events that caused him to lose his job, he continued to blame the manager, his coworkers, and the customer for his termination. He did not feel remorse for his wrongdoing.

In therapy, it was important for Bobbie to look at his actions without blaming anyone else. Then he needed to experience the remorse for his behavior. His inability to feel remorse was keeping him stuck in the process of self-forgiveness. Bobbie was eventually able to look at his part, feel regret, and have some remorseful reflection over this job experience. He could then begin seeking new employment with consideration for not repeating his mistakes. Blame was blocking him from remorseful reflection.

To summarize, we can only be accountable for our own behavior. If we have done wrong, it doesn't matter what others have done incorrectly. We have no power over others' behavior. In blaming others for our mistakes, we lose the value of accountability. It's important to have some remorse or regretful reflection over the errors we have made. We do not want to stay there a long time, but it is a necessary stage of healing. We can surrender to the emotions associated with remorse and regret.

Step 3 – Surrender

I think of surrender as a form of ***release.*** The process of identification of wrongdoing and then feeling the remorse of the situation may leave anyone drowning in emotions and even self-pity. Releasing or letting go of self-recrimination is significant to the healing process.

If you have a God or Higher Source that you can release all these feelings to, you can imagine yourself handing over the situation, the guilt, the shame, the remorse, and the past actions to that Source. A criminal that surrenders themselves to the police is essentially releasing control of their situation to another power. The need to "*wave the white flag*" and surrender control of the situation is significant on a spiritual level.

From a spiritual perspective, when I am holding tight to anything and refusing to release it, I am not allowing for a spiritual surrender. Human power cannot heal or change the level of connection I feel to what I have done wrong. When I am controlling the inability to forgive myself, I am holding myself hostage to that situation. Releasing can come when I believe I can surrender this wrongdoing to another power or Source.

Perhaps I can surrender by praying to the God of my life. If my God is a traditional Christian God, I can visualize a release to the heavens. And similarly, if my God is another religious Divine Being, I can visualize a release and letting go of my wrongdoing. If my Higher Source is the God of Nature, perhaps I can go outside where I can visibly see my Source and release the whole situation. If my Source is God of the Universe, I can visualize releasing the situation out into the universe and let it go. Letting go and surrendering what I have done wrong can initiate the change I feel. If I continue to hold on to the feelings, the flashbacks, and the self-recrimination, I am attempting to ***control the memory*** of the situation.

I will also need to surrender to the reality of the situation and find acceptance in what I did, or I will feel no peace. To find the inner peace that accompanies self-forgiveness, I must find my way toward acceptance. In the bigger picture, I will be seeking self-acceptance prior to being able to forgive myself. I must surrender to the reality of the situation.

Step 4 – Acceptance

The acceptance step is significant in forgiveness of others. It is also very important to find acceptance in self-forgiveness. This may mean finding self-acceptance at a deep level. Acceptance does not mean that I am now okay with what wrongs I have done. It does not mean that I endorse my previous behavior. It does not mean that I justify what I have done previously. In the situation with Bret and Martha, they both have identified what they did wrong. They have surrendered to a tremendous amount of regret and bad feelings associated with their mistakes. ***But they cannot change what they did.***

"Self-acceptance is knowing that we all have our flaws and our strengths"

This is key to understanding the concept of acceptance. Knowing that the past mistake is unchangeable allows us the opportunity to embrace what happened and ***find acceptance in what feels unacceptable***. Acceptance means that Martha will embrace her deepest regret in the treatment of her daughter. She has identified all the facts of what happened. She feels the pain of what happened. Martha may have surrendered her series of mistakes toward her daughter to her Higher Source. But she cannot change what she did. Finding the place of acceptance does not mean that Martha is condoning her previous behavior. It does not mean that Martha likes what she did in the past toward her daughter. It just means that she cannot change the past.

Acceptance does not mean approval, justification, or endorsement of a past behavior. It means that it cannot be changed and therefore, we are faced with the task of embracing that we did what we did. It means that while we regret and have surrendered to the remorseful reflection of what we did, we still are unable to change it.

Acceptance does not mean that Bret is justifying or endorsing his past behavior with a coworker. He is not giving himself a pass for future betrayals of others. Bret does not like what happened and how the course of his life changed because of what he did. Bret is feeling regret and has surrendered to many emotions associated with his past behavior. Bret cannot change the past. He must find ***acceptance in the unacceptable*** and embrace the truth of his wrongdoing that is ***unchangeable.***

In the preceding example of Bobbie, he has identified his wrongdoing in the workplace. He now feels remorse and has surrendered to the reality of what he did. Bobbie cannot change what he did, nor can he change the past. Although he knows his behavior is unacceptable, he must find the place of acceptance and embrace the unchangeable nature of the past.

There is an element of self-acceptance that you will need to encounter when reaching this step toward self-forgiveness. Self-acceptance is knowing that we all have our flaws and our strengths. Embracing who we are as fallible human beings is a necessary part of finding acceptance in our mistakes. This means that we must be very honest with ourselves and look hard at who we are. This is not always easy. There may be layers of truth of who we are when we look honestly at ourselves. This may be a good beginning as we assess what we need to accept about ourselves.

Step 5 – Repairing and Amending

There are many situations that we cannot repair, fix, or reconcile. This is an unfortunate truth. Reconciliation of any situation requires that both parties agree to find peace with each other.

> *In the case of Bret, his wife was not willing to talk to him and only communicated when Bret had a visitation with the children. Bret decided to attempt to repair what he had done by writing an extensive apology in a letter. He also made several attempts to contact his wife and apologize to her for his mistakes. She was not ready and was not willing. Bret's wife returned his letter unread and cut him off in any attempt to verbally talk about his wrong.*
>
> *Bret had to accept that not only did he hurt his wife and family, but that he may never be able to amend his wrong. In therapy, we worked out a plan for Bret to amend and repair his wrongdoing by engaging in his own personal behavior change. He was now consciously aware of his honesty in all other situations and committed to being a trustworthy person in future relationships.*

Martha was also unable to repair her relationship with her daughter fully. She continued to attempt to call and communicate with her. Her daughter was not very receptive to her calls. Over time, however, her daughter began talking more and allowing for her mother to formally apologize for their past together. Her daughter agreed to meet with Martha once a month for lunch and to reconcile their relationship. Eventually, Martha's daughter got married and had a daughter. Martha was an amazing grandmother and amended her relationship further by being a warm, kind, and loving grandma.

Repairing or amending a relationship is more than stating, "I'm sorry." There must be a willingness to change and not repeat the same mistakes. Reconciliation may not always happen such as in the case of Bret. However, changing behavior and not repeating the previous mistakes is a part of the repair. There needs to be a willingness to ***"come full circle"*** and be a ***better version of yourself i***n the future.

Step 6 – Self-Compassion

Remorse for our actions can put us in a dark place if we stay there too long. We can surrender and accept our wrongs and still be in a place of self-hatred. It is important, however, to acknowledge the emotions associated with reflection of our mistakes in judgment. Self-compassion is a healing type of response to remorseful reflection. If surrender and acceptance of the situation have not taken away the bad feelings, it is time to find compassion for the self.

Some of us are good at feeling compassion for others but have little compassion for ourselves. Harsh judgment and criticism of your behavior is unnecessary and can provide shame-based feelings. The shame-based narratives may sound like *"I am a bad person"* or *"I am damaged"* or *"I fall short of God's expectations."* This type of self-criticism creates greater suffering than necessary.

Yes, we make mistakes. Yes, you may have done something that you feel is unforgiveable. You may be in a state of remorse and regret over your errors in judgment. Now it is time to find understanding and mercy for yourself.

Making mistakes is a part of the human experience. If you feel deep regret for an action that you engaged in, and you have identified all the facts associated with what you did wrong, you may now be stuck in a remorseful state. It is time to feel compassion for yourself. You can recognize your imperfection and begin to be gentle with yourself. You are not worthless.

A part of the human experience is making mistakes and sometimes having erroneous judgment. Harsh judgments of yourself are not of value to you. Put the bat down and discontinue the emotional beatings of yourself. Practice self-compassion.

Step 7 – Self-Forgiveness

It is now time to be in a place to forgive yourself. If you still do not feel the forgiveness of yourself and feel you are experiencing the "unforgivable," you may want to repeat all the previous steps. You may want to seek professional help or find a compassionate friend with whom you can share your emotional pain. You will want to learn from your experience and learn from your mistakes. You can potentially behave in a more considerate way in the future and make better choices. You are forgivable. "*You are forgiven.*" It is now time to work on forgiving yourself.

Releasing

There is tremendous power in our ability to release and let go of unwanted and old ideas. The fact that releasing is a powerful practice might seem counterintuitive. Holding on and controlling a situation or a memory is seemingly more powerful. But control is an illusion. Even when you think you are in control, you really are not. You most likely feel a desire to control something when you are plagued with fear. Fear can dictate behaviors that are ineffective, and fear can promote poor judgment.

There is a saying that goes, "Fear is the lack of faith." I think it is more important to consider that acting in faith in the face of fear is acting with courage. We will often feel fear and need to draw on the strength we find in faith. There is some power that can help me through any situation. I may believe in karma, science, the laws of the Universe, or God from a Christian or Muslim perspective. But there is a Higher Source that is bigger than you.

There is power in the act of releasing. Releasing the memories of a situation, an old idea, or releasing an emotion is a form of liberation. You are freeing yourself to let go of something that is no longer serving you. You are escaping from the hold of the old idea.

When you release an emotion, you are allowing yourself to feel deeply and freely. In therapy, there is a term, *"catharsis,"* which refers to the release of emotional tension and thereby feeling an emancipation from those feelings. People will often feel refreshed and restored. Holding on to emotions can have the effect of being held hostage to them. It can also have a "pressure cooker" effect on you, and eventually will explode in an inappropriate way.

The principle of release is significant to this chapter on spirituality because it can help to visualize that you are releasing your old ideas, painful memories, and pent-up emotions to a Higher Source. Your desire to control or hold tight to old ideas may reflect that it is unsafe to release them.

You can visualize that you are releasing these things to God, to your Divine Being, your Higher Source, the Universe, or your God of Nature. You are entrusting these things onto which you are holding to another, greater Source than yourself. You are letting go. The following is an exercise that you can incorporate when you feel yourself attempting to control something or someone, or holding on to old ideas that are no longer serving you:

- *Find a quiet place where you feel safe.*
- *Close your eyes and take three deep and cleansing breaths.*
- *Hold out your hand and visualize that the person, memory, or old idea about yourself is in your hand.*
- *Close your hand and hold the image in your hand, clutching it tightly.*
- *Open your hand and release it.*
- *Imagine that your Higher Source is receiving it from you.*
- *You are free.*

Repeat this daily until you feel you have released it. It is common to feel the release and then to find yourself obsessed with a situation, person, memory, or old idea again. It is okay. Return to the activity and visualize the release. Visualize your freedom that comes as you are released from the bondage of that idea. Know that your Higher Source has it and will take care of it for you. You no longer must feel the chains of the imprisonment of those thoughts or ideas. You can ***release***.

Tense and Release

A way to initiate a physiological release is to practice a progressive muscle relaxation exercise of ***"tensing and releasing."*** The process of progressively relaxing muscles can provide a sense of peace and calm. You can also visualize that you are releasing your old ideas, unwanted memories, or emotional stress. Recall that high levels of stress and trauma are stored in ***somatic memory.*** This means that your body stores these things. The practice of tensing and releasing can help trigger a physiological release.

You can use the following exercise for release:

- *Find a quiet place free of distractions, where you feel safe.*
- *Close your eyes and take three deep and cleansing breaths.*
- *Scan your body for where you are holding the most stress or tension.*
- *Visualize that your body is carrying the emotion, memory, or old idea that you want to release.*
- *Beginning with your feet, tense and then release the muscles.*
- *Tense your calf muscles, and then release them.*
- *Moving up to your thigh muscles, tense and release/relax those muscles.*
- *Now your buttocks, tense them and release the muscles.*
- *Moving up your back, tense and release your back and torso muscles.*
- *Tense and release your shoulders.*
- *Tense and release your arms, and then your hands.*
- *Now your face...tense the facial muscles and then release them.*
- *Notice your body. Does it feel relaxed and calm?*
- *Visualize that you have released that thing you want to let go of.*

You are free.

The ability to release and let go is significant to feeling spiritually connected. When you are constricted and your mind is full of negativity, you are not free. When you are not free, you are not able to feel connected to your Higher Source. Release the thoughts, emotions, and somatic tension that block you from feeling connected to your Higher Source and to others.

The Spiritual Journey

I have hiked a lot of trails, and I appreciate some of the beautiful things I have seen. In many ways, hiking up a mountain is much like the spiritual journey we are all on. The various hikers are going at different paces and on different trails. While hiking, I have imagined that each journey is much like walking the path of spirituality. Our personal decision to engage in a growth process is much like making the decision to take a long hike.

Visualize that you are walking up a huge mountain. There are many paths that lead to the summit, and you are on your own journey. Others are also walking on various trails – some intersect and some run parallel. Some lead back to the bottom of the mountain and some people circle the perimeter.

As you are walking on your personal path, there are times when you encounter others, even walk alongside them. There may be times when you get off the path, and eventually find your way back.

You will stop to admire the view at different places. You will likely find a meaningful observation point. As you ascend, you will likely notice something sacred within you that you hoped to find.

This is spiritual growth. We are seeking. We are hoping to clear the way to see better or deeper. We are hoping to find new perspectives and new awareness. We will find those things if we continue the search. We will be looking more clearly at ourselves and what we need to do to get closer to the truth.

Your journey to the top of the mountain is uniquely yours. I hope to see you at the lookout or the summit. I hope to walk alongside you at times. As I get further up the mountain, I can see the presence of a Higher Source in the Divine, in nature, other people, and in the path itself.

14.a Reflection

- Describe your thoughts and feelings associated with the concept of a "Higher Source" or a power that can help you with your human difficulties. Also describe your Higher Source if you have one.

____

____

____

____

____

____

- Does the concept of forgiveness challenge you to retreat from the journey of healing (not forgive) or move forward (forgive)? Explain your answer.

____

____

____

____

____

____

- Are you able to forgive yourself for past mistakes, or are you on the path toward self-forgiveness? Describe your journey toward self-forgiveness.

14.a

- What are some of your barriers toward releasing the past of your or others actions?

Chapter 15

Final Thoughts

Trusting Yourself

"There is a universal, intelligent life force that exists within everyone and everything. It resides within each one of us as a ***deep wisdom, an inner knowing****. We can access this wonderful source of knowledge and wisdom through our intuition, an inner sense that tells us what feels right and true for us at any given moment."*

— *Shakti Gawain, Living in the Light*

Trust is the ability to believe in something or someone. We may have difficulty in trusting others if we have been betrayed or let down. We may also have difficulty in trusting ourselves because of our errors in judgment or mistakes that feel unforgiveable. Increased self-confidence may begin with embracing the truth of who we are and the mistakes we have made and then letting go of further assaults on self.

Transformation and change begin with accepting and embracing who we are. Then we can emerge and ascend from that place to the next level. Claiming our higher self moves us closer to trusting ourselves. Trust in others begins with trust in self. Are you willing to claim your higher self?

The process of trusting yourself may have already begun for you. If you have worked on the previous chapters of this book, you have probably come to understand yourself in a deeper and more complex way. You may have gained personal insight into your life that you did not see previously. Your perspective of self may now be more three-dimensional, rather than seeing everything that happens as "cause and effect."

My hope is that you now have increased awareness and more extensive vision into your life. If you have not completed the previous chapter activities, my hope is that you will. These activities will bring you greater self-knowledge and, in return, increased peace and feelings of stability. Perhaps you can now draw parallels to your personal reactions to life experiences and your past. The personal reflections may have encouraged you to want to explore further and consider getting therapy to dig even deeper.

Blockage to Deep Wisdom and Inner Knowing

The quote at the beginning of this chapter by Shakti Gawain refers to the inner knowing and the internal truth that we all possess. Our inner nudges can sometimes be blocked by ***misinformation*** about ourselves or by being ***externally focused***. When we are full of false narratives about who we are, we are not able to trust ourselves and it becomes difficult to sort through the misinformation and the truthful nudges that come from an "inner knowing." When we are completely externally focused, we often miss our internal cues.

Misinformation

Several of the earlier chapters of this book utilized inventories to access the belief system (see Exercises 6.a through 6.d). Our ***beliefs*** about ourselves will often generate the ***narratives*** we tell ourselves. When the narratives are clouded by false information about self that are derived from a faulty belief system, it is time to clear the wreckage so we can access our personal truth without distorted perceptions. This will open the door to *"inner wisdom"* and *"knowing."*

Clearing away the wreckage and clutter can pave the way to greater insight. This insight establishes awareness that is holding a lamp to the truth about yourself and life situations.

I liken this idea to the visual that we all have a brave, courageous, wise, and spiritual seer inside of ourselves. That seer or wise person is dormant for those of us who are blocked by misinformation and false ideas about ourselves. Your inner critic voice may be drowning out the voice of the wise prophet inside of you. Your narratives about yourself can be loud and derail the truth. It is time to be directed by your own brand of personal genius. We all possess a different form of genius and unblocking it can bring you a greater sense of self-confidence and self-satisfaction.

Unleash and unblock your courageous and wise seer within you. Let that voice become louder and you will begin to have the ability to trust yourself, your judgment, and your personal truth. Beware to not be misdirected by an internalized false prophet or a dark entity. Your inner wise person will have the light of truth. Your wise counsel will not be making harsh judgments of you or others.

"Your inner critic voice may be drowning out the wise prophet inside of you."

External Focus

Some of us may not be in touch with our own personal wisdom and insight because we tend to be externally focused. When we are always looking outside of ourselves, we cannot see what is within. We cannot hear the voice of our inner wisdom if we are focused on only external messages.

Many of us have been programmed to only look outside of ourselves for answers. In some situations, it is necessary to look outside of ourselves. The entire education system is learning through external resources such as books, teachers, and learning institutions. That is something that is critical to understanding and the learning process.

When turning to therapy it seems that we are looking outside of ourselves for answers. However, a well-trained psychotherapist will guide you to looking for your own personal truth to any situation. A psychotherapist will have you consider your values and will assist you with eliminating misinformation or false narratives.

We live in the Age of Information. We have access to unlimited information on any topic through exploring things on the search engine of our computers. Seeking answers from hard data is something that is useful and can be categorized as "looking outside of yourself."

However, many of us grow up in chaotic and dysfunctional households, where we learn to look only outside of ourselves for answers. Many of us have been told while growing up that our feelings are inaccurate by parental messages such as, "*You shouldn't be angry,*" or "*Don't be sad,*" or "*Don't feel that way.*" This will cause a person to look outside of themselves as adults for someone to tell them how they feel. They have internalized the idea that, "***What I feel is not true. My mother told me so. The person I looked up to and depended upon told me my feelings are wrong. So, tell me how I am feeling.***"

This is often the beginning of not trusting your own perception. This is often the beginning of not trusting yourself and your inner wisdom.

Some children grow up around chaos and conflict in their home environment. This may also lead to being focused externally rather than on one's own internal cues. Justin is an example of someone who did not trust himself and grew up in an extremely chaotic home.

> *Justin's earliest memories were of his parents arguing and the violence between them. His father drank excessively and became violent with family members regularly. Justin describes his father as ignorant and angry, and he was physically abused by his father several times a week from as far back as he can remember. There were multiple memories of the family kowtowing to Justin's father because they did not know when he would rage.*
>
> *Justin became* ***externally focused*** *because he was always on "high alert" to his father's mood. Justin left home at age 16, but he took his memories of the family violence with him. Justin came to therapy to work through his traumatic childhood. He was unable to access his feelings because he had spent so many years dissociating from his feelings.*

> *He watched his external environment to determine his experience. If others laughed, he knew he could laugh. If others were sad, he knew he was supposed to be sad. In therapy Justin worked hard to access his feelings and to listen to his internal cues. Justin's process was to learn to trust himself and tap into his inner voice. There were layers of defenses and distrust that Justin had to work through. He was gradually listening to his internal world.*

Hopefully you have begun to listen to your inner voice and trust yourself. This may be a process where you will want to find a therapist to guide you. Psychotherapy is intended to lead you to find your inner truth. I hope that you have begun this journey with or without a therapist. ***Trusting yourself is a process.***

I am hopeful that if you engaged in the inventories and self-assessments of the previous chapters, you have learned more about yourself. The ability to be honest with ourselves sometimes means looking at things we do not like.

In truth, we are all on a path from brokenness toward wholeness. Some people stay stagnant and do not venture on the path toward self-improvement. That is their journey. Some people may be blocked by addictions. Various types of addictions possess the soul and block people from the freedom that can come from looking honestly at the self.

The journey of change takes courage and if you are on the path toward personal growth, you are a champion. You are no longer satisfied with your life as it is and are wanting more. You are wanting more personal satisfaction, greater understanding, and awareness of why you feel, think, and do the things that you do.

This journey can often be uncomfortable. Looking at the past and seeing how it is affecting your present day is not always easy. Drawing parallels to our past and seeing how past hurtful experiences are affecting our present-day relationships can be both liberating and painful. The alternative, however, of being stagnant and not changing throughout a lifetime on the planet can be dull and motionless.

Trust

The ability to trust begins in the first year of life. We are programmed to learn to trust our primary caregivers and depend upon them. This is our initial opportunity to feel safety, security, and stability. As adults, we may or may not have had the experience of feeling trust in others and the world around us because of caregivers and life experiences.

But this is not the end of the road. This is not the grand finale and the established destiny of our lives. We have the power to change and alter a negative outcome by exploring our beliefs and narratives that have caused us to see the world in a distorted way. If you have not yet embarked on this journey toward having greater clarity in your life, this is your opportunity. The chapters of this book can be a route to clearing the way to a more affirming reality.

Although trust begins in the first year of life, you can renegotiate your personal ideas about trust. As you begin to see the misperceptions and misunderstandings you have had along your life's journey, you may want to reclaim your personal power. As you reclaim what was yours all along the way, you can begin to find greater trust in yourself.

Trusting yourself does not mean that you will now be mistake-free or perfect in your decisions. Trusting yourself means feeling a greater sense of confidence in who you are. It means having the ability to overcome any faulty decision you make. It means that what others think about you is not nearly as accurate as your self-assessment, as you have cleared away the negative self-perceptions that plagued you in the past.

Trusting yourself incorporates the idea of being reliable and accountable for your actions. You can be counted upon, and you will have a sense of responsibility for the way you live your life and in what you say. When you act with integrity, you are setting the stage for accountability.

You are now able to listen to your inner voice and trust the nudges you feel. You will still have unlimited personal freedom, as responsibility will offer that. Being irresponsible only provides a setup for loss of freedom. Responsibility for self gives you freedom.

My hope is that by reading this book you will be able to practically apply the ideas to live a more gratifying and enjoyable life. I truly believe that we are meant to feel passion for life. When we clear our path of negativity, self-criticism, and judgment, we are likely to feel the passion and love for our lives.

Your life is yours to live. The picture that you paint on your "canvas" that represents your life can be paradise if you choose to paint that story for yourself. You are the artist of your canvas. Today you can paint the next layer that represents your new narrative. Paint with confidence and trust in yourself. *Paint with love for yourself.*

15.a Reflection

- Is the voice of your inner critic or the wise prophet louder in your head? Has your work in this book helped you to find your inner prophet?

___

___

___

___

___

___

___

- Do you have barriers or blockages to hearing your inner wisdom and internal voice? If so, what would you like to release and let go of?

15.a

- In what ways do you feel a sense of transformational change as a result of doing the self-assessments and inventories in this book? Describe any new sense of freedom or trust in yourself.

Glossary

Affect: The responsive, emotional feeling that precedes cognition.

Anxiety: An emotion characterized by an unpleasant state of inner turmoil and includes feelings of dread over anticipated events.

Attachment: The physiological and psychological bond that exists between an infant and their caregiver.

Awareness: A concept about knowing, perceiving and being cognizant of events.

Belief system: A system in which the subjective attitudes exist that a proposition is true. A set of subjective attitudes that influence behavior.

Cognitions: The mental action or process of acquiring knowledge and understanding through thought, experience, and the senses. It encompasses all aspects of intellectual functions and processes such as perception, attention, thought, imagination, intelligence, the formation of knowledge, memory and working memory, judgment and evaluation, reasoning, problem solving and decision making.

Cognitive behavioral therapy (CBT): A psycho-social intervention that aims to reduce symptoms of various mental health conditions, primarily depression and anxiety disorders.

Cognitive Dissonance: The perception of contradictory information and the mental toll of it. The psychological stress that occurs when a person participates in an action that goes against one's feelings, ideas, beliefs or values.

Cognitive Processing Therapy (CPT): A manualized therapy used by clinicians to help people recover from post traumatic stress disorder (PTSD) and related conditions.

Complacency: A feeling of contented self-satisfaction with the way things are, that prevents people from trying harder.

Conscious awareness/conscious beliefs: Beliefs that we are consciously aware of.

Core beliefs: Strong, long-term beliefs that a person has the help them understand how the world works and who they are.

Depression: A state of low mood and aversion to activity.

Dialectical behavior therapy (DBT): An evidence-based psychotherapy that began with efforts to treat personality disorders and interpersonal conflicts.

Dissociation: The experience of having one's attention and emotions detached from the environment.

Endorphins: Peptides produced in the brain that block the perception of pain and increase feelings of wellbing.

Environment: Constructed surroundings that provide the setting for human activity, ranging from the large-scale civic surroundings to the personal places, as well as the culture, the people and institutions with whom an individual interacts.

Existential: An aspect of the philosophy of existentialism which explores the issue of human existence. Existential philosophers explore questions related to the meaning, purpose and value of human existence.

Eye Movement Desensitization and Reprocessing (EMDR): A form of psychotherapy designed to alleviate the distress associated with traumatic memories such as post traumatic stress disorder (PTSD)

False narrative: Inaccurate or incorrect stories or tales of an account of a series of related events or experiences.

Forgiveness: The intentional and voluntary process by which one who may initially feel victimized or wronged, goes through a change in feelings and attitude regarding a given offender, and overcomes the impact of the offense including negative emotions such as resentment and a desire for vengeance.

Grounding: A strategy for coping with stress or other negative emotions through focusing on a visual or physical touch sensation.

Hyper-arousal: Excessive arousal. An abnormal state of increased responsiveness to stimuli that is marked by various physiological and psychological symptoms such as increased levels of alertness, hypervigilance, panic, rage.

Hypervigilance: The elevated state of constantly assessment potential threats around a person. Often this occurs as a result of trauma.

Hypo-arousal: An arousal state that lies on the low end of a continuum. An under-responsiveness to stimuli and one's environment that may include disconnect, dissociation, depression and apathy.

Influencers: Someone that affects the behavior of an individual or a group.

Influences: Something that affects the behavior of an individual or group.

Insight: an introspection where an individual gains an understanding of cause and effect based on the identification of relationships and behaviors within a scenario.

Intention: a mental state where the agent commits themselves to a course of action.

Internal reality: The sum of all that is real or existent within an indivudal's thoughts and perceptions.

Maladaptive coping: Unhealthy or negative ways of coping that has adverse consequences of only short- term results.

Manifest: The act of an event, action, or object that shows or demonstrates an idea.

Mantras: A sacred utterance, a numinous sound, a syllable, word or phonemes, or group of words believed to have spiritual powers or calming effects.

Meditation: A practice in which an individual uses a technique – such as mindfulness or focusing the mind on a particular object, thought, or activity – to train attention and awareness and achieve a mentally clear and emotionally calm and stable state.

Metathesiophobia: Excessive fear of change

Mindfulness: The practice of purposely bringing one's attention to the present-moment experience without evaluation.

Mistaken beliefs: • Self-defeating beliefs: Deep rooted beliefs or assumptions that we hold about ourselves, other people and in life. Most often they are incorrect and unhelpful and tend to defeat one's sense of capability.

Narrative: an account of a series of related events or experiences.

Neocortex: A set of layers of the mammalian cerebral cortex involved in higher-order brain functions such as sensory perception, cognition, generation of motor commands, spatial reasoning and language.

Neurochemistry: The existence of chemicals, including neurotranmitters and other molecules that control and influence the physiology of the nervous system.

Neurocognitive disorders: A category of mental health disorders that primarily affect cognitive abilities including learning, memory, perception and problem-solving.

Neuroplasticity: The ability of the neural networks in the brain to change through growth and reorganization.

Neurotransmitters: A signaling molecule secreted by a neuron to affect another cell across a synapse.

Parasympathetic nervous system: One of the three division of the autonomic nervous system. It is responsible for regulating the body's unconscious actions. Also is responsible for the "rest and digest" activities.

Perceptions: The organization, identification, and interpretation of sensory information in order to represent and understand the presented information or environment.

Phobia: An anxiety disorder, defined by a persistent and excessive fear of an object or situation.

Physiology: The scientific study of functions and mechanisms in a person. The chemical processes and substances that occur within living organisms.

Polyvagal theory: A psychological construct pertaining to the role of the vagus nerve in emotion regulation, social connection and fear response, introduced by Stephen Porges

Primal wounds: The emotional pain and hurt an individual carries due to intentional or unintentional infliction of hurt by primary caregivers.

Private conversations: The internal conversations or narratives a person has that reflects their belief system

Private logic: Subjective and private beliefs which serve as a referece for attitudes, subjective and phenomenological views of self, others and the world.

Psychotherapy: (also psychological therapy, tak therapy or talking therapy) is the use of psychological methods, particularly when based on regular person interaction, to help a person change behavior, increase happiness, and overcome problems.

Redecision therapy: A type of cognitive behavioral therapy where a person can "re-decide" on an earlier decision.

Schizophrenia: A mental disorder characterized by continuous or relapsing episodes of psychosis.

Self-defeating beliefs: Deep rooted beliefs or assumptions that we hold about ourselves, other people and in life. Most often they are incorrect and unhelpful and tend to defeat one's sense of capability.

Self-examination: The process of assessing oneself in a methodical way.

Self-perception: The way in which a person perceives themselves in their environment and in the context of relationships

Sympathetic nervous system: One of the three divisions of the autonomic nervous system that functions to regulate the body's unconscious actions. Specifically, the primary purpose is to stimulate the body's fight or flight response.

Transcendence: The aspect of a god wholly independent of the material universe

Transformation: A fundamental change in an individual

Trauma: Exposure to an incident or series of events that are emotionally disturbing or life-threatening with lasting adverse effects on the individual's functioning and mental, physical, social, emotional, and/or spiritual well-being.

Trauma Resilience Model (TRM): A model of trauma therapy that is biologically based with components of visualizations.

Unfinished business: Something that a person needs to deal with or work on.

Vagus nerve: A cranial nerve that carries sensory fibers that create a pathway the interfaces with the parasympathetic control of the body.

Validation: Compliance in a social activity to fit in and be a part of the majority. Also the external acknowledgment of an individual for their behavior.

References

Adler, A. (2013). *Understanding human nature.* Routledge. (Original work published 1928)

Beck, A. T. (1976). *Cognitive Therapy and the Emotional Disorders.*Penguin Books.

Beck, J. S. (2011). *Cognitive behavior therapy: basics and beyond* (2nd ed.). U.S. Guilford Press.

Bowlby, J. (1969). *Attachment and loss* (Vol. 1). Basic Books.

Bowlby, J. (1982). Attachment and loss: retrospect and prospect. *American Journal of Orthopsychiatry, 52(4),* 664-678.

Chodron, P. (2002). *When Things Fall Apart: Heart Advice for Difficult Times.* Element Books.

C., Joy Bell (2014). *The sun is always snowing: the scrapbook.* Amazon.

Cohen, W.E. & Inaba, D. S. (2004). *Uppers, downers, all arounders* (5th ed.). CNS Publications, Inc.

Early, B.P. & Grady, M.D. (2017). Embracing the contribution of both behavioral and cognitive theories to cognitive behavioral therapy: maximizing the richness. *Clin Soc Work J 45*, 39–48.

Ferguson, E. D. (2001). Adler and Dreikurs: cognitive-social dynamics innovators. *The Journal of Individual Psychology, 57*(4), 324-341.

Festinger, L. (1957). *A theory of cognitive dissonance.* Stanford University Press.

Festinger, L. (1959). Some attitudinal consequences of forced decisions. *Acta Psychologica, 15*, 389-390.

Frankl, V. (1959). *Man's search for meaning.* Beacon Press.

Gupta, S. (2021). *Keep Sharp: Build a better brain at any age.* Simon & Schuster.

Hesse, Hermann (1982). *Siddhartha.* Bantam Books.

Kabat-Zinn, J. (2005). *Coming to our senses: healing ourselves and the world through mindfulness.* Hachette.

Keller, H. (1946). *Let us have faith.* Doubleday & Company.

Krishnakumar, D., Hamblin, M., and Lakshmanan, S. (2015). Meditation and yoga can modulate brain mechanisms that affect behavior and anxiety: a modern scientific perspective. *Anc Sci, 2,* 13-19.

Kubler-Ross, E. (1970). *On death and dying.* Collier Books

Lennox, C. E. (1997). *Redecision therapy: a brief, action-oriented approach.* Jason Aronson, Inc.

Menon, V. (2011). Large-scale brain networks and psychopathology: a unifying triple network model. *Trends in Cognitive Sciences, 15(10),* 483-506.

Nepo, M. (2020). *The book of awakening.* Red Wheel/Weiser LLC.

Porges, S. W. (2017). *The pocket guide to the polyvagal theory: the transformative power of feeling safe.* WW Norton.

Porges, S. W. (2022). Polyvagal theory: a science of safety. *Frontiers in Human Neuroscience, 16,* 67.

Siegel, D. J. (2010). *Mindsight: the new science of personal transformation.* Random House.

Sullivan, R. M. (2013). The neurobiology of attachment to nurturing and abusive caregivers. *Hastings Law Journal, 63(6),* 1553-1570.

Sullivan, M.B., Erb, M., Schmalzl, L., Moonaz, S., Taylor, J.N., & Porges, S.W. (2018). Yoga therapy and polyvagal theory: The convergence of traditional wisdom and contemporary neuroscience for self-regulation and resilience. *Frontiers in Human Neuroscience, 12.*

Index

Made in the USA
Middletown, DE
03 May 2024